P9-DXR-623

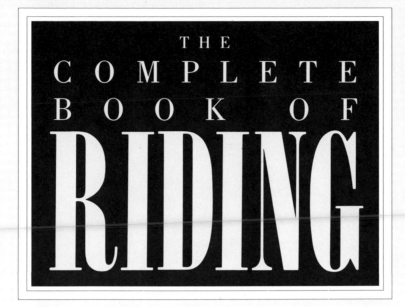

THE

COMPLETE

BOOK OF

RIDING

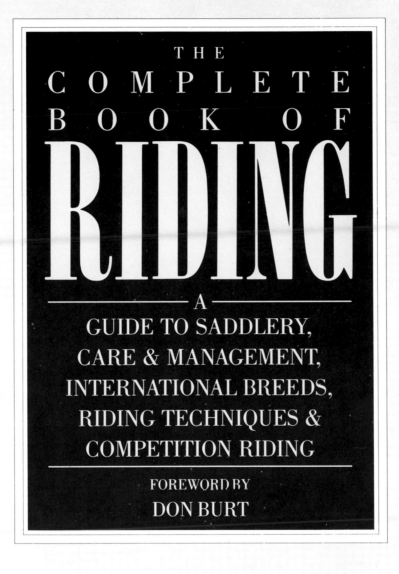

THE
COMPLETE
BOOK OF
RIDING

A
GUIDE TO SADDLERY, CARE & MANAGEMENT, INTERNATIONAL BREEDS, RIDING TECHNIQUES & COMPETITION RIDING

FOREWORD BY
DON BURT

GALLERY BOOKS
An Imprint of W. H. Smith Publishers Inc.
112 Madison Avenue
New York City 10016

First published in 1989 by
The Hamlyn Publishing Group Limited
a division of the Octopus Publishing Group
Michelin House
81 Fulham Road
London SW3 6RB

First published in the United States in 1989 by
Gallery Books
an imprint of W.H. Smith Publishers, Inc.
112 Madison Avenue
New York 10016

© Bookbourne Limited 1989

ISBN 0 8317 1537 5

Produced by Mandarin Offset
Printed and bound in Hong Kong

Gallery Books are available for bulk purchase
for sales promotions and premium use. For
details write or telephone the Manager of
Special Sales, W.H. Smith Publishers, Inc., 112
Madison Avenue, New York, New York
10016. (212) 532-6600

FOREWORD

As incredible as it seems, the horse has been a part of our lives a scant 6,000 years – not much time when you consider the length of human history. Once domesticated, the horse was first driven, then ridden. The skills and techniques used in training, riding, and caring for a horse have evolved over the centuries; man and horse have been learning from each other all the while. In time, thoughtful people felt the need to write about horsemanship and horsemastership and to share their knowledge with others.

The Complete Book of Riding is an example of the work of just such thoughtful and knowledgeable people. Elwyn Hartley Edwards and the experts who assisted him can be proud of this contribution to the literature.

Although the book focuses primarily on all the great disciplines and sports involving the ridden horse (polo, hunting, dressage, racing, show jumping, endurance riding, trekking), it also offers us a wide range of information about the horse. As a lifelong horseman, I realize that in order to understand and appreciate the horse, we need to know as much as possible about him. This extraordinary book will go a long way toward satisfying that need because it features in-depth coverage of such topics as the history of the horse, the specifics of approximately fourscore breeds, care and breeding, tack and equipment, and stable management, among others.

This is a book to be read and enjoyed by horse-enthusiasts of every kind, and will be a welcome addition to your equestrian library.

DON BURT

CONTENTS

TACK & EQUIPMENT

Owning horses and ponies also involves possessing equipment and clothing suitable for the type of activity which one wishes to pursue. In addition, horses have to be stabled and the stables equipped with the appropriate fittings; and since, in the modern world, mobility is of the essence, the means of transporting horses is a further and major consideration.

Horse vans were in use in England as long ago as the 17th century, being used very occasionally to convey especially valuable animals to Newmarket when that town, under the influence of King Charles II, was becoming the principal center of English racing. Motorized horse vans, usually horse ambulances, were in use during World War I, but the appearance of the now ubiquitous trailer was delayed until midway between the two World Wars.

The origin of the wheeled horse-drawn vehicle, however, goes back almost to the invention of the wheel itself. Solid wheels, dated at about 3500 BC, have been found in Sumerian graves excavated in the Tigris–Euphrates valley, and spoked chariot wheels were in use in Mesopotamia a thousand years after that. In fact, the chariot was the principal prototype for many of the lighter carriages which appeared in the following centuries. The Mediterranean type of racing chariot discovered in the tomb of Tutankhamen is, indeed, very reminiscent of the modern racing sulky, harness racing being the modern equivalent of the chariot racing popular in ancient Greece and Rome.

Without any doubt, though, the greatest influence on the development of the wheeled vehicle was that of the Hungarians. It was their one-time rulers, the early Huns, who first brought wheeled transport into Europe. Later, in AD 451, Attila the Hun had a wagon-laager at the epic battle of Châlons in northeast France, the momentous engagement which signaled the final phase of the Roman Empire.

The Hungarians were later operating advanced wagon-train systems when the rest of Europe relied on pack transport, and it was in the Hungarian village of Kocs, in the Komorne area, that the first road coach (*Kocsi szekér*) was produced, in the late 15th century. Interestingly, a design feature of the Hungarian coach – the front wheels being smaller than the rear ones to give a tighter turning circle – is exactly the same arrangement as that on a wagon buried with the Sumerian King Abargi in the third millennium BC.

In terms of practical usage and supreme quality of materials and construction, carriage harness (and indeed coaches and carriages, too) reached its zenith in that short period in history between 1820 and 1845 which has been called coaching's "golden age." The refinements made to harness in 19th century Europe, however, stemmed from far earlier innovations made, as always, in Asia.

It was the inventive Chinese who made the greatest and most significant developments in both harness and carriage design. They were using sophisticated vehicles, surprisingly modern in appearance, by 1300 BC. They were the inventors of the single-horse vehicle fitted with lateral shafts, and by 250 BC were using a breast harness identical to those in use today. The Chinese were the first to drive horses in tandem, and after that they produced the breeching strap. Finally, it was the people of the world's then most advanced civilization who gave us the horse collar, which has been hailed as one of the greatest inventions ever made because, by allowing the possible tractive force to be used to the greatest effect, it made an enormous contribution to the development of horse-drawn transport.

Not surprisingly, the principal method of horse control – the bit – made an early appearance on the equestrian scene. Initially, control was achieved by means of a leather thong encompassing the lower jaw; after that came bits of hardwood, then of bone and horn. Metal bits, jointed in the mouthpiece, were in general use by 1200 to 1300 BC. They became increasingly sophisticated in the ensuing centuries, but essentially no significant alteration in the basic system of control has been made in something like 3000 years.

The first "saddles" were no more than animal skins or cloths thrown over the horse's back. They gave a degree of comfort to the rider but hardly contributed much to his security. It was not until the dawn of the Christian era that the Sarmatians, nomads again, from the steppes north of the Black Sea, were building a type of saddle based on a shaped wooden foundation (a tree) which comprised front and rear arches joined by wooden bars on each side of the horse's spine. The stirrup took far longer to evolve, but by the 8th century AD it was in general use in Europe, having been common in central Asia for two or three hundred years before that.

The greatest influence on saddle design was the dip-seated saddle of the medieval knight. It survives in an adapted form as the Western saddle, derived from those of the 16th century conquistadors, and in a streamlined version – the *selle royale* of the Renaissance – it forms the basis of the modern dressage saddles.

For many years the "center of the universe" in terms of the wholesale production of saddlery, horse "furniture" (such as buckles and metal fittings) and bits (including many of the Western types) was the town of Walsall in the English Midlands, while the London saddlers, like the tailors of Savile Row, were reckoned to be pre-eminent in the "bespoke" business.

But for reasons both economic and social, Walsall lost its position as a world leader in the early 1960s and today it is German saddlery that heads the field, although the trade of lorimery (the making of bits, spurs and other metal items) has returned, ironically, to the East, the greater part of equestrian hardware being produced in Korea and Taiwan.

CHOOSING A SADDLE

The most important item of a rider's equipment, and certainly the most expensive, is the saddle. Properly designed and constructed, it will help both you and your horse to realize your performance potential. But a bad saddle, which interferes with the horse's natural movement and makes it difficult for you to sit in balance, will have the opposite result.

Looked at in that light, your choice of saddle should be governed by the ability of its design and construction to fulfil a group of basic requirements:

● The saddle should conform comfortably to the structure of the horse's back, without in any way inhibiting the animal's natural movement

● The saddle has to suit you as well as your horse, particularly regarding the size of seat and the length of your legs. The design should also allow you to position your weight, without undue effort, as nearly as possible over the horse's center of gravity, or balance (You are then said to be "in balance")

● The design of the saddle should suit the purpose for which it is intended, for instance, general usage, jumping, distance riding and so on

● The materials used and the construction of the saddle should be of a sufficiently high quality to ensure that it is safe to use, and is durable within reasonable limits.

The first of these requirements concerns the fit of the saddle. For example, when the rider is in position, the horse's spine must be free from pressure both laterally and along its length. In practice there should be sufficient space between the pommel arch and the withers for the insertion of three fingers, and there should be complete clearance at the cantle.

To ensure that there is no lateral pressure on the horse's spinal vertebrae, the channel dividing the two halves of the saddle panel must be sufficiently wide throughout its length. If it becomes closed, there will be pressure on the spine and this pressure will cause the horse discomfort, encouraging a hollowing of the back and a subsequent restriction of movement. Pressure on the withers or at the cantle will have a similar effect and in every instance there is the likelihood of the saddle causing abrasion. Interference with the spinal complex is also a principal cause of erratic jumping and/or refusals.

Clearly, a tree (the foundation on which the saddle is built) which is too wide in the pommel arch will press on the withers, and the fault will be compounded rather than corrected by excessive stuffing of the panel. However, too narrow a fitting is just as bad. The "points" of the tree — the extremities of the front arch which project below the stirrup bars — will then pinch below and on either side of the withers with the same results. Trees are usually made in wide, medium and narrow fittings, and there is an extra-wide fitting for pony saddle trees.

It is also important that the weight is distributed over the whole bearing surface of the panel. If the weight is concentrated over a small area, as a result of the panel being stuffed unevenly, pressure points are created which cause discomfort or soreness, affecting the movement of the horse. This will happen if the panel is stuffed too high at the front or the rear, or more on one side than the other, or, which is by no means impossible, by a tree which has been twisted out of shape in some way. Pressure points are also caused by uneven stuffing resulting in lumps in the panel surface.

While meeting these conditions, the saddle should nonetheless fit the horse's back closely. If it is overstuffed to stand more than usually clear of the spine, there will be a side-to-side rolling movement of the saddle and the friction will cause soreness.

A saddle which is cut too far forward, so that the knee roll of the panel rests *on* the shoulder rather than behind it, will also cause significant interference to the horse's movement. In fairness, the fault isn't always the saddlemaker's; very often it is caused by the shoulder being too upright, a serious fault in a riding horse.

The second consideration, that of positioning the rider "in balance," depends on an understanding of the principles involved. It has been established by experiment that the center of balance or gravity of the horse at rest is at the intersection of two imaginary lines, the one drawn vertically to the ground from a point some four inches behind the highest part of the withers and the other drawn horizontally from the point of the shoulder to the rear.

The center, in the middle of the horse's body, is fluid, its position depending on the balancing

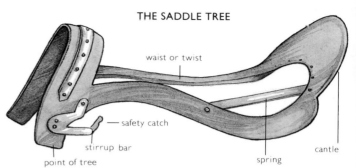

THE SADDLE TREE

waist or twist

safety catch

stirrup bar

point of tree

spring

cantle

The saddle tree is the frame on which the saddle is built. Trees are usually made of laminated wood, and may include steel springs.

JUMPING SADDLE

The jumping saddle is designed to allow the rider to use a shorter stirrup leather and to sit well forward. The saddle is almost always built on a spring tree, and has a fairly deep seat.

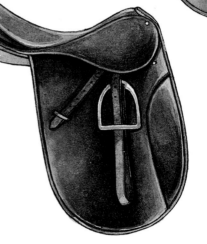

DRESSAGE SADDLE

The dressage saddle enables the rider to use the leg and weight aids with great precision. The leathers are long, and only a light flap and sweat flap come between the rider's leg and the horse.

SADDLE PAD

The saddle pad or numnah is fitted beneath the saddle. Made of cotton, linen, sheepskin or a synthetic material, it protects the horse's back from abrasion by the saddle.

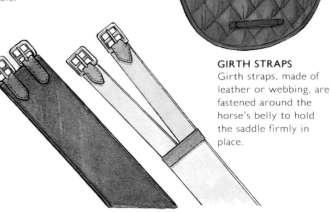

GIRTH STRAPS

Girth straps, made of leather or webbing, are fastened around the horse's belly to hold the saddle firmly in place.

PARTS OF A SADDLE

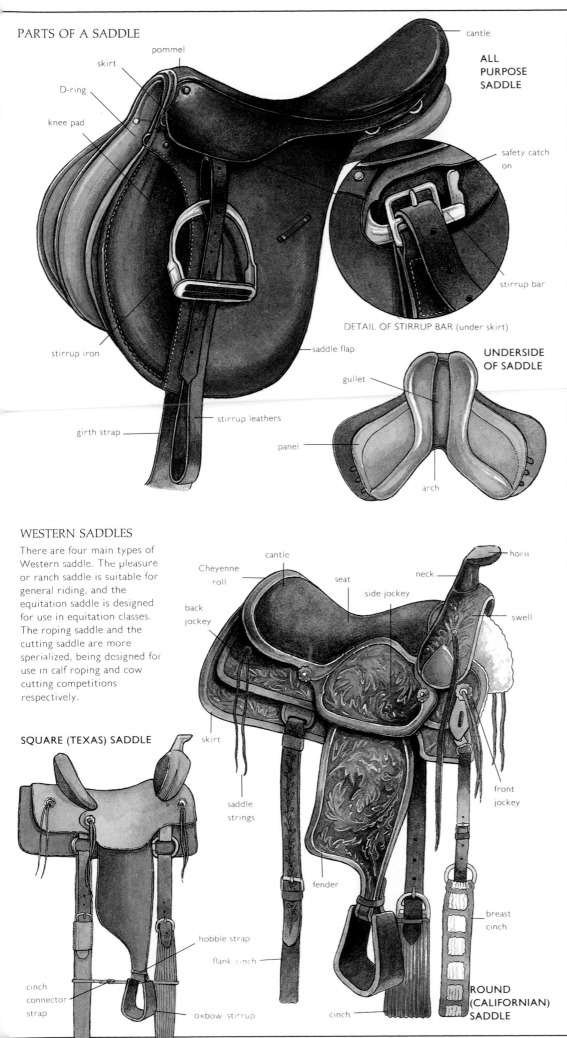

ALL PURPOSE SADDLE

- cantle
- pommel
- skirt
- D-ring
- knee pad
- safety catch on
- stirrup bar
- stirrup iron
- saddle flap
- stirrup leathers
- girth strap

DETAIL OF STIRRUP BAR (under skirt)

UNDERSIDE OF SADDLE

- gullet
- panel
- arch

WESTERN SADDLES

There are four main types of Western saddle. The pleasure or ranch saddle is suitable for general riding, and the equitation saddle is designed for use in equitation classes. The roping saddle and the cutting saddle are more specialized, being designed for use in calf roping and cow cutting competitions respectively.

SQUARE (TEXAS) SADDLE

- cantle
- Cheyenne roll
- seat
- side jockey
- neck
- horn
- back jockey
- swell
- skirt
- saddle strings
- front jockey
- fender
- breast cinch
- hobble strap
- flank cinch
- cinch connector strap
- oxbow stirrup
- cinch

ROUND (CALIFORNIAN) SADDLE

agents, the head and the neck. If the latter are stretched forward in extension, as when galloping or jumping, the center moves forward. In collection, when the head is flexed at the poll, the neck held high and the croup lowered as the hocks become more actively engaged under the body, the center moves slightly to the rear.

It follows that for the weight of the rider to be the least possible encumbrance to the horse it has to be held in alignment with the latter's sense of balance. In front of that point the rider overweights the forehand; behind it, the weight restricts the movement of the hindquarters, the "engine room" of the horse.

Thus the design of the jumping saddle has to position the rider well forward, while that of the dressage saddle, at the other end of the spectrum, must allow the weight to be positioned more to the rear. It would be no use buying a dressage saddle for jumping, or a jumping saddle for dressage.

Similar considerations apply when you are buying a Western saddle. You should choose one that is suitable for the type of riding you intend to do with it.

For instance, a proper roping saddle is essential for roping competitions, but because it is designed to sit immovably on the horse's back, and is heavy and rigid, it is unsuitable for general riding. The cutting saddle, however, can be a good alternative to the conventional pleasure saddle for general riding. Its lightness, and the freedom of movement offered by its flat seat, make it popular with many pleasure riders.

All in all, price is aligned to quality. In a first-class, highly priced saddle the leather will be soft, supple and well finished; the stirrup bars will be made (and stamped accordingly) of the far more reliable forged steel rather than of cast steel. Furthermore, it is reasonable to assume that the methods of construction used are in line with the quality of the materials.

However, your choice of saddle will be governed to some degree by the price you can afford to pay, and if you can't afford the very best there are alternatives. Try for a secondhand saddle by a reputable maker or disregard the conventional and buy a saddle made from synthetic materials. It won't last as long, but it will be easy to maintain, usually well designed, and far superior to most of the lesser-quality leather saddles.

ALL-PURPOSE SADDLES

The all-purpose saddle is at the center of the saddle spectrum, the extremes (excluding the racing saddle) being the dressage at one end and the jumping saddle at the other. It is for that reason the most practical choice for the majority of riders, because it is a saddle which the average rider can use quite satisfactorily for going across country, show jumping or for riding a dressage test. Judicious adjustment of the leathers will place the rider centrally and over the center of balance in any of these activities at the sort of level to which most of us aspire.

Most all-purpose saddles of conventional construction will be made on a spring tree rather than on the older type of rigid tree. Both have advantages and disadvantages which are worth thinking about.

Traditionally, saddle trees are made of beechwood. Once they were shaped by hand, but the modern trees are made from strips

The all-purpose saddle is a practical choice for most riders. The three shown here are a Wintec synthetic saddle (top), and leather saddles from Balaton (right) and Polegate Saddlery (left).

bones to be more easily transmitted than would be possible in a tree of rigid construction. Furthermore, the spring tree "gives" with the movement of the horse's back.

The spring tree is thus something of a precision instrument and for that reason needs to be treated with care. It would be possible, for instance, for the tree to be twisted by the rider mounting incorrectly. Should he seek to pull himself up by holding the right hand on the cantle, the tree will easily be pulled out of alignment.

The rider will then sit out of balance and the weight will be concentrated on one side of the saddle, possibly giving rise to soreness and injury to the horse.

The rigid tree, made without springs, lacks the resilience of the sprung variety but has the advantage of being stronger.

The synthetic saddles sometimes employ conventional spring trees, but more usually they are made of nylon, which has a considerable degree of resilience but which will not be twisted easily.

The essential differences between the all-purpose saddle and the dressage and jumping saddles are found in the shape of the tree, the position of the bars, which in modern saddles are recessed so as to obviate painful lumps under the thigh, and the extent to which the panel and the overlying flap are inclined to the front.

In addition, since the all-purpose saddle will be in use for far longer periods of time than a jumping saddle — a rider may expect, for instance, to be in the saddle for up to five hours at a stretch during a day's hunting — the panel needs to be made so as to provide a larger bearing surface over which the weight can be distributed.

The "twist" or waist of the tree in a jumping saddle can be closed to give an artificially narrow grip to the thighs but this, of course, also compels the panel to be narrower and its bearing surface reduced in that area. It is not of much consequence in a pure jumping saddle, but it could cause problems in a saddle used for some hours at a time.

The position of the bars, and to a very large degree the line of the panel and flap, depend upon the inclination of the head or pommel.

In the jumping saddle the inclination of the head takes the bars and the panel well forward to allow for the shortened leather

and the advancing center of balance over fences. The all-purpose saddle is less exaggerated, the position of the bars and the line of the panel, knee rolls and flap allowing the rider to use a longer leather. ("Knee roll" is really a misnomer. The forward roll on the panel is actually a support for the thigh just above the knee rather than for the knee itself.)

In recent years the principal design faults in the manufacture of all-purpose saddles have been excessively dipped seats and panels cut too far forward.

The former tend to tip the rider too much on the fork and to concentrate the weight in the forward waist area and, in addition, they limit the rider's freedom of movement.

The forward cut flap, even if it does not interfere with the movement of the shoulder, is of no use to the rider wishing to employ a longer leather for schooling or dressage tests and may even cause him to ride too short across country. In general, the better quality leather saddles and the synthetics avoid these failings. There is, too, a growing trend in the design of modern saddles against the accentuated dip and towards a slightly flatter seat.

Most of the modern all-purpose saddles have panels which are stuffed with wool and which can therefore be regulated quite easily to make minor adaptations to the fit.

There are saddles, however, principally those of French make, which are fitted with panels made of thick felt covered, as usual, with leather. So long as the original fit was correct, these panels will require a minimum of adjustment. A degree of latitude is nonetheless provided by a relatively thin wool stuffing laid over the felt between the latter and the leather panel covering.

German saddles and those following the German style are for the most part made on trees with cut-back pommels. The idea is that heads of this shape accommodate high withers more easily.

At one time trees were made with quarter, half and full cut-back pommels. The fashion today is for the quarter cut-back pommel; in fact, the cut-back pommel is really more a matter of fashion than of utility. High-withered horses can be fitted just as easily with the conventionally sloped pommel as with one that is cut back and it is, of course, a stronger construction.

of the same wood which are laminated in molds with resin. This method ensures a consistent product which is also lighter and stronger than a hand-shaped tree. The tree is reinforced with metal and in the spring tree two pieces

of sprung steel are laid along the frame from the pommel (or head) to the cantle.

The spring tree gives a resilience to the seat which is more comfortable for the rider and allows the influence of his seat

JUMPING & RACING SADDLES

Jumping saddles are built to allow the rider to use a shorter leather and to position his weight well forward in accordance with the shifting center of balance as the horse jumps. To allow for this, the panel is swept to the front, and in the classic pattern the head of the tree will be sloped so as to bring the stirrup bars a little forward of the position they occupy in an all-purpose saddle. The tree (almost always a spring tree) is long enough to accommodate the rider when the latter, using his shortened leather, has his seat in the saddle. A fairly deep seat is desirable but the dip must not be too exaggerated.

The classic jumping saddle, from which the less forward inclined all-purpose derives, was that developed in the 1950s by Count Ilias Toptani and the pattern is still marketed under his name. The Toptani saddle was a successor to the jumping saddles developed in the Twenties and Thirties, notably those produced by Pariani of Milan and the Santini designed by Major Piero Santini, the disciple of Federico Caprilli (who advocated the "forward seat" style of jumping) and the principal interpreter of his theories. Both came very close to conforming to the principles of the forward system propounded by Caprilli, but Toptani was the first to appreciate that it was the position of the stirrup bars which contributed to the easy maintenance of a balanced forward position over fences.

Toptani, trainer of the victorious Mexican Olympic jumping team of 1948, based his design, very correctly, on the tree. Up to that time the conventional saddle of the English hunting type was made on a rigid tree in which the head formed a vertical line with the frame; the seat itself was nearly flat and in many patterns it was almost impossible for the rider to sit other than towards the cantle, out of balance with the horse and behind the movement.

Toptani introduced a dip to the seat, he had the twist narrowed and he sloped the head at an angle of about 45 degrees to the frame by bringing the points, and therefore the bars which are attached to them, *forward*. The ends of the points, which in the older type saddles projected inches below the bar, terminated immediately below in Toptani's models, being finished with a shaped piece of leather. These "flexible points," as they were called, removed the annoying bulk under the rider's knee and gave the saddle a greater fitting range.

In addition, Toptani introduced the practice of the recessed bar, which lies virtually flush with the tree, and he used spring trees in his saddles, an innovation which had, in fact, been introduced by Pariani some twenty years previously.

The Toptani panel, following the line of the head, was cut well forward and the old-style flap leather, thick enough to last two lifetimes or more, was replaced by leather of far less substance, while the whole saddle was much lighter in weight.

The forward rolls on the Toptani panel increased the rider's security and helped maintain his leg position. At the rear of the sweat flap, behind the girth straps, there was another roll which became known as a "thigh roll." In fact, its purpose was to prevent the girth straps from slipping to the rear and it had nothing to do with positioning the leg.

A saddle which did attempt to secure the rider's leg position was the French Danloux pattern, named after the famous Colonel Danloux, one of France's leading show jumpers in the years before World War II.

The panel of the Danloux (termed a Saumur or French panel), unlike the stuffed wool panel of the Toptani, was made of felt. It was broader in the bearing surface through the waist and while it incorporated a flattish forward roll it was designed to

The saddles in the top row are (from the left) a Polegate Saddlery Friston show jumping saddle, a Shires racing saddle from NJ Ainge and a Schroder steeplechase saddle. The two in the bottom row are a racing saddle (left) and a steeplechase saddle, both from the Australian saddlers Bates.

give support to the thigh above the knee and it terminated well above that joint. To fix the leg position a substantial leather covered pad, nearly triangular in shape, was built into the rear of the sweat flap so that it fitted behind the leg close up to the crook of the knee.

The Danloux pattern, or saddles similar in style, is now making a comeback, but for the most part the market in this field is still dominated by the German influence. The German saddles, which came to prominence in the 1960s, are very well-finished, but to many people they are rather clumsy and heavy-looking.

The object in the making of flat-racing saddles is to keep the weight to an absolute minimum, and a saddle weighing not much more than 1 pound when mounted (fitted with leathers, irons, girth etc) is not concerned with the conventional principles of design and fit. Indeed, saddles of this weight provide little more than a convenient anchorage for the stirrups.

Most of the modern styles of lightweight racing saddles are made on glassfiber or nylon trees. They are not fitted with stirrup bars, the leathers being looped around the bars of the tree itself on either side. The "leathers," indeed, are made not from that material but from light web or nylon, while the "irons" are of aluminum. A single girth strap is used in saddles of this weight.

Traditionally, these lightweight saddles were covered in the thinnest pig- or calf-skin, the panels being no more than a suggestion of fine wool covered in silk. The horse's back is protected by a withers pad placed under the front arch, but since the saddle is in use for so short a space of time, fitting in the conventional sense is of no consequence. To-day, increasing use is made of synthetic materials and they are ideally suited to the purpose, even for the larger and heavier steeplechase saddles which may weigh from 6 pounds upwards, some of them, for lightweight jockeys trying to make point-to-point weights, being up to 22 pounds.

These heavier saddles, apart from being cut very well forward in the flap, are built in the conventional manner but, of course, the tree needs to be flat, the usual sort of cantle being an uncomfortable thing on which to land if one should be somewhat "left behind" over a fence.

DRESSAGE AND SHOW SADDLES

There is a close resemblance between the dressage and the show saddle, but there the relationship ends, for the purposes for which the two saddles are designed could not be farther apart.

Of all the riding saddles the dressage version is the most specialized. Obviously, it has to conform to the usual rules of fitting, but otherwise its concern is with the most effective positioning of the rider in relationship to the movement and the rider's ability to influence the horse through the natural aids.

Dressage involves the shortening of the horse's base in the collected movements, the forehand being lightened while the weight is carried increasingly over lowered hindquarters and actively engaged hocks. The precise positioning of the rider's weight in accordance with the center of gravity is critical to all dressage movements and is of paramount importance in the design of the dressage saddle.

To apply the leg aid effectively, while maintaining the suppleness of the small of the back and the upward forward push of the pelvis, a long leather is necessary, allowing the pointed knee to be placed farther down the saddle with the lower leg drawn somewhat to the rear.

The position of the bars in the dressage saddle, which govern the placement of the body weight, has therefore to be to the rear of what is desirable in the jumping saddle, or even in the all-purpose saddle.

It is permissible for that reason to employ a tree with a vertical head, although many modern dressage saddles are made on the ubiquitous quarter cut-back tree. In some versions an extended bar is used which, because of its length, places the position of the leather just that much farther to the rear. (It is important in a dressage saddle, and also in an all-purpose saddle, that there should be no artificial narrowing of the tree at the waist. Carried to excess this practice, although it prevents the upper thighs being spread, makes it difficult for the rider to adopt a deep seat well down in the saddle.)

The flap and panel, with its light front roll, follows the line of the pommel and is usually cut in a slight forward curve just in advance of the vertical. Some saddles go to the extreme, cutting the flap line virtually behind the vertical, but there is no real advantage

in this exaggerated shape and much to be said against it, for it encourages all but the most expert to be thrown off the seat bones and onto the fork.

The tree may be rigid or of the more usual spring variety. A deep seat is necessary, but it should not be so short as to encase the rider and prohibit his movement.

So that nothing but the light flap and sweat flap should come between the rider's leg and the horse, dressage saddles are frequently fitted with extra-long

girth straps which are fastened to a special short girth, the girth buckles then being placed below the level of the horse's elbow where they are well out of the rider's way. In some instances, dressage riders use stirrup leathers which are adjusted by means of a buckle, covered with a light leather guard, which is placed just above the eye of the stirrup iron instead of being on the stirrup bar where it can be felt by the rider's thigh even with recessed bars.

The show saddle has no such

considerations for the rider's seat and position. It is designed almost entirely for the purpose of showing off the horse to the best advantage.

In its extreme form it is built on a nearly flat rigid tree fitted with either a vertical or cut-back pommel. The panel is often of the "skeleton" type, a half-panel (without any forward supporting rolls) which is sometimes called a Rugby panel. (It is so named because this type of panel, which allows the leg to be very close to

The dressage saddle (left) has a light flap that follows the line of the pommel. The show saddle (right) has a straight flap.

the horse, was first introduced by polo players at Rugby, England, once a center for the game.)

The panel is made of thin felt so that, in conjunction with the flat seat, there is no interruption of the natural line of the horse's back.

The flap is either cut vertically or just in advance of that line, but sometimes it may be cut to the rear of the vertical. The reason for the flap being so straight is to show off the excellence of the horse's shoulder or to make an average shoulder, or even a not

very good one, look better than it is in reality. Not for nothing is this known as the "Saddle of Deception."

The positioning and use of the girth straps on a show saddle is a matter of some importance. Usually, the saddle is fitted with three straps on each side. If it is thought necessary to have the saddle sit farther to the rear, thus accentuating the appearance of length in the shoulder and front, the two forward girth straps are used. If the saddle needs to be

brought a little to the front the girth is fitted to the center and the rear straps.

The saddle can be made to sit even farther back if a point strap is used. This is an additional girth strap fitted from beneath the point of the tree. Used in conjunction with the first of the ordinary girth straps, it affects the saddle's position quite materially.

This type of show saddle persists in the classes for children's show ponies and its American equivalent, the 'cow mouth' (a

very full cut-back) flat seated show saddle, is still *de rigeur* in the saddle-seat classes for the gaited horses such as the American Saddlebred. Otherwise, there is an increasing tendency in the English show ring to use the less extreme types of dressage saddle or what is known as the working hunter saddle, in effect an all-purpose saddle with a slightly straighter flap and panel than usual.

Such saddles are more comfortable and they position the rider more correctly and effectively.

BRIDLES & BITS

Despite there being a great many types of bit, all can be classified under one or another of five main bitting groups. These are: snaffle; Weymouth or double bridle; Pelham; gag; and the family of bitless bridles which are frequently described, incorrectly, as hackamores.

There are numerous variations on the basic snaffle, which represents the simplest form of control, but the principal differences occur between the mullen mouthpiece and the jointed mouthpiece, and in the type of bit ring employed.

The mildest of all the bits is that with a half-moon or mullen mouthpiece made of rubber (the least severe), nylon, vulcanite or metal. Somewhat stronger is the jointed mouthpiece which exerts what is called a "nutcracker" action across the lower jaw. The effect is mitigated if a spatula or ring replaces the central joint, as with the French bradoon. It is made more severe by the use of bits incorporating rollers set either across or around the mouthpiece, or by those which have serrated or twisted mouths.

Bit rings are either 'loose' or 'fixed' as in the eggbutt and most of the cheek snaffles. The former, in which the ring runs through a hole in the butt-end of the mouthpiece, allows increased movement within the mouth which is believed to encourage salivation and the subsequent relaxation of the lower jaw. The fixed rings obviate the possibility of the lips being pinched.

The action of the snaffle varies according to the position of the head and neck. In the young horse, who may be expected to carry the neck low and extended, the action is upward against the corners of the lips.

In the later stages of training, when the head is held somewhat in advance of the vertical, the action is divided between the lips and the bars of the lower jaw. (The bars of the mouth are the sensitive areas of gum between the molars and the incisor teeth.) As the head approaches the vertical carriage in the advanced horse the bit acts increasingly across the lower jaw.

The addition of a drop noseband goes some way toward altering the complexion of the bit. As well as closing the mouth and preventing any evasion of the bit's action, it causes (as a result of pressure on the nose in response to the rein action) a lowering of the head and a retraction of the nose which brings the bit increasingly into play across the jaw.

The most complex bridle in its action, and the most sophisticated, is the Weymouth or double bridle. Two mouthpieces are employed, a light bradoon, having the action of the snaffle but used in an upward effect against the lips, and a curb bit fitted with a curb chain.

The mouthpiece of the curb is made with a tongue port at its center. As a result the tongue, which would normally lie at least in part over the bars, rises into the port allowing the bearing surfaces of the mouth to act directly on the latter. The action is downward to the rear and supported by pressure exerted on the poll.

This latter occurs when the curb assumes its working angle of about 45 degrees in the mouth. The eyes of the bit, attached to the bridle cheekpieces, are then moved forward on an arc and consequently transmit downward pressure on the poll through the crownpiece. At the same time the curb chain tightens in the curb groove, causing a relaxation of the lower jaw and a retraction of the nose. Using a double bridle a skillful rider can *suggest* a head carriage with far greater *finesse* than with any other bridling arrangement.

The severity of the curb bit is governed by the length of the cheek; the longer the cheek the greater is the possible leverage. The longer the cheek above the mouthpiece the greater will be the pressure exerted on the poll and vice versa. A deep port allows a greater degree of direct pressure on the bars. A shallow one or a plain mullen mouth removes much of the pressure from the bars to the tongue, which can be an advantage in the case of a horse with very sensitive, thinly covered bars.

These points apply equally to the Pelham, which is usually made with a mullen mouthpiece but can be fitted with a ported one. The Pelham, however, seeks to obtain much the same result as the Weymouth by using two reins with one mouthpiece. In theory this is hardly possible, but in practice many horses go well in this type of bit, probably because the action is soft and definite.

Fitted with a port mouth and a cheek of reasonable length, the Pelham can give good results in the hands of an experienced rider.

The gag bit is really no more than an extension of the snaffle group. The cheekpieces, either of rounded leather or cord, pass through aligned holes in the bit rings. Pressure on the rein causes the mouthpiece to be raised up in the mouth and as a result the head is lifted. That is the principle involved and the bit does increase the rider's control, particularly on a strong horse bearing down on the hand. Nonetheless, it could be argued that the upward action of the bit produces a corresponding and contradictory downward pressure on the poll. For this reason, among others, it is advisable to fit two reins to this bridle, riding on the direct rein until it is necessary to operate the gag rein.

A bitless bridle acts purely upon the nose, pressure being applied through cheekpieces of various designs and severity. It can work very well in skillful hands or when a mouth injury makes conventional bitting impossible.

Its origin is with the infinitely more sophisticated hackamore system of the Western horseman. This employs a progression of

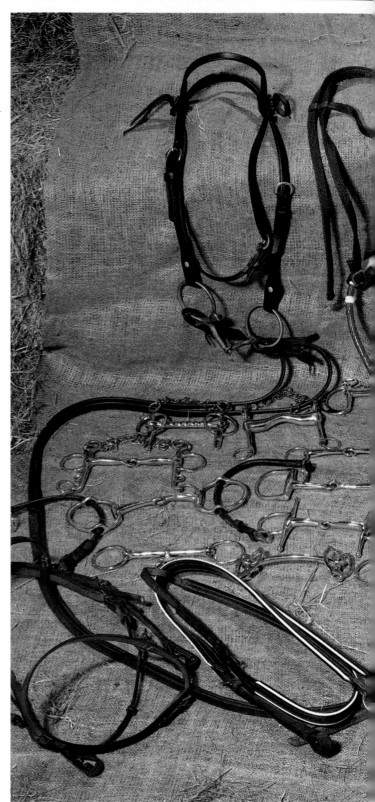

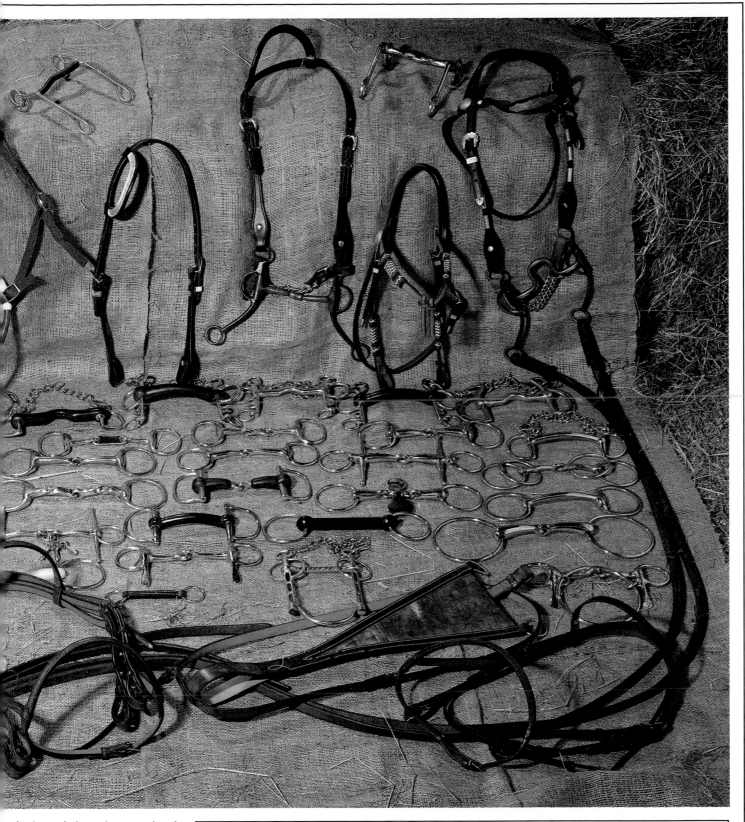

finely balanced nosebands (bosals), each one lighter than its predecessor, and culminates in the potentially severe spade or curb bit. The horse is virtually mouthed from his nose and the finished Western horse can be ridden in complicated maneuvers at speed in a light curb bridle used with a floating, or looping, rein. It could be argued, with some justification, that the method is far closer to the original "classical" concept than that now practiced in Europe.

Bridles (top of picture): from left to right — bridle with snaffle bit; nylon bridle with bosal; show bridle; bridle with shank snaffle; show bridle; bridle with high ported curb. Bits: top row — short cheek Liverpool; fixed cheek dressage Weymouth; Kimblewick; vulcanite Kimblewick; rubber covered Pelham; short cheek Pelham; vulcanite Pelham; Kimblewick. Row two — jointed Pelham; Weymouth bradoon; Dr Bristol; French snaffle; eggbutt snaffle; mullen Kimblewick. Row three — Cheltenham gag; Myers D-snaffle; twisted eggbutt snaffle; rubber covered D-ring snaffle; Fulmer; Wilson loose ring, with a mullen eggbutt snaffle below it. Row four — full cheek eggbutt snaffle; full cheek snaffle with players; vulcanite D-ring mullen; loose ring tongue layer, with a loose ring rubber snaffle below it. Bottom row — loose ring Barmouth with players; in-hand mullen with horseshoe cheeks; apple scented plastic loose ring snaffle; half spoon eggbutt snaffle; nickel Liverpool with bar; loose ring racing snaffle, with a half spoon Dexter below it. Martingales: a padded martingale (with white stripe) and a bib martingale (with wedge-shaped panel).

WESTERN SADDLES

As Western folklore has it, the cowboy's most treasured possession was his saddle. If you want to ride Western today, the right choice of saddle is essential for your own comfort and that of your horse. Apart from your horse, your saddle is the most expensive piece of equipment you will buy, so it pays to take time and trouble choosing it.

There are four basic types of Western saddle – the pleasure or ranch type saddle, the cutting saddle, the roping saddle and the equitation saddle. The pleasure or ranch saddle is most suitable for general Western riding, but all Western saddles have the same basic components. These are the

tree, swell, horn, cantle, skirt, rigging and seat.

The tree has solid bars which help to prevent pressure on the horse's back, rather than the spring tree found in most English saddles, and it also distributes weight over a wider area. There are numerous styles of tree available, with variations in the height of the gullet, cantle and slope of the seat.

The idea that a Western saddle will fit any horse is a fallacy and you should be as careful in its selection as you would be in choosing an English saddle. For example, an Arabian horse, with its short back, should have a saddle with Arab bars, which will produce a shorter saddle, but one that will still have the correct length of seat for the rider. A Western saddle, like an English saddle, should have a clear channel along the spine and should not create pressure on the withers.

The swell, at the front of the saddle, can be either smooth and round, or more prominent, which helps lock the thigh in position and gives more security. The horn on a working saddle needed to be strong enough to secure a calf by dallying (wrapping) a rope around it. However, most riding saddles today do not carry such big, high horns and they are unnecessary in an all-purpose saddle.

The seat of your saddle can be of smooth leather or suede and the cantle low, medium or high. Again, traditional saddles had very high cantles and deep seats to give a great deal of support to the rider. When roping a calf, the high cantle also provided a rest for the rope, rather than the rider's thigh. A high cantle makes mounting and dismounting more difficult and today, most ranch saddles have a medium cantle.

The skirt may be square-edged or rounded, according to personal preference, and the rigging, to which the cinch (girth) is attached, can be in several positions. Full rigging is positioned directly below the swell; seven-eighths, which is commonly used, is slightly farther back, then the three-quarters and finally the center position, which is rarely used.

Saddles may be made of plain leather, stamped leather in either floral patterns or basketweave, or, in more expensive styles, hand tooled leather.

The stirrup leathers are attached to a slot in the tree and covered by the fenders which give protection to the rider's leg. Stirrups may be plain or leather covered and should be wide enough to comfortably accommodate the rider's foot.

The four basic types of saddle have different features to make them suitable for particular tasks.

The roping saddle is extremely heavy and robustly made to take the strain of calf roping. Intended purely for competition riding, it would be unsuitable for general riding because it is designed to be as immovable as possible. The roping competitor is timed from the moment he leaves the chute, through roping his calf, dismounting and tying up the animal. To avoid any possibility of catching the competitor's foot, or causing a drag on the stirrups, these are a heavy, box-type design with wide, stiff fenders. Thus the roping saddle severely restricts the rider's leg and seat aids, due to its sheer weight and rigidity.

The cutting saddle is another specialized saddle, designed for cow cutting competitions, and is in many ways the opposite of the roping saddle. It has very much lighter stirrup leathers, with oxbow stirrups which are designed to prevent the foot from slipping out when it is thrust home.

The stirrup bar is curved to hold the foot, since a lost stirrup could be disastrous in a cutting competition, but this type of stirrup obviously should not be used for general riding.

The horse turns fast and low to the ground in cutting competitions, and the rider is permitted to hold the horn for support and to push his weight back, thus the horn on a cutting saddle is taller and thinner than on other Western saddles. The seat is generally flat, to allow the rider freedom of movement. Most riders "read" the cow as well as the horse does, so are constantly anticipating where the cow will go and simultaneously following the movement of the horse.

Unlike a roping saddle, a cutting saddle can conveniently be used for general riding and many riders appreciate its lightness and freedom of movement.

The pleasure saddle, which is commonly used for general riding and pleasure horse competitions, is a lightweight saddle, about 36 to 38 pounds in weight. It should have a slight, but not high rise to the front of the seat and the cantle should not be too high.

The ranch saddle is a plainer, more workmanlike version of the same design, with a stronger horn to allow a rope to be dallied around it, but still allowing plenty of freedom of movement to the rider. There are many variations on the same theme, for example reining saddles, which may have a flat seat or a slight rise, but at this point personal preference is the main criterion.

Finally, a saddle to be avoided for general riding is the equitation saddle, a design that came into fashion for young riders in equitation classes. A variation of the pleasure saddle, it has a deep seat, but a high rise in front which tends to lock the rider too far back in the saddle, and although it creates an attractive appearance, it curtails the effective use of the seat and leg aids.

Four Western saddles. Top left is a 'Billy Cook' cutting saddle, and to its right is a 'Double R' ranch/roping saddle. The two saddles below them are both pleasure/show saddles, a 'Circle Y' on the left and a 'Double R' on the right.

LONG DISTANCE SADDLES

The main criterion which determines the design of saddles for long distance or endurance riding is the amount of time for which they are in use. This may be anything up to twenty-four hours at a time and, obviously, an ill-fitting or damaged saddle would have far greater adverse effect on the endurance horse than on a horse wearing it for an hour or two. In addition, an endurance saddle must spread the load over the horse's back as effectively as possible with no uneven pressure.

Another effect of a badly fitting saddle is to restrict the horse's freedom of movement, as he tries to compensate for the discomfort. In endurance competition it is essential that nothing should impede the horse's way of going, as the stress applied when one area of the body continually has to compensate for pain in another area will ultimately cause an injury, if not permanent damage.

Many riders use an ordinary all-purpose saddle for long distance riding and this can be satisfactory, provided the design does not place excess local pressure on the withers. The endurance rider spends most of his time out of the saddle, his weight being carried

down through his legs to the stirrups, so it is particularly important that the front of the saddle does not bear down on the withers.

A well-fitting saddle should not require the addition of a saddle pad. However, for long distance work, where there is pressure on the horse's back over a prolonged period of time, some extra protection is advisable. The "cool back" type of pad is ideal, as are sheepskin and the modern synthetic fabrics. Thin cotton, or anything which is likely to wrinkle, and materials which do not absorb the horse's sweat, are unsuitable.

Specialized endurance saddles are made to many different designs in the various endurance riding countries, but one feature they all share is the effort to distribute the weight carried evenly over the horse's back and this is achieved by means of extended panels. The length of these panels varies from saddle to saddle and care must be taken, if you have a short-backed horse, that the panels are not so long that they extend over his loins, which is the weakest part of the back.

In the United States, lighter

weight Western saddles are often used and another old favorite is the McClellan saddle, though neither are ideal for modern endurance riding.

In Britain, efforts have been made to introduce specialized saddles and three distinct patterns are available from different manufacturers.

First on the scene was the Paragon, from John Goodwin International Ltd, tested by endurance riders and combining the features of Western saddles and British cavalry saddles. The Paragon is a substantial saddle, strongly made, with long flaps, a high cantle and a rigid, deeply padded seat for additional comfort when spending long hours in the saddle.

However, many riders felt the weight of the Paragon to be a drawback and John Goodwin has now produced the Paladin, which weighs in at just under $11\frac{1}{2}$ pounds and incorporates the same features for comfort and durability as the Paragon, though placing the rider's weight slightly farther forward.

The Endurance–LDR by the Equestrian Products Innovation Company Ltd, represents the

fruits of extensive research to build exactly the kind of saddle needed by endurance riders. Several amendments have been made to improve upon the original design and this saddle now has the fans integral to the tree, which is specially designed to allow a good riding posture, plus comfort, without loss of contact with the horse – a frequent problem with saddles intended for all day riding.

There is a high cantle, to increase support and security, but the pommel has been lowered, which improves comfort and allows the rider to get his weight forward when riding up steep hills. The cutback head, high gullet and military-style panels are designed to reduce localized pressure while maximizing weight distribution over the horse's back. Other features include nonstretch, individually mounted girth straps and recessed stirrup bars. Stirrups can be hung in the conventional manner, or underneath the saddle flap to avoid pinching the rider's calf.

There are ample D-rings for the attachment of essential equipment and the saddle is available in the usual sizes in narrow, standard

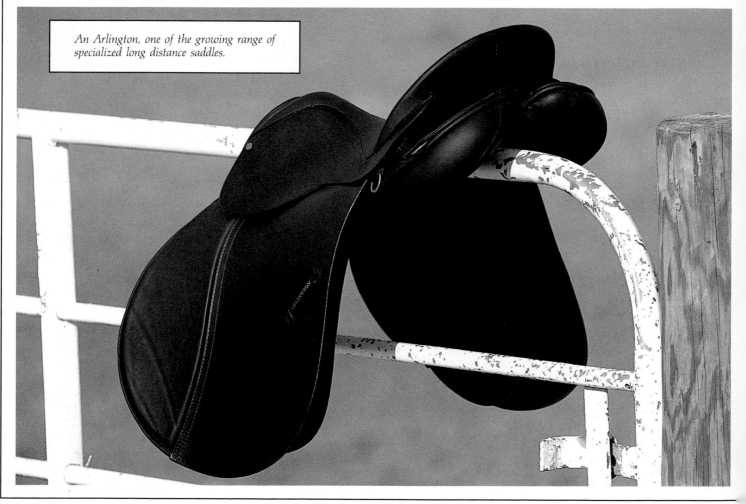

An Arlington, one of the growing range of specialized long distance saddles.

The Paragon is a substantial saddle with a deeply padded seat to maximize the comfort of the rider.

and broad fittings. This saddle has been used by top riders in the famous Tevis Cup ride in California and has won numerous saddlery awards.

The third British saddle is the Glenn Hellman lightweight (less than 9 pounds) long distance saddle, the only British-made long distance saddle based on a rigid tree, as used by top British rider Valerie Long, on her Arab stallion Tarim. A rigid tree, according to designer Glenn Hellman, causes

less friction than a spring tree – although it may be less comfortable for the rider – as it moves less on the horse's back. These saddles are completely hand made, the trees being fashioned individually to suit the horse. The removable panels are made of felt, as are the pigskin-covered flaps. There are no knee rolls, the entire design maximizing contact with the horse and encouraging a forward position.

The growth of the sport is

encouraging new developments in saddle design every year and there are one or two other British designs, notably in synthetic materials, plus many produced on the continent and in the United States. The American style lightweight endurance saddle is based on the Western pattern, but with a far less cumbersome design. Traditional Western saddles have three major drawbacks for long distance riding. They are heavy, they extend too far over the

horse's back and the stirrups are often stiff and hamper the rider's leg movement.

Americans tend to favor string girths, while in Britain the foam padded, cotton backed variety is popular. A major problem for endurance riders is the amount of time spent with the weight out of the saddle, with resultant pressure on the balls of the feet. An attempt is now being made to overcome this in America, by a spring-loaded stirrup design.

BASIC TRAINING EQUIPMENT

Principal among the items of equipment used in the early dismounted schooling of the horse is the lunge cavesson. The padded nosepiece, which has to fit very closely, carries three swivelling rings, one on the nose and one on each side. It may also be fitted with additional dees. The crownpiece is kept in place by a cheek strap which when correctly placed prevents the former from being pulled uncomfortably across the eye. It provides the trainer with a very powerful means of control should it be necessary.

The second item of lunge equipment is the lunge line, which is usually attached to the center of the three nose rings. It is most often made from tubular cotton webbing and may be as long as 35 feet. Tubular cotton web is strong and less likely to cause burns should it be pulled through the hand. (Nylon is sometimes used for lunge lines but is not as satisfactory. It has great tensile strength, but it makes the rein too light and is a very abrasive material which can cut the hands.)

The lunge line can be fastened either with a buckle and billet or a strong snaphook. Both fastenings should be swivel mounted to prevent the line being twisted.

The lunge whip, which acts as an extension of the trainer's arm and is used to encourage the horse to go forward into the cavesson and rein, is an essential. It is never used to hit the horse, but it must be long enough to reach him. For that reason the thong and lash need to be at least 7 feet long. Nylon whips are usually the most satisfactory as they are light and well-balanced – both important considerations.

Prudent trainers provide themselves with a pair of gloves, in case the rein is pulled through the hand, and insist on the young horse wearing protective boots on all four legs. Young horses, undeveloped physically and lacking coordination, are very likely to sustain knocks while being worked in a circle.

Initially, this is all the equipment which is required, but once the horse has learned to circle quietly in either direction the training has to be extended, and this involves the use of side reins, a body roller to act as a point of attachment and possibly a crupper also.

A schooling roller, preferably of strong leather, needs to be well padded on either side of the withers, so that it does not rub, and should, ideally, adjust on both sides for the sake of convenience and correctness of fit. It should have three large rings on each side, the lowest being placed halfway down the body. This allows for the side reins to be placed at different heights as appropriate to the horse's level of schooling. A ring in the center of the pads at the rear is necessary if a crupper is to be used.

A crupper helps to keep the roller in place and the addition of a breast girth for the same reason is also helpful and will obviate any need for the roller to be fastened too tightly.

Side reins, and in some respects the presence of the crupper, too,

help the horse to acquire a balanced outline and carriage. They should not be used, however, to force the carriage of head and neck by being adjusted tightly. The ideal is for the side reins to show a slight curve when the horse is in motion.

Many side reins are made with an inset of elastic or with rubber inserts so that when attached to a bit there is a "give-and-take" action. There is a danger, however, of the "take" part causing the horse to evade the bit by drawing back and behind it. For this reason many trainers, including those at the Spanish Riding School in Vienna, use plain leather reins.

The use of side reins, and the "making" of the mouth, involves the horse in wearing a bit. Very often this will be a straight bar "mouthing" bit fitted with "keys" at its center. The object is to encourage the horse to make saliva and relax his lower jaw, which he does by playing with the "keys." Once more, however, there is a danger of the horse coming behind the bit by retracting the mouth, whereas the real objective is for him to seek and maintain contact with his bit.

It is probably advisable, however, in the early stages to fit a mullen mouth bit rather than a jointed one. A bit of this construction, if properly fitted, prevents the horse from getting his tongue over the mouthpiece, a serious evasion that may be difficult to cure.

As the training progresses the horse may be driven in long reins. This method allows the trainer to work the horse in changes of direction and to accustom him to the simple rein aids, including those for the changes of pace, the halt and the reinback. It is considered by many to be an essential element in the "mouthing" of the young horse.

Long reins are very similar to lunge lines and about the same length. In the so-called English method, the inside rein, when the horse is working in a circle or in part of one, passes from the bit ring through the dee on the side of the roller and then to the trainer's hand. The opposite rein passes through the roller dee in the same way but is carried around the hindquarters before returning to the trainer. The horse can be worked in a circle or can be driven directly from the rear.

There are other methods of long reining. The French, for instance, use a driving collar, taking the reins from the mouth through the hame terrets and then downward through the lower dee on the roller. The reins then pass to the trainer who drives the horse forward and into the bit from a position directly behind the hindquarters. The Danish manner, in which the reins pass through the terrets of a driving pad, allows the horse to be driven either in a circle or straight forward and is the most flexible method for the skilled trainer.

In the Spanish Riding School the trained horse is shown in long reins passing directly from the bit to the trainer's hands, the trainer standing behind and close to the horse's hindquarters.

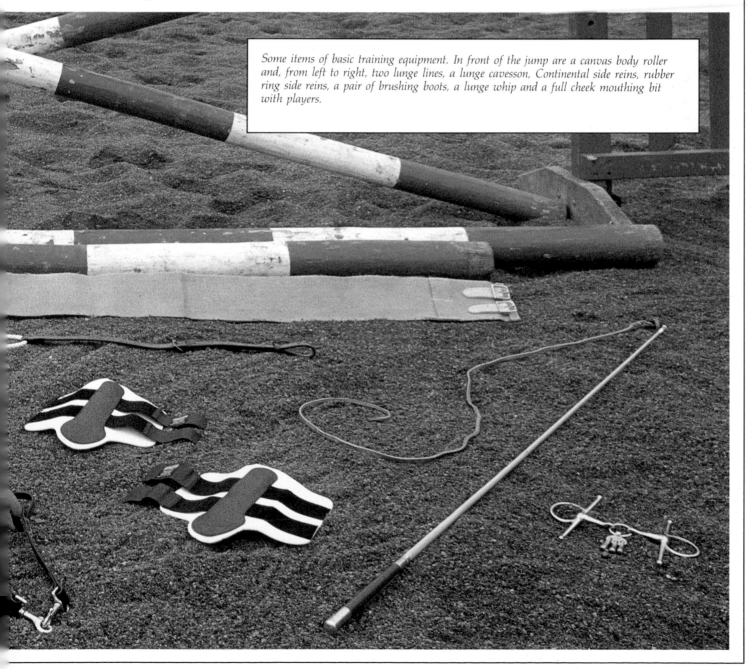

Some items of basic training equipment. In front of the jump are a canvas body roller and, from left to right, two lunge lines, a lunge cavesson, Continental side reins, rubber ring side reins, a pair of brushing boots, a lunge whip and a full cheek mouthing bit with players.

DRIVING HARNESS AND VEHICLES

The growing popularity of driving, both for pleasure and in competitions, has led to a corresponding growth in the production of vehicles and harness, and to the introduction of new materials and technologies.

A set of harness has two purposes: to allow the horse to pull the vehicle efficiently and comfortably, and to allow the whip (the correct name for the driver) to control the horse. It is vital for both these purposes that the harness fits perfectly (all sets of harness have a small amount of adjustment) and is strong enough not to come apart under stress.

Leather is the traditional material for harness, and is essential for showing and in the Presentation phase of combined driving. Its advantages are its good looks, strength and ability to absorb sweat, and its suppleness, which means it won't rub the horse. Its disadvantages are that in order to be smart, strong and supple it must be properly cared for, which can be quite a time-consuming chore, and it is relatively expensive.

Over recent years alternative materials have been tried, and there are several companies manufacturing harness in webbing or coated nylon. The advantages are that they are strong, very easy to clean and relatively inexpensive. The disadvantages are that they are less supple and absorbent than leather and do not look as good. Although not suitable for showing, this type of harness is ideal for beginners, for exercising and, in particular, for cross country driving, where everything is likely to get caked in mud.

The parts of a set of harness are shown in the diagram. The traction is transmitted from the horse's shoulders to the vehicle through the collar, hames and the traces, which are attached to hooks on the front of the vehicle. Some harness sets have a "breast collar," which is cheaper and easier to fit than the full collar shown here, but not as good when pulling heavy weights.

The shafts, which merely keep the horse going in a straight line in front of the vehicle, are supported by the pad or saddle. This is held in place by the girth, crupper and back strap, and it carries the back band to which is attached the tugs that actually carry the shafts, and the belly band which stops the shafts from going up in the air.

The breeching — strapped to the shafts, through dees to stop it

moving along them — allows the horse to brake the vehicle by "sitting" in the breeching to hold it back. The horse is controlled by means of the bridle, bit and reins, which are very similar to those used for riding, except that the bridle has blinkers so the horse can't see the moving wheels, different bits are preferred and the reins are longer.

The harness required for driving a pair of horses (two horses side by side), a tandem (two horses, one in front of the other) or a team (two pairs of horses, one in front of the other) is basically the same, with minor alterations to allow for different connections to the vehicle and different arrangements of the reins.

There are many types of driving vehicle, traditional and modern, two-wheeled and four-wheeled. Traditional vehicles, either originals or reproductions, are used for showing and presentation. They can be divided into five main groups — governess carts, gigs, dog carts, phaetons and wagonettes and brakes — although there is a good deal of variation within each group.

Governess carts are usually two-wheeled, and are the cheapest traditional vehicles to be found. They have enclosed bodies with seats running lengthwise and facing in, and are entered by a low step and a door at the rear. Because of the rather precarious and uncomfortable driving position, and the difficulty of getting out in an emergency, they should only be used with a very quiet horse and an experienced whip. Also, they rarely do well in show classes, as they are not considered very elegant.

The most elegant and popular type of vehicle for a single horse is the gig. Gigs have two wheels, usually a forward-facing seat to accommodate the whip and one passenger, and shafts mounted level with the floor and outside the body. Onto these basics are built many styles of body.

Dog carts can be either two- or four-wheeled, the two-wheeled carts being used for a single horse or a tandem and the four-wheeled being used with shafts for a single or tandem or with a pole for a pair or a team. Back to back with the forward-facing seats for the whip and one passenger, there is a backward-facing seat for two more passengers.

Phaetons all have four wheels and forward-facing seats for the whip and one passenger, but apart

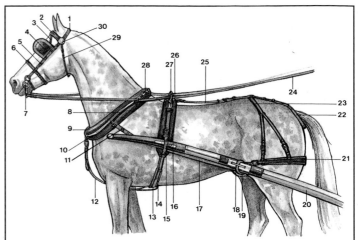

1 headpiece; 2 browband; 3 blinker strap; 4 blinker; 5 cheekpiece; 6 noseband; 7 bit; 8 hames; 9 collar; 10 bottom hame strap; 11 hame tug; 12 false martingale; 13 girth; 14 belly band; 15 tug; 16 back band; 17 tug stop; 18 trace; 19 breeching dee; 20 shaft; 21 breeching; 22 crupper; 23 loin strap; 24 rein; 25 back strap; 26 saddle; 27 terret; 28 top hame strap; 29 throatlatch; 30 rosette.

RIGHT Leather harness must be properly cared for.
FAR RIGHT Blinkers stop the horse from seeing the moving wheels.

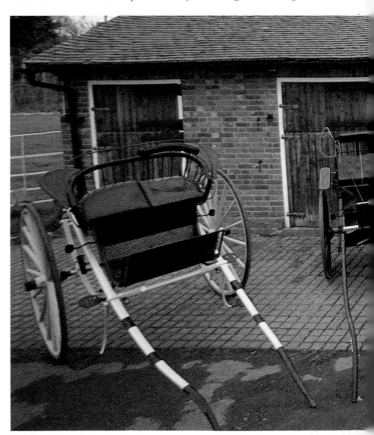

from this they can vary enormously from low, elegantly curved vehicles for ladies to big, robust vehicles for men. They are very popular, and original vehicles are now very expensive, but many modern versions are available. They are particularly suitable for weddings.

The distinction between wagonettes and brakes (or breaks)

has become somewhat blurred. Both are four-wheeled vehicles having a raised box seat for the whip and behind this, two seats set lengthwise facing each other, the larger vehicles perhaps having additional seats facing forward/backward (reversible) as well. They are entered by a rear door or, in the larger ones, by a door near the front. The smaller vehi-

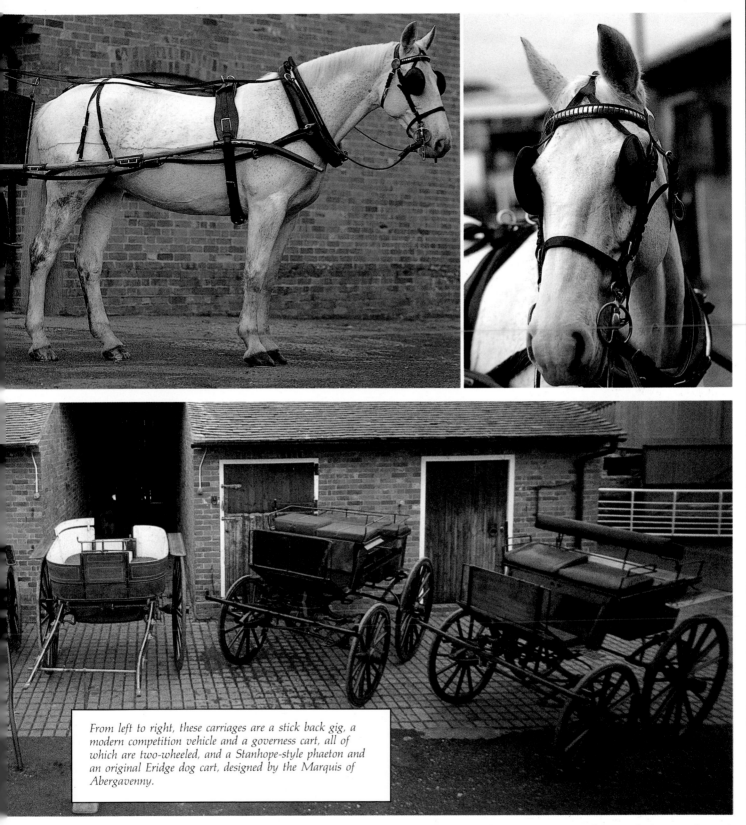

From left to right, these carriages are a stick back gig, a modern competition vehicle and a governess cart, all of which are two-wheeled, and a Stanhope-style phaeton and an original Eridge dog cart, designed by the Marquis of Abergavenny.

cles look smart for Private Driving with a pair or team.

The increased interest in competitive driving has added impetus to the production of vehicles made in modern materials, using modern technologies and often of somewhat unorthodox appearance. A steel frame gives strength and forms the outline of the vehicle, and the metal body panels are bolted on, making them easy to replace if damaged. Wheels are made of wood, steel or aluminum, or a combination of two of these. Most vehicles have either drum or disc brakes, and the suspension, too, owes a good deal to the horseless carriage, the old-fashioned springs being replaced by modern systems incorporating shock absorbers.

For competitive driving it is possible to use one vehicle for all phases, smart enough for use in the Presentation phase yet tough enough to cope with the Marathon. Alternatively, a traditional vehicle can be used for Presentation and perhaps Dressage, while for the remaining phases a more unorthodox modern vehicle can be used, which instead of a rear seat has a platform and "grab handles" for the grooms.

Your choice of vehicle depends on several factors — your personal preferences, how much you can afford, the type(s) of driving you intend to do, and the size and weight of your horse. It is, however, most important that the vehicle fits your horse correctly and is comfortable for him to pull.

HARNESS RACING SULKIES

Harness racers are bred selectively for speed and stamina, the Standardbred epitomizing the ideal. Nevertheless, to attain the top speeds of which the individual horse is capable it must be shod so as to achieve the maximum length of stride and perfect synchronization between the pairs of legs, whether used diagonally or laterally. The harness must be strong enough, but very light and carefully designed so that no restriction or discomfort is caused. Great attention has to be given to the bitting arrangements and those devices used to fix the head directly to the front. Horses that carry the head to one side or the other cannot reach maximum speed and are more than likely to interfere (knock one leg or foot into another) when moving at 35 mph to 45 mph.

Pacers are equipped with carefully adjusted hobbles to keep them steady and to encourage them to maintain the gait. The pacing gait is a natural one, inbred in most of the Standardbred strains, and it is in no way forced by the use of the hobbles. Hobbles came into use soon after their invention in 1885 by one John Browning, a harness-racing buff who earned his living as a railway conductor.

Shadow rolls, of various shapes, plus blinkers, overchecks, martingales and nosebands, are all more or less critical to the performance, depending upon the

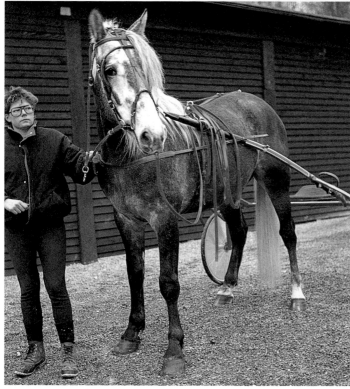

idiosyncrasies of the individual, but the most important piece of the harness racer's equipment is the sulky itself.

The sulky is a light, two-wheel vehicle built to carry one person seated between the wheels. It has been suggested that the origin of the name was first concerned with the driver's antisocial tendency to prefer his own company. Be that as it may, the sulky certainly derived from a heavy, wooden-wheeled vehicle built with strong crossbars on which the driver supported his feet. In Colonial times it was driven over rough ground that would have been impassable to less robust vehicles.

The first lightweight sulkies, built with a pair of very large wheels, appeared in 1804 when races, or "brushes," between individuals on roadways (and later on rough tracks) were becoming the fashion of the day. They brought about an increase in speed, but it was not until the 1890s that the great advance in the design of the sulkies, and a far more notable increase in speed, took place.

Bicycles were then being fitted with smaller, pneumatic tires and at about the same time the ball-bearing wheel was being perfected in England.

The first sulky to combine both was made in England, where, in

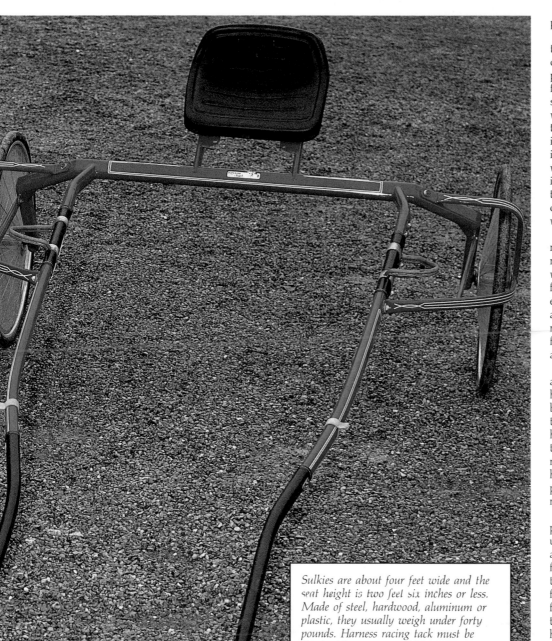

Sulkies are about four feet wide and the seat height is two feet six inches or less. Made of steel, hardwood, aluminum or plastic, they usually weigh under forty pounds. Harness racing tack must be fitted with great care (left).

persuaded to look to the front.

The shadow roll is no more than a noseband generously covered in a roll of sheepskin. Its purpose is to prevent the horse from lowering his head and seeing shadows or marks on the track which might make him shy, break the gait as a result and possibly interfere with the other horses. It is used most commonly on pacers, who are considered to be more inclined to spookiness than trotters, possibly, it is suggested, on account of the hobbles they wear.

The adjustment of the shadow roll, as with every item of harness racing equipment, has to be made with absolute precision if it is to fulfill its purpose. It has to be exactly high enough to discourage the lowering of the head but not so high as to obscure the forward vision and affect the action.

The fitting of hobbles requires a similar accuracy. In simple terms, hobbles are padded loops joined by an adjustable horizontal strap; the loops encircle the fore and hind legs above the joint and on the same side, that is, near fore and near hind and vice versa. They are held in place by four hangers passing over the back between the neck to the hindquarters.

The straps, nowadays made of plastic and nylon, stretch a little in use and therefore have to be adjusted constantly. If they are fitted too high they will restrict the muscles at the top of the leg, if fastened too tightly they limit the freedom of the stride; if they are too loose, on the other hand, the horse, missing the usual slight degree of support, will begin to roll in his gait.

Harness horses are expected to take a fairly strong hold, which is acceptable enough, but if a horse pulls so hard as to make control difficult it is necessary to use some form of restraint. An overcheck rein, running up the face and back to the harness saddle, will usually provide a solution and, carefully adjusted, allows the head to be positioned to the greatest advantage. Otherwise, there is a range of overcheck bits either used as auxiliaries to the driving snaffle or incorporated into its design.

Both trotters and pacers can suffer serious injury from feet striking into the limbs at speed. To protect the horses against the effects of striking there is a large selection of ingeniously designed and accurately constructed protective boots.

fact, there was no harness-racing tradition, and was imported to the United States by a veteran driver, Budd Doble. It was first driven, to hoots of derision, at a Detroit track in 1892, the driver being Ed Geers, a harness-racing man who was also an avid cyclist. He silenced the critics by winning his race decisively and setting a new track record. The pneumatic-tired sulky had arrived and the records began to topple.

No further improvements were made to the racing sulky until the mid-1970s when Joe King, an aeronautical engineer, perfected the so-called modified rig. It was made of lightweight steel instead of wood and fitted with shorter, straighter shafts. It weighed around 30 pounds and the number of recorded 2-minute miles increased dramatically – in 1974 the number was 685; two years later, when the modified rig was in full production, it had risen to 1849.

The basic driving bridle is an open one (one without blinkers), and is fitted with one or other of the wide range of harness snaffles available. The bit is frequently fitted with guards to prevent soring the mouth and a number are made with sliding mouth-pieces, and so on, which dissuade the horse from hanging to one side or the other.

Harness trainers select their tack with care and are enormously expert in the use of bits and related equipment. For the habitual offender who persists in racing with his head to one side, they will often have recourse to a head pole, fastened from the saddle pad to the bridle. Head poles are telescopic and can be adjusted to the required length.

Blinkers will also help to keep a horse straight, and one effective device on the blinker principle is the Murphy blind, which cups inward around the front of the eye. If the horse turns his head the blind obscures his vision on whatever side it is fitted and he is soon

STABLES & FITTINGS

Picture a stable in your mind's eye and what you most likely see is the image of a horse's head appearing over a Dutch door with a dark space beyond. But how should that space be arranged? Does your mental picture describe contentment — or an inadequate shack?

A stable should be of adequate size for the horse to move around, lie down and roll without injuring himself. A space of at least 10 feet × 10 feet is adequate for a pony, while for larger horses 14 feet × 12 feet is ideal, and a large stable is always useful for sick or convalescent horses, or foaling mares.

Comfortable shelter is needed, so a stable should be warm in winter, but cool in summer. For this reason, galvanized steel is not a suitable roofing material, although it is frequently used. Your stable floor should be easy to clean, without cracks or holes where urine can lie and cause unpleasant smells and ultimately more damage. Concrete is the simplest flooring for new stables and should be finished with a nonskid surface. Clay floors are warm, but are difficult to manage hygienically. Obviously, drainage is important and the floor should be graded to ease drainage, with any gulleys protected from being blocked by shavings or straw.

One of the most vital aspects of good stabling is draft-free ventilation. The combination of dusty hay or bedding and poorly ventilated accommodation is the most frequent cause of equine respiratory problems, which are all too common. There are various ways of improving the natural ventilation in existing buildings, for example, by fitting air inlets at low level in the back wall, with hoppers, fanlights or rooflights to provide high level outlets. Mechanical ventilation systems can also be used.

There are several types of stable design which provide easily managed accommodation. Traditional European-style stabling, built around a courtyard, with thick stone or brick walls and tiled or slated roofs is both attractive and practical. (In much of the United States, however, wood was and is the preferred building material.) Today, it would be advisable to raise the stable ceilings from their traditionally low level, by taking out the loft area. Hay and straw should be stored elsewhere to minimize risk of fire.

ABOVE The traditional British type of stabling is built around a courtyard, and has stone or brick walls with tile or slate roofing.

RIGHT The inside of a stable should be clean, light and well ventilated.

If you look carefully at traditional stabling, you will see rounded coins (external corners) to doorways, solid hardwood panelling and partitions which are resistant to damage from chewing or kicking, and sensibly designed mangers and hay racks, without low-level projections or dangerous edges. It makes sense to learn from the experience of those to whom the horse was an everyday means of transport or beast of burden, and to incorporate these features in modern designs in today's materials.

TOP The American barn system of stabling has stalls built on either side of a wide drive-through space.

ABOVE Stalls facing onto a stable yard. The top halves of the doors can be left open to allow the horses to look out.

Traditional stables were often built for economy of space, and although horses can be kept satisfactorily in this manner, it is not ideal for their mental well-being, especially as today's pleasure and competition horse is required to be mentally alert and interested in his work.

Stalls are generally preferred today but, even then, it is advisable for your horse to spend as much time as possible in his natural environment, which is outdoors.

Stables can be built of any suitable building materials — stone, brick, cinder block or wood — and many owners today opt for prefabricated wooden ones, which can be custom made and erected on a prepared site. Most manufacturers of this type of stabling provide a design service and will also advise on ground preparation and drainage and the laying of a suitable floor. Roofing is a matter of personal choice, or of local planning regulations. Asbestos shingles are frequently used and nowadays are available in a variety of colors. Slate or tiled roofs are attractive but, of course, more expensive. Whatever the covering, the roof ideally should be insulated for extra warmth and to prevent condensation.

In the United States, the typical barn has stalls on either side of a wide center aisle and openings at either end. The advantages of this system are that it is companionable for the horses and everything can be done indoors. The disadvantage is that if one horse catches an infection, it is very difficult to prevent it from spreading to the others.

A fresh, clean water supply must be available. Automatic drinking bowls are convenient, but they make it impossible to tell how much any individual horse is drinking and require regular maintenance. Buckets are more usual, but make sure your supply is in a central location to minimize carrying. Water pipes should be protected against freezing up.

Electricity lines must be protected from inquisitive horses who may chew them, and outlets and light switches should be placed outside boxes, out of reach of horses. Light fixtures should be the wall type, positioned at high level.

Nowadays, numerous safe and durable stable fittings can be bought quite cheaply, including mangers, hay racks, bucket holders and tie rings. Alternatively, mangers and hay racks can be built in. The important point is that there are no dangerous projections or sharp edges to catch a horse's face or legs.

Tie rings must be securely fixed so that they do not come away from the wall, should the horse pull back, while rings for attaching haynets must be high enough so that when empty the haynet does not dangle within reach of the horse's feet.

Doors are usually double, with the top half open for the horse to look out. Padlocks or bolts should be used and a kickover bolt at the bottom is convenient. Doors should open outwards and windows should not project into the stable area when open. Any glass should be protected by a metal grille.

It is better not to store tack and feed in the same room, especially if you have a boiler for barley or linseed as the steam will create a damp atmosphere which could damage your tack. However, it is useful to incorporate a sink, with a hot and cold water supply, so that equipment can be cleaned without taking it into the house.

Hay and straw should be stored slightly away from your stables and downwind so that the dust and spores are carried away. Your manure pile should be downwind, with adequate drainage, but easily accessible from the stables with your wheelbarrow — and there should be good access for removal of the manure when necessary.

HORSE VANS & TRAILERS

Once you start competing, even if only in local riding club events, you will soon need some form of transportation for your horse. The choice of vehicles is bewildering – do you opt for a trailer which you can tow behind a car you already own, or do you go for a small horse van? Once that decision is made, how do you choose among the many makes on the market?

The first thing to do is to assess your particular needs and make a list. A horse van, for example, saves you the worry of towing and may provide living accommodation where you can sleep overnight if you are away at a show or event. However, a trailer can be unhitched, freeing your towing vehicle for normal use and does not require separate licensing, or plating. Some larger trailers include living space nowadays.

The main limiting factor in the choice of a trailer is the towing capacity of your vehicle and you should take advice as to whether its curb (unloaded) weight is sufficient to cope safely with your loaded trailer.

Also, remember that a front unload trailer, with two ramps, necessarily weighs more than a rear unload model with a single ramp. The less substantial of many imported lightweight trailers are those which have been produced purely to meet the British preference for the front unload design. However, if your towing capacity is limited, a rear unload trailer could be a better choice.

Before you buy a vehicle for transporting your horse, check any legal requirements that might exist. For example, do you need a special license to drive that size vehicle? Do you need special license plates? Also, when you travel out of state, certain documents will be needed for any horse you are transporting, usually a valid negative Coggins and a health certificate from a veterinarian. Inquire well beforehand what is required.

The most important factors to consider, however, are the safety and comfort of your horse when traveling.

From the safety point of view, keep your horse van or trailer regularly serviced and properly maintained. In trailers, the floor is a particularly vulnerable area, both to wear from the horses' feet and, more dangerously, to rot from wet and urine. Modern materials and sealed rubber matting can help prevent this, but in older trailers, or those of more traditional construction, the floor should be regularly checked for safety and renewed when necessary.

Some lightweight trailers can seem unstable – a point to consider if you have horses of a nervous disposition who are reluctant loaders. The fact that a trailer is high sided, with a high center of gravity when loaded, makes features to improve stability important and most modern trailer designs have independent suspension.

The more expensive trailers on the market, using the latest technology, also have the best built-in stability features, but if you have problems with your particular make of trailer, stabilizing devices, which fit onto the towbar, are available. Also check that your vehicle's towbar is fitted at the correct height.

There are basically two kinds of trailers on the market today – those of traditional painted steel, aluminum or wood construction, and those using modern high-technology materials, which are designed for easy maintenance. In some makes the chassis and other metal parts are galvanized as a standard feature, in others, galvanizing is available as an extra. Phenolic resin-treated panelling requires no painting, and the latest trailer body designs are constructed of glass-reinforced plastic (GRP), producing extremely lightweight and airy trailers. Automatic reverse braking systems overcome the need to get out of your vehicle and make adjustments whenever you want to reverse.

If you decide to buy a horse van, your choice is even wider than if you opt for a trailer. Horse vans range from a modest two-horse size to those capable of carrying a dozen race horses. Various standard designs are available built on a variety of chassis. Even a small horse van, cleverly designed, will incorporate some means of providing human sleeping accommodation and essential living facilities, even if this means encroaching into the equine traveling area once the occupants are unloaded.

A two-horse van will usually allow both horses to travel facing forward, while a larger vehicle may have other arrangements. Horses will usually travel quite happily partitioned in a van, which obviously provides more stability than a trailer and, as a general rule, the more securely the horses are partitioned, the safer the driving.

However, some horses like to spread their legs out against the swaying motion of a trailer and if you're transporting just one horse in a double trailer, he might be happier with the partition removed. If the partition is left in, put the horse on the left side as this will help it resist the centrifugal force created by the road camber.

Many special features are available, but look for these basics: strong, safe partitions, adequate padding, a strong breast bar in trailers, adequate kicking boards, nonskid flooring, interior lighting and spring assisted ramps.

When driving a horse van or towing a trailer, the most important thing is to give yourself plenty of time to maneuver. Whenever you have to negotiate a narrow space, square the vehicle up first, think about the length of vehicle behind you, keep it straight and give plenty of signals. Use your side mirrors and don't forget to allow for overhanging trees or buildings. Give your horse a smooth ride and he won't object to travel.

The interior of a horse van or trailer should have strong, safe partitions and the floor should be surfaced with an easily cleaned, nonskid material.

If your towing capacity is limited, a rear unload trailer (top left) is a good choice. Spring assisted ramps (above left) are desirable on larger vehicles, and strong partitions (above right) are essential. Many large trailers (above) include sleeping accommodation.

CLOTHING

The rider is wearing a Christy hard hat, a How's Racesafe stock, Caldene show jacket and breeches and Lovesome leather boots. Next to her are an Owens jockey helmet, Aigle rubber boots and Regent jodhpur boots, HAC-TAC denim jodhpurs, Harry Meyer jodhpurs and Shires suede chaps.

Clothing for English riding has evolved over a long period, and by looking at the different competitive disciplines it is easily seen that, beyond the few overall safety rules (see pages 142–3), riding wear differs considerably according to the demands of the sport concerned. Hunting dress, for example, may admirably meet the needs of someone riding to hounds on a cold winter's day, but would be an impossible burden to a jockey.

For competition riding, notice what others wear in the sport and aim for a correct turnout. However, most of your riding will probably be schooling at home, or hacking, and in recent years the market for casual riding wear has expanded considerably to provide practical, comfortable clothing that really meets the needs of today's rider.

A safety-approved hard hat is, of course, essential and many riders who, in less safety conscious days, were accustomed to riding hatless, today would not even think of sitting on a horse without a properly fastened safety helmet.

The purpose of the stock or hunting tie is to protect the neck in a fall, and although this protection might be limited, it is useful to wear a stock for cross country riding. Also, if you are riding in a hot, dusty climate, a neckerchief might be useful, to keep dust out of your nose and mouth.

Sweatshirts are perfect for casual riding, worn over a shirt or T-shirt. They are warm enough for cooler days but stay comparatively cool in hot weather and bits of hay and straw do not cling to them.

Jeans, trousers that get bunched up and those with thick seams between the rider's leg and the saddle can be uncomfortable. Jodhpurs and breeches are preferable and nowadays come in many practical colors, as well as the customary light shades, and stretch denim has probably provided the toughest and most convenient wear for everyday

This Western rider is wearing a Resistol felt hat, a PanHandle Slim's shirt, Levi's jeans and Tony Lama boots. Next to him are a Resistol straw hat, a pair of Tony Lama boots and show chaps from RPM Malvern.

slipping through the stirrups, and many riders find that a pair of short yard boots are ideal footwear for activities such as exercising and schooling as well as for doing the mucking out.

Wet weather wear is a matter of personal preference. Some choose full-length raincoats, others prefer waterproof trousers or leggings. Whatever your choice, there is no shortage of styles available and the qualities of modern synthetic fabrics are constantly being improved in terms of waterproofing and of their "breathability," which allows perspiration to evaporate away. Gloves are a must in cold weather and should be either string or leather, to give the best grip on the reins.

Clothing for Western riding has also evolved over many years, and is directly descended from the essentially practical gear used by the cowboys of the Old West. For Western riding, colors should be coordinated, both for tack and the rider's dress.

A man's outfit consists of a Western style shirt, cords or jeans and, ideally, chaps, either fringed or plain edged. Gloves should be leather, not string, and a good quality hat, although expensive, will be a good investment if you want to do much showing. Women can wear brightly colored equitation outfits, matching or color-coordinated, consisting of a shirt or blouse, vest, pants and hat. Chaps, if worn, should match or complement the rest of the outfit. You should buy the best quality clothing that you can afford, but tastefulness and choosing a color combination that suits your horse are generally more important than spending a lot of money.

Good boots are essential. They should have all-leather uppers, but the soles and heels may be either leather or synthetic. The heels should be solid, not hollow (which is too weak), and the boots should have a steel insert in the arch to give extra support, and good stitching on the shaft to prevent it from sagging.

Boot decorations, toe shape and heel height are largely a matter of personal preference, but if you intend to use the boots for trail riding, where you will be spending time out of the saddle on rough ground, the boots must be tough and comfortable to walk in. Another essential for trail riding is the slicker or Western raincoat, which will cover the saddle and most of the horse's back as well as the rider, and should be stowed behind the saddle when not being worn.

TYING A STOCK

1 Put your top shirt button through the hole in the stock. Pass one end of the stock around your neck and through the slot at the back.

2 Pull the two ends forward, not too tightly.

3 Make a simple slip knot and straighten.

4 Turn the top end under and put it over your shoulder.

5 Bring the other end through the loop. Pull both ends to make the knot.

6 Hunting style: cross and pin.

Dressage: pull knot tighter, drape over and pin.

exercising and yard work.

Recently, a type of tracksuit adapted for riding has been introduced, which is comfortable and ideal for schooling your horse at home, or at an event before you change into your competition gear.

Many people find suede or leather chaps indispensable, both for warmth in winter and to protect clothing from dirt. If you find that the stirrup leathers pinch your calves when you wear short boots, but perspiration is a problem in long rubber riding boots, invest in a pair of half-chaps, which can be worn over jodhpur boots or yard boots and will protect your legs without being too hot.

Made-to-measure riding boots are the ultimate horse rider's luxury, but are best kept for important occasions. Cleaning is a time consuming chore and such boots will suffer if you continually get them wet and muddy. Rubber riding boots are more practical for general wear and during wet weather. Your footwear must have heels, to prevent your feet

HORSE CLOTHING & GROOMING KIT

With the rider outfitted and ready to go, what might the horse need, in addition to his basic tack?

Leg protection is the first thing to consider — sound limbs are essential for the working horse and his legs are always vulnerable to accident. Bandages help support the tendons and protect the legs from knocks, and are particularly useful when schooling a young or unfit horse. They must be fitted smoothly, over leg pads, from just below the knee to just above the fetlock.

Boots are easier to fit and, although they may give less support, will give good protection from injuries due to impact. Many styles are available — choose one that is well made and easy to clean.

Tendon boots are similar to brushing boots, except that they are often open fronted. Their purpose is to protect the front leg tendons, should the horse strike into himself when jumping. Over-reach boots are also advisable for jumping, although when worn for cross country work, they tend to become inverted, so the design must be chosen carefully.

For roadwork, especially with young or excitable horses, or valuable show animals, skeleton knee boots are a useful precaution.

When traveling, hock and knee boots, usually made of wool melton or felt, with leather straps or Velcro fastenings, are worn, with shipping boots or bandages and overreach boots. Traveling and stable bandages are fitted from just below the knee to just above the coronet. "All-in-one" shipping boots, which cover the leg from above the knee to the coronet, are also available.

Rugs and blankets will be used for traveling and in the stable, to keep the show horse clean and the clipped horse warm. Show horses are rugged through the early part of the year to encourage early shedding of the winter coat.

Traditional wool blankets are still the most popular choice, but there are also many excellent modern synthetic under-rugs on the market. Stable rugs, worn on their own or over blankets, are either traditional jute, lined with wool or a wool mixture and usually fastened with a single surcingle around the girth, or quilted synthetic materials, many with special thermal properties. The latter are frequently fastened by crossed surcingles, the preferred method today, which avoids the risk of putting any pressure on the horse's spine.

Finally, your horse will need a turnout, or New Zealand rug, which may be flax, cheaper canvas or, again, a modern "breathable" synthetic. The most important point is to see that the rug fits well, so that it does not rub the horse's shoulders or withers and does not slip out of place when your horse has a roll, or kicks up his heels in his pasture.

The basic grooming kit consists of various brushes and combs, plus sponges, a sweat scraper, hoof oil and a hoof pick.

The dandy brush, usually made of wood with stiff bristles, is used for the initial removal of surface dirt from the legs, feet and flanks of the horse, but is too coarse to be used on sensitive parts such as the belly, face and between the thighs. It shouldn't be used on the mane or tail, either, as it will damage the hairs.

The body brush has an oval body and short, relatively soft bristles, and a strap across the back through which you slip your hand to give you a better grip. This firm grip is essential because the brush is used with firm pressure to remove grease from the horse's coat, and using the body brush would be awkward and

tiring without the strap.

The body brush is used in conjunction with the curry comb, a square piece of wood or metal fitted with a handle and having rows of metal teeth. The curry comb is never used on the horse; its only job is to scrape the grease from the body brush. However, rubber or plastic curry combs, which are oval with concentric rows of soft teeth, can also be used directly on the horse – for removing loose hair when the horse is shedding his coat.

The water brush is like a smaller, finer version of the dandy brush. It is so called because it is used wetted with water, for laying the mane and tail neatly after brushing (or combing with a mane comb) or before braiding or bandaging.

You need at least two small sponges in your basic grooming kit, one for cleaning your horse's eyes and nostrils, the other for cleaning around his dock. These two sponges should be kept apart from each other, and the one you

use for cleaning around the dock should never be used for cleaning around the eyes and nostrils, otherwise you risk causing infection in these sensitive areas.

The sweat scraper has a curved blade which acts like a squeegee to remove excess water or sweat from the horse's coat, while the hoof pick, as its name suggests, has a curved point with which you can pick out your horse's hoofs. Once you have picked out and cleaned the hoofs, you can brush them with hoof oil. This not only

makes the hoofs look good, it also strengthens them and reduces the chance of their becoming brittle or cracked.

One other essential part of your grooming kit is a rub rag, which is sometimes used, folded into a pad, for rubbing down the horse after it has been brushed to give a final finishing touch to the grooming. The rub rag, which is a rectangular piece of (usually) linen, is also very useful for drying off the horse's ears if he comes in wet.

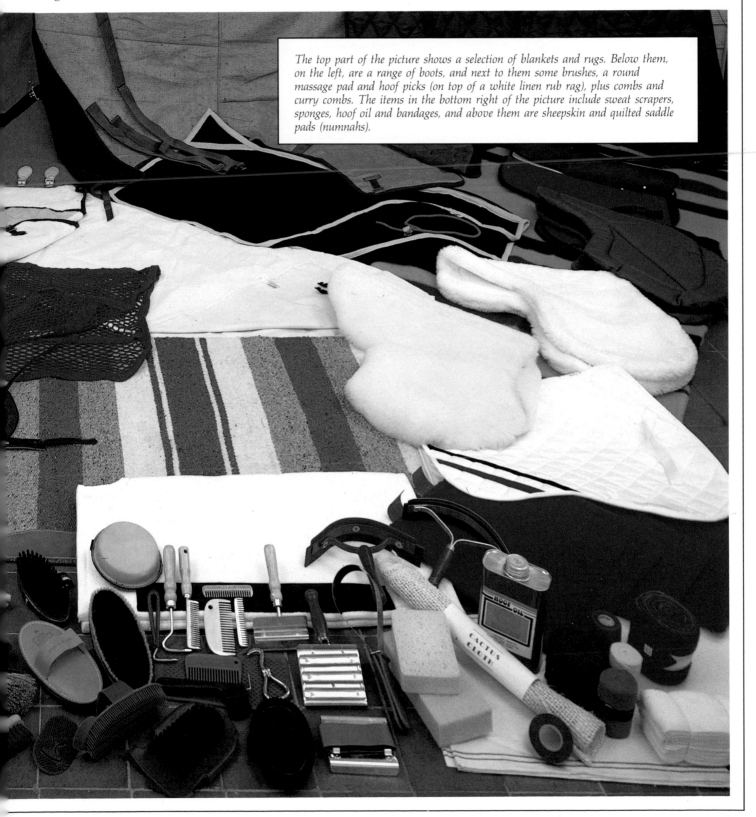

The top part of the picture shows a selection of blankets and rugs. Below them, on the left, are a range of boots, and next to them some brushes, a round massage pad and hoof picks (on top of a white linen rub rag), plus combs and curry combs. The items in the bottom right of the picture include sweat scrapers, sponges, hoof oil and bandages, and above them are sheepskin and quilted saddle pads (numnahs).

CARE &
BREEDING

"Care" is one of the many English words which have two different meanings, depending on the preposition which is used after it. For example, one can take care of something — or someone — or one can care for them, which is not the same thing. One can take care of all sorts of things one doesn't particularly like, or care for. To be pedantic, the dictionary not only confirms these two meanings, but also states that the word itself actually has two different root derivations.

To take good care of horses, it is important also to care for them as animals. Most people who own dogs or cats do so because they like one or the other, and enjoy looking after them. It is therefore sensible that only if we like horses should we own them, and take care of them; if we don't, then looking after them will seem only a burdensome chore. In fact, it can give as much pleasure as riding, which after all only occupies a small portion of the time we spend with our horses.

This is probably especially true of pony-mad children who, if given the chance, will enjoy everything to do with their ponies, such as feeding them, grooming them and taking them in and out of the pasture. They and the ponies develop feelings of companionship and mutual trust.

It is the latter which develops with the day-to-day care of the horse and which is the basis on which to build good rider-horse partnerships. Because we don't keep horses in our houses as we (mostly) do our dogs, we tend to forget that the more we are with them, do for them and understand them, the better they — like our dogs — will understand us, accept our discipline and serve us.

Nor should we think that, because they don't give us a rapturous welcome every time they see us, they are incapable of any kind of affection. Certainly they are capable of likes, dislikes and preferences. A horse that will stay quiet in its stall when its owner or handler comes in, shows complete trust in that person, which is an equine way of showing affection.

Horses will also, after many years of separation, recognize with friendly nickerings someone who has cared kindly for them, even if others in the meantime may have abused their trust in humans.

Depending on how they have been handled by men, or by women, some horses show a distinct preference for one or the other. What is puzzling is how these horses, before the man or woman has spoken to them, know the difference. Both sexes must look alike to them; women don't usually go about the stables in flowing skirts and picture hats. Possibly, and probably, it is smell — and it's a good thing that our smell sense is not as acute as theirs!

Taking care of horses, one soon comes to realize that every one is an individual, with its own character, moods, likes and dislikes: its equine character. But we should not anthropomorphize our horses, that is, think of them as having human intelligence and reactions. They are intelligent, but as horses, not as humans. Some are more intelligent than others, and individual intelligence will always develop the more the horse is handled and taught, as happens also with dogs.

Horses do, however, have many feelings and emotions which are akin to ours. They can experience fear, boredom, jealousy, loneliness, friendship with particular individuals of their own kind, and attachment to places and people. An endlessly fascinating way to learn more about the natural behavior patterns of horses is to watch them when they are at liberty, in company.

Everyone knows that it takes dogs some time to settle into a new home and accept a new master. The same applies to horses. A newly bought horse should be given time to adjust to its surroundings, to new equine companions, and a new handler and rider. It is bound, at first, to suffer from what in humans would be called homesickness.

Today, many owners board their horses; many others employ grooms. The more that owners know about horse care, the better they will be able to check that their horses are properly cared for. There's an old saying that 'The eye of the master keepeth the horse fat.' This doesn't only apply to the horse's food, but also to its general well-being and outlook on life.

When a horse becomes too old to work, unless one can afford to keep it in comfortable retirement, it is far kinder to have it put down than to turn it out in a pasture, throw food to it now and then, and hope it will enjoy doing nothing. It will not only miss the daily routine to which it has become accustomed, but the human care it has come to expect. Even more unkind is to send an old horse to a sale, where it will be bought for meat.

It may be distressing to humans to have horses put down, but surely animals which have given us years of pleasure should not have to end their days in fear and loneliness.

POINTS OF THE HORSE

All horses have the same "points," that is, they are all made on the same basic skeletal frame; they have the same arrangement of bones, joints, muscles, ligaments and tendons. But the sum total of these points, the horse's conformation, will vary according to the breed or type, ranging from the Shetland, the tiniest working equine, through the Thoroughbred, the fastest, to the heavy draft horses, which are the most powerful.

Different breeds have various specialized conformation characteristics, but every well-made equine will be pleasing to the eye, giving a picture of balance, proportion and, when moving, grace.

For a riding horse, it is important that it have good gaits, in particular an active, long-striding walk. It must therefore have what is called a "good shoulder," a sloping one which allows the forelegs to stride out freely. A straight shoulder will give a shorter, less comfortable stride. This is not as important with draft horses, which need strength to pull, not speed to cover the ground quickly.

The neck should be slightly arched along the crest, not hollowed ("ewe necked"), which will tend to make the horse carry its head in the air. The head should be set onto the neck with a clean jowl line; too thick a jowl makes it hard for the horse to relax the poll and come lightly into the hand.

The eyes should be large, clear, alert and kind. The muzzle, although with Arabs it is often quite small, should be broad, not flattened, and the nostrils should be capable of considerable dilation. Most horses and ponies with Arab blood have "dished," slightly concave profiles. Others, but not ponies, have concave "Roman nose" profiles. A good horse does not need to have a pretty head, but it must be a pleasing one, with the bone structure well defined.

The withers also should be well defined, because if they are too flat or thick it will be difficult to keep the saddle from slipping. The back should appear in proportion. Although many good horses have fairly long backs, over-long ones can predispose to back trouble, as there is bound to be a certain weakness over the loins. Cobs have noticeably short backs (are "close coupled"), allowing them to carry considerable weight for their height. A mare's back is usually slightly longer than a

gelding's or a stallion's. The ribcage should be well rounded, because flatter ribs do not allow so much lung expansion.

It is the hindquarters which initiate the horse's movement — the engine, you might say, is at the back. These therefore should be strong, with a well developed thigh and second thigh, or gaskin. The hocks should be well let down, that is, the angle from stifles to hocks should allow them to stand square in line down from the buttocks, not tilted under, or stretched out behind.

The tail should be set fairly high; it is, after all, the end of the spine. When the horse walks, the tail should be carried gracefully and swing lightly with the body's movements. A horse with a low-set tail and a rather sloping croup is called "goose rumped;" this is not always a disadvantage – some such horses are very good jumpers – but it is not good for a show horse.

The body of the horse should be deep through the girth, which means there is plenty of room for the heart, for lung expansion and for the stomach, and the underline of the belly should not slope upwards too sharply. Above all, the body should not appear too heavy for the legs, nor the legs too long for the body.

The cannon bone should appear to be slightly shorter than the forearm. It is the measurement of the cannon bone, taken just below the knee, which determines, up to a point, the weight the horse can carry. If a horse is described as "light of bone," that means that the measurement is less than it should be for the animal's make and shape. However big it may be, it will not be able to carry as much weight as a considerably smaller horse with better bone. The British native ponies have exceptionally good bone for their size, which is why the larger breeds can carry quite heavy adults more happily than would a much bigger, but lighter-boned, horse.

The pasterns should be sloping, but not exaggeratedly so, allowing the foot to rest on the ground at an angle of about 45 degrees. Straight pasterns do not absorb as much of the impact when the foot comes to the ground and as well as being less comfortable for the rider they are jarring to the leg. Pasterns that are exaggeratedly sloping put a strain on the tendons of the legs.

The feet should be well shaped

and be two pairs: the front hoofs should be rounded, while the hind pair should be more oval. Seen from the front, there should be plenty of room between the two forelegs, which should be straight, with the feet standing squarely and the hoofs turning neither in nor out. Looking at the horse from behind, the hind legs should fall straight and naturally on either

side of the buttocks. They should be neither too wide apart, nor too close together, either of which will impede the straightness of action of the hind legs. Nor should the hocks be "cow hocks," turned in toward each other.

No horse or pony can ever be perfect, but the better the conformation of an animal the better will be its action.

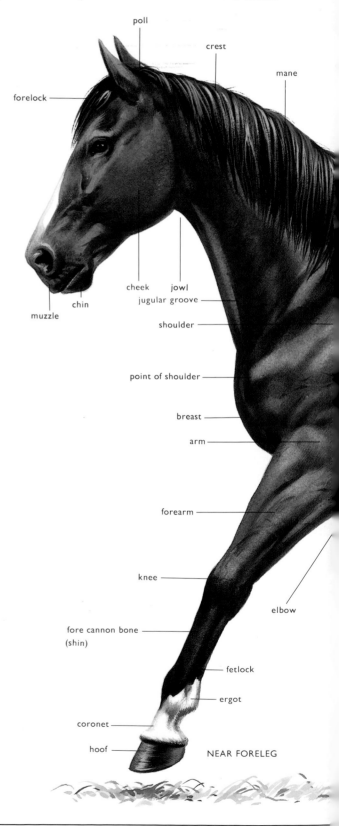

poll
crest
mane
forelock
cheek
jowl
chin
jugular groove
muzzle
shoulder
point of shoulder
breast
arm
forearm
knee
fore cannon bone
(shin)
elbow
fetlock
ergot
coronet
hoof
NEAR FORELEG

CHESTNUT The small, horny outgrowth on each of a horse's legs is known as a chestnut or castor. A horse's chestnuts are as individual to it as fingerprints are to people, so color photographs of them are useful aids to identification if the animal is stolen.

MEASURING A HORSE
The highest point of a horse when it is standing upright (apart from its ears) is its poll. As the height of the poll can vary according to how the horse is holding its head, the height of a horse is measured in a vertical line from the ground to its withers. Horses are measured in "hands," one hand being 4 inches (about 10 cm). If a horse is more than an exact number of hands high, the extra inches are given after a decimal point, for example 14 hands 2 inches is 14.2 hands high (hh).

distance from withers to ground

POINTS OF A HORSE Each distinct part of a horse is called a "point," and collectively the points define the conformation (the physical shape and lines of the horse), which varies from one breed to another and to a lesser extent between individuals of the same breed.

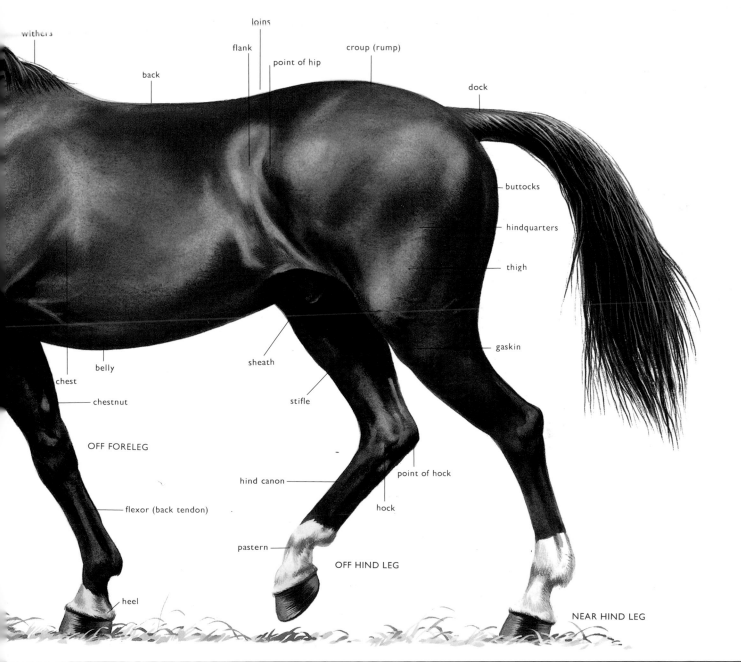

withers

loins

flank

back

point of hip

croup (rump)

dock

buttocks

hindquarters

thigh

gaskin

sheath

belly

chest

chestnut

stifle

OFF FORELEG

hind canon

point of hock

flexor (back tendon)

hock

pastern

OFF HIND LEG

NEAR HIND LEG

heel

HORSE ANATOMY

In common with all vertebrate creatures the horse has a framework of bones combining to form a skeleton. The bones form a rigid support for the body mass and their movement, in response to the contraction of muscle and the consequent activation of the joints, produces *locomotion*.

Joints are formed at the juncture of two bones, the articular surface of which is of greater density than elsewhere in the bone. An additional preventative against wear is the separating layer of gristle (*cartilage*) between the bone surfaces. The whole is held together by *ligaments* attached to each bone. The ligaments act to govern the extension of the joint, preventing movement beyond the latter's proper limitations, which might result in strain or rupture.

Muscles, which cover a large part of the body, cause movement in the joints, and thus in the whole structure, by means of their attachment to the bones. Movement occurs when muscle is contracted. The points of attachment are then brought closer together and so induce movement in the joint. Those muscles contracting to flex a joint are termed *flexors*, the opposite effect being achieved by *extensor* muscles.

Muscles are highly elastic but they would easily become torn unless equipped with supporting *tendons*. A tendon is a tough, inelastic "rope" running through the muscle's length, one end being fastened to the bone and the other being virtually braided into the substance of the muscle.

Muscle, when not in contraction or extension, retains a state of slight tension (*tonus*) which prevents movement that would cause joints to be flexed or extended so violently as to cause structural damage. (Lack of tone leads to uncoordination, which can produce violent movement, resulting in

THE SKELETON

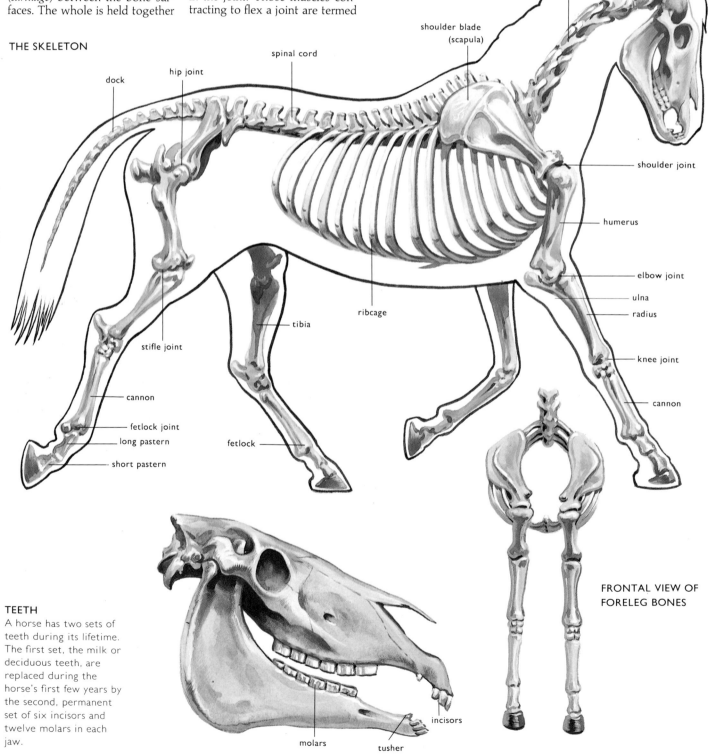

TEETH

A horse has two sets of teeth during its lifetime. The first set, the milk or deciduous teeth, are replaced during the horse's first few years by the second, permanent set of six incisors and twelve molars in each jaw.

FRONTAL VIEW OF FORELEG BONES

MAIN ORGANS AND MUSCLES

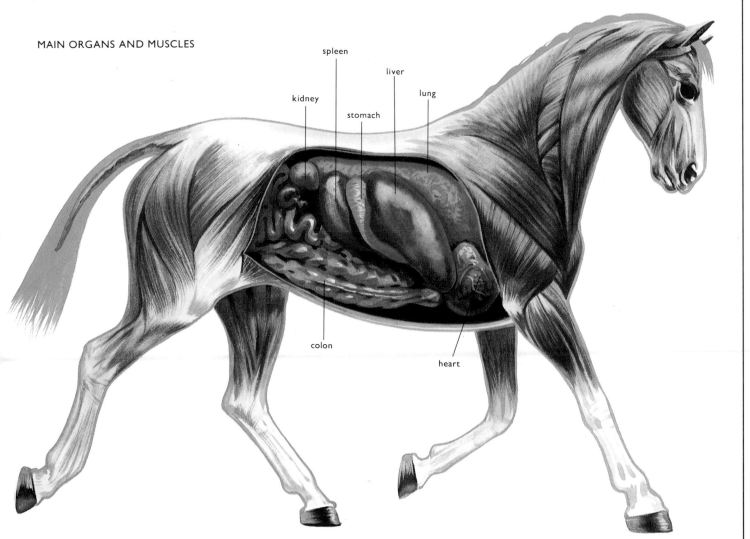

spleen

kidney

liver

lung

stomach

colon

heart

undue strain being put on the joint components. It occurs commonly in tired or unfit horses.)

A particular property of muscle, very relevant in the schooling of horses, is that the ability to contract is equalled by the extent to which it can be extended. It follows therefore that exercises designed to stretch muscle will result in their increased ability to contract and, consequently, the more efficient will be the flexion of the joints they control. Voluntary muscles (those whose action the horse can control) act in pairs to flex or extend a joint, but they also oppose each other or act in compensation.

In attempting to achieve the desirable rounding of the topline, for instance, a matter of much concern in the schooling of the young horse, the big back muscles are stretched, acting as extensors, the lowering of the neck causing the *cervical ligament* (extending from poll to sacrum) to be stretched in turn over the fulcrum provided by the withers.

The effect is completed by the hind legs being drawn further under the body to provide greater propulsion, an action that must be accompanied by a raising of the abdomen. It is accomplished by three muscles on the side of the abdomen and three running from the fifth and ninth ribs to the pubis acting as flexors and in opposition, therefore, to the extensors of the back.

Involuntary muscles (which act without the conscious control of the horse) occur in the internal organs, like those causing movement in the bowels, and the independent cardiac muscle which is connected with the heart function.

The spine or *vertebral column* comprises seven *cervical* (neck) vertebrae; eighteen *thoracic* (dorsal) vertebrae; six *lumbar* vertebrae and five fused bones which form the *sacrum*. There are eighteen *coccygeal* (tail) vertebrae.

To each of the thoracic vertebrae a pair of ribs is attached. The first eight pairs (*sternal*) are attached to the *sternum* (breastbone) and are called "true" ribs, the remaining ten (*asternal*) are attached only to vertebrae and are known as "false" ribs. The *thorax*, or rib cage, contains the organs of circulation and respiration, the heart and lungs.

Concussion caused in movement is a prime cause of lameness in the horse. Concussion is absorbed throughout the limb, particularly in the joints, but absorption occurs primarily in the feet and pasterns.

The principal anticoncussion area is formed by the elastic *frog*, the triangular-shaped elastic formation in the sole, which as well as absorbing the initial jar opens the angle of the "bars" adjoining it and causes blood to be returned up the leg in the process of circulation.

The foot itself has an insensitive outer covering of horn, encasing the sensitive inner foot which comprises the *phalangeal* and *navicular* bones, the sensitive sole and *laminae*, the sensitive frog and the digital cushion.

In the mature horse there are six incisor and twelve molar teeth in each jaw. Male horses develop four canines or tushers behind the incisors at the age of four. The horse is not said to have a "full mouth" until the age of six, when the milk teeth have been replaced by permanent ones.

Digestion begins in the mouth, food being rolled by the tongue and then ground by the molar teeth. The action stimulates the release of saliva from the glands under the tongue and in the jaw, which helps to reduce the food to a paste.

The muscles of the gullet then force food into the stomach where it is kneaded still further by the action of involuntary muscles. Gastric juices reduce the food still more and the resultant paste is passed into the small bowel, into which are emptied the ducts from the pancreas and liver to add their secretions to the process. Once reduced to liquid form the food is absorbed into the body.

The capacious large bowel receives unabsorbed matter, constant movements of the gut extracting further nutrients before the waste is excreted.

The horse breathes through the nostrils alone, the air passing through the larynx and windpipe into the lungs. At rest, the natural contractions of the ribs and lungs are enough to expel "tidal" air. In exertion, however, which demands "forced breathing," the process is assisted by the flank muscles which cover the ribs and belly, compressing those parts so as to force out the used air.

STABLE MANAGEMENT

By nature, horses are active, freedom-loving, gregarious animals. It is unnatural for them to spend, as most domesticated ones do, long periods of time confined in stables. To adjust successfully to this man-imposed way of life, they need from man not only physical care, but an understanding of their equine character needs and instinctive behavior patterns.

In the wild they were hunted animals, so they are far more highly strung than man and suspicious of the new or the unexpected, and their reaction to an imagined danger is still to take refuge in flight. However, years of domestication have allowed them to accept, willingly if properly handled, the domination of man as once they accepted that of the herd leader, and the warmth and comfort of their stable or stall as security.

But if you abuse a horse in that stable, shout at it, hit it with broom or fork handles or worse, or beat it if it doesn't at once do what you want, then because it cannot escape it will sooner or later retaliate with teeth and heels. Most horses that are difficult in the stable have been made so by bad human handling. So work quietly and calmly about the horse in the stable, and use your voice to tell the horse what you want it to do; horses can learn words as quickly as dogs can.

The stabled horse needs space, air and light. A stall of 12 feet × 12 feet will allow it to move about freely and to lie down or even roll around if it wants to; 10 feet × 10 feet is big enough for most ponies. The door of the stall should be in two halves, so that the top half can be left open both to give the horse air and to allow it to look out and watch the goings-on in the yard. This need only be shut if sleet or a blizzard is blowing directly into the stall, when the window can be opened instead. The window should open in, and should be protected by wire netting or bars.

The stall will need a tie ring, set at about shoulder height, for tying the horse and for the haynet, although hay can instead be fed in a corner rack, fixed about 4 feet from the floor. Because they are more easily kept clean, it is more hygienic to give short feeds in bowls or buckets or in the excel-

As far as possible, you should try to follow the same feeding and stable management routine every day.

lent modern portable mangers which can be hooked over the door. Automatic water bowls are fine, except in very cold weather when the supply pipes can freeze up, but if you use water buckets they should be heavy, so that they're not easily knocked over. Stable bricks make a good floor but are expensive, so roughened concrete is more usual. Whatever the floor is made of, it should slope slightly toward the front.

Bedding can be of straw, peat moss, sawdust or wood shavings, or of specially prepared shredded paper. Wheat straw is the best, but combine-harvested barley straw is also satisfactory because there are no scratchy awns (bristles) left in it. Oat straw is palatable to horses and they may eat it; peat moss, sawdust and shavings will not be eaten, but they can pack into the horse's feet and then must be meticulously picked out.

Shredded paper is bacteria-free, so it makes excellent bedding for horses with respiratory or bronchial problems. Whatever material you provide for a night bed, make sure that you spread it deeply enough, because a horse lying on bare concrete is liable to develop capped hocks.

The management routine for a stabled horse will vary according to the work the horse is doing, but is roughly as follows. Give the first feed, plus fresh water and a small haynet, between 7 and 7:30 am. When the feed is finished, tie the horse and muck out the stall. If the bedding is straw, bank it around the sides of the stall to air it and sweep the floor clean; if the bedding is of other material, remove all the droppings and wet patches. Then untie the horse.

At about 9 am tie the horse again and remove the droppings. Brush the horse and, if you're going to exercise it, pick out its feet and tack up. On return from exercise, remove the tack and let the horse drink. If it hasn't urinated while out, and if bedded on straw, put some down from the sides; horses will not urinate on a bare floor. Replenish the haynet, tie the horse and groom it thoroughly, then give it its second feed and refill the water bucket.

Thorough grooming is best done after exercise, but if the

LEFT Some of the basic features of a typical small stable.

BELOW As well as keeping the floors of the stalls clean, make sure that the stable yard is swept regularly.

horse has come in wet, or rather hot, cover it with a sweat rug, or a day rug inside out (so the inside doesn't get wet), and groom it later.

If you're going to ride the horse again in the afternoon, you should first repeat the morning's procedure. Horses not working can be left to rest, and should be given good bedding. Or they can be lead out in halter for a pick of grass, or, better still, turned out if there is a convenient paddock. All stabled horses benefit from such periods of freedom and enjoy the often playful companionship of their own kind.

Between 4:30 and 5 pm lay the night bed (if straw), or clean up droppings and wet patches (if other bedding) and add more bedding if necessary. Put up a fresh haynet, then tie the horse and groom thoroughly if not done earlier. Then provide fresh water, cover the horse with its night rug or rugs, untie it and give the third feed. Later, not earlier than 7 pm, refill the water bucket, put up the night net of hay, check that the rug is in position and, if the horse is on a lot of concentrates, give a fourth feed.

Horses, like ourselves, can suffer from boredom. The stable vices of cribbing, wind-sucking and weaving are really boredom neuroses, the horse giving itself something to do to pass the time. This is why stalls should always be arranged so the horses can see not only one another, but also what's going on in the yard, and why all stabled horses, however well exercised, should be turned out now and then, preferably in the company of other horses.

The horse is by nature a freedom-loving herd animal, and periods of being turned out with other horses will allow it to enjoy the pleasures of companionship and of being its natural, uninhibited self. These periods benefit its mental as well as physical health. The old adage 'a healthy mind in a healthy body' is as valid for horses as it is for human beings.

Cribbing can be discouraged by painting wooden surfaces with creosote or a commercial preparation, and a strap fitted around the horse's throat makes it difficult for it to wind-suck. Weaving is, maddeningly, infectious — one weaver will soon have others imitating it. It can often be discouraged by hanging a large turnip on a rope from the top of the inside of the door, so that as the horse swings its head, it bangs against it.

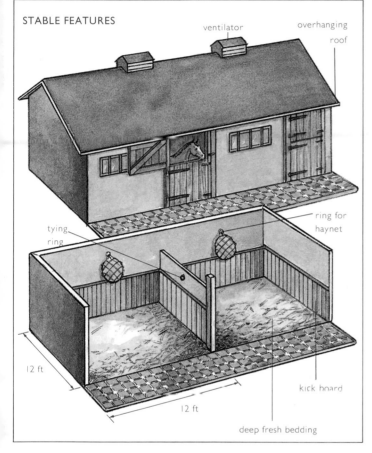

STABLE FEATURES

ventilator

overhanging roof

tying ring

ring for haynet

12 ft

12 ft

kick board

deep fresh bedding

FEEDING

The three basic rules for the correct feeding of horses are feed little and often, do not work immediately after a full meal, and provide plenty of fresh water.

The reason for the first one is that the horse is a grazing animal, and in its natural state it would be eating small amounts more or less all the time. Its digestive system is adapted to this kind of feeding, unlike the digestive systems of meat eaters such as dogs, cats and ourselves, which can cope with big meals at widely spaced intervals.

The horse has a small stomach and capacious intestines. When it is eating, as soon as the stomach is about two-thirds full, the food begins to pass into the intestines for digestion. This process occurs naturally when the horse is grazing on grass or munching hay, both of which it eats slowly and which take a considerable amount of chewing.

When it is working, however, it needs some energy-producing "concentrate" food. It is this which must be given not in one large meal, but in several relatively small ones. Concentrate food is very palatable and so a horse will eat it more quickly than grass or hay. Too large a feed will distend the horse's stomach and impede the natural balance of ingestion and digestion. About 4 pounds of concentrate food is the most a horse's stomach can cope with successfully; the more concentrates a horse needs, the more individual feeds.

After a concentrate feed a horse's stomach and intestines, being full, will take up more room, distending the belly not only outward but also forward toward the diaphragm, which in turn presses on the lungs. Pressure on these causes distress and labored breathing, so a horse should be given an hour for digestion before being asked to work.

Originally, the third rule was "water before feeding." This was in the days when it was customary to take horses out to water at a trough. But if clean fresh water is always available, a horse will seldom drink too much or at the wrong time, although it is sensible, after work, to give it the chance to drink before putting its feed in the feed pail. A hot, tired horse may want to drink a lot; let it do so, but give it a hay net to

Horses should be fed at the same times every day, and clean water should always be available.

pull at and a rest before its hard feed.

Horses are fastidious drinkers, so buckets, drinking bowls or outdoor troughs should be kept scrupulously clean. On average, a horse will drink about 8 gallons of water a day although, like people, some drink more and some drink less than average.

To calculate how much food a horse needs, it is a help to know how much a horse at liberty might eat in 24 hours: a 15-hand horse, for example, would eat about 24 pounds. For horses of other heights, add or subtract 1 pound of food for every inch above or below 15 hands.

This amount will be made up of both bulk (hay and/or grass) and concentrates. If a 15-hand horse is

fully worked it will need 10 or 12 pounds of concentrates, which means it will need 14 or 12 pounds of bulk. If it is lightly or only occasionally worked, it will need only 5 or 6 pounds of concentrates but 19 or 18 pounds of bulk. It is important to keep the balance right — an increase of concentrates means a decrease of bulk, and vice versa, so that the total weight intake remains the same.

This is only a rough guide because horses, like people, are individuals: overweight horses need dieting, while those in poor condition will need carefully selected concentrates plus as much bulk as they will eat. It is, however, a useful working hypothesis. Horses doing no work at all can

keep healthy on a "maintenance diet" of bulk alone, but the moment they are worked they will be expending more energy which must be replaced.

To replace this energy, and keep the horse physically fit for the work asked of it, its diet must contain a correct balance of protein, fats, starches and sugars (energy and heat producing), salts, water (existing in all foods, even those known as "dry"), fiber (vital to its digestion and found in most foods, but particularly in hay) and vitamins.

The single food providing the best dietary balance for the horse is oats. Oats should be fed bruised, but with discretion as they can have an over-exhilarating effect, and not to children's

ponies. Barley is almost as good, with the advantage that horses do not "heat up" on it. It can be fed bruised or flaked, or boiled, in which case the whole kernels are used.

Corn is less fibrous than oats or barley but when fed along with other grains, or pellets, is a good winter feed as it contains a lot of starch, fats and sugar. Bran has little nutritional value, but it provides bulk and fiber and it can be added to feeds like oats or concentrates to encourage slower eating. Bran is, however, useful for making mashes. Sugar beets, shredded or in cubes, must be soaked in water for up to 24 hours before use, and although a little is useful as a feed additive, it should not be fed on its own.

Hay must always be clean and sweet; moldy or dusty hay can cause respiratory problems.

There are a number of commercial brands of pellets and coarse mixes, specially balanced in different grades for horses in all kinds of work, and all including vitamins and minerals. If fed according to the manufacturer's instructions, the advantages of feeding them are that the product is guaranteed to be always the same, the bags are easily handled, and additives may not be necessary.

Some of the best additives, if feeding traditionally, are seaweed extracts, cod liver oil and garlic powder. Carrots, sliced lengthwise, are another useful dietary supplement, and most horses love them. Some also like rutabagas or turnips, which can be put whole in the feed pail or thrown out in the pasture.

The four types of hay are timothy, clover, mixed and meadow, the most usual being mixed, which is taken from specially seeded pastures. Timothy is very nutritious but somewhat woody and it's hard for old horses to chew. Meadow can be very good or very bad, and clover is hard to make well. Never feed moldy or dusty hay, and give stabled horses the largest portion of their hay ration at night.

Stabilize feeding times as far as possible. If you're giving three feeds a day, give them early morning, after work and in the evening; if four feeds, early morning, after work, late afternoon and late evening. If a change of diet is considered, change it gradually; and worm your horse regularly — there is no point in feeding parasites.

GROOMING & SHOEING

Grooming is an important part of horse care. It keeps the skin and coat healthy, stimulates the circulation and, because most horses enjoy it, can be a pleasant time for both horse and handler.

A stabled horse should be groomed thoroughly every day. The dandy brush is used to remove surface dirt after the horse has worked or been turned out, but don't use it on the more sensitive places such as the face, the belly and between the thighs, or on the mane or tail. Because it is hard, it will break the hairs.

The body brush removes grease and really cleans the coat, and in its turn it is cleaned with a metal curry comb. The water brush is used for the mane and tail, to remove stable stains and when shampooing the horse. A rubber curry comb is useful when the horse is shedding (changing) its coat, which it does twice a year. Used firmly with a massaging, rotary motion, it will bring out masses of loose hair.

A small sponge is useful for cleaning the nostrils and wiping around the eyes, but use a separate one for cleaning around the dock. A mare should have her udder sponged now and then, especially in hot weather, and the sheath of a gelding or a stallion should be cleaned at least twice a month. If it becomes clogged, it can make letting-down difficult or even painful; get an experienced person to show you how to clean it. A rub rag will give the coat a final polish and it can also be used, folded into a pad, for "strapping," which consists of energetically hitting the muscles of the horse's neck and hindquarters to tone them up.

When you're grooming in very cold weather, the horse can be "quartered." Undo the front fastenings of the horse's rug, fold it back and groom the front end, and then replace it. Then undo the roller or surcingle, fold the rug forward and groom the hindquarters.

It is best, even in cold weather, not to wear gloves when you are grooming. Only bare fingers can feel any bumps, lumps or scratches, and the gritty granulations there may be on the legs, around the fetlocks, pasterns and on the heels. These can develop into mud fever or cracked heels and are caused by dirt or mud being left on and thus blocking the pores. They can be gently worked off with the fingers and the area smeared with vaseline.

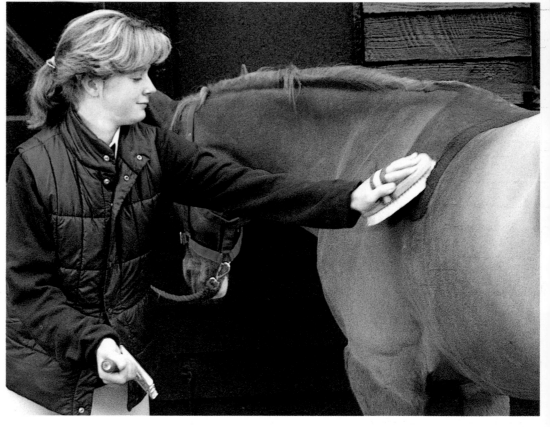

A good way to clean muddy legs is to put stable bandages on them when the horse comes in, which will dry the mud, and then to brush the legs thoroughly when the bandages are taken off. Any tangles in the tail should be worked loose with the fingers before brushing, and a tail bandage put on after grooming will help to keep the tail lying neatly between the buttocks.

The horse's feet should be picked out both when grooming and when the horse returns from work. Hoof oil put on after cleaning out the feet not only makes the hoofs look nice but also is good for the horn, particularly if it is applied right up to where the hoof grows out of the coronary band, which is similar to the human cuticle.

Cleaning out the feet provides a good opportunity for checking the shoes. If a shoe is loose, or the clenches (the bent-over points of the nails) have risen, then the farrier (blacksmith) is needed.

Never try to economize on shoeing. Find a good farrier and stick with him, and get him to pay you a regular monthly, or at most five-weekly, visit. Most horses need the farrier every four to five weeks, because even if the shoes are not worn or loose, the feet will have grown and the shoes will need a "remove." Farriers are busy people, and although they will always do their best for their regular clients, they can't be expected to turn up immediately to shoe a horse that should have been done weeks before.

Farriery is a highly skilled profession. Every qualified farrier has considerable veterinary and anatomical kowledge, in particular of the structure of the foot and the tendons and ligaments of the leg supporting it, and can make and fit various kinds of remedial shoes for horses with foot or leg problems.

Stabled horses working in winter will need clipping — a full clip if working hard, and perhaps mostly indoors. They will then need both a night rug and an underblanket. Hunters or horses in outdoor work are usually given hunter clips or blanket clips. The hunter clip leaves the hair on the legs and the saddle patch, while the blanket clip leaves the hair over the loins as well as on the legs.

A trace clip will be enough for horses used mostly for weekend riding. The hair is clipped from the belly, between the thighs and from the underside of the neck. This clip is also useful for ponies and cobs worked in winter.

All clipped horses need New Zealand rugs when turned out. At night, hunter and blanket clipped horses need full rugging, but a single night rug is enough for a trace clipped horse. Horses should

Using a body brush and curry comb to clean and remove grease from a horse's coat.

be clipped only when the winter coat has come through, which is usually by mid October; a second clip may be necessary, but it should not be given later than February. Clipping helps to keep the horse cool when worked hard, and makes it easier to groom it and to keep it clean.

Horses that live out can be groomed thoroughly in summer. In winter, however, even if being worked, they should only be brushed over with the dandy brush to remove dirt and sweat. The body brush will remove from their coats too much of the natural oils that help to keep them warm and dry.

Particular care should be taken to keep their legs clean and mud free and, after riding, to dry off and brush the saddle patch and behind the elbows where the girth lies. Sweat left to dry and congeal in either place can, because of the thick winter coat, cause saddle sores or girth galls (abrasions). Keep manes and tails untangled and brushed out, and when doing so keep a lookout for lice. Strange as it may seem, lice can appear in winter on even the best conditioned animals. If found, two or three liberal sprinklings of medicated powder should kill them off.

TYPES OF CLIP

THE FULL CLIP, the clipping of the entire coat, is used mainly for show horses. Electric clippers are best, but keep them sharp.

HUNTER CLIP
In the hunter clip, the hair is clipped from all parts of the coat except the legs and the saddle area. These parts are left unclipped to give them some protection.

BLANKET CLIP
The blanket clip, which leaves the hair over the loins and on the legs, is for horses kept out by day but brought in at night.

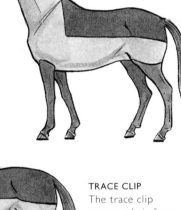

TRACE CLIP
The trace clip removes hair from the belly, between the thighs and under the neck. It was originally used for harness horses.

Regular combing of the mane will keep the hairs in good condition and stop them getting tangled or matted.

BRAIDING A MANE

1 Damp the mane and divide it into the number of braids you want, fastening them with rubber bands. Remove the band from the first, and braid it.

2 Secure the braid with a rubber band, then push a needle with double, knotted thread through the end.

3 Roll the braid up to the crest, and push the needle through from bottom to top and back again until the braid is secure. Repeat the procedure for each braid.

Your horse's shoes should be checked by your farrier every four to five weeks, and you should check them yourself every day.

SHOES
Shoes prevent hoof wear or splitting. Grass tips protect the toes of horses out at grass.

Hunter shoe

- frog
- nails
- sole
- wall
- groove
- toeclip

Grass tip

HOOFS
The hoof of a horse has an outer wall of horn which grows down from the coronary band and is an extension of the skin of the leg. Hoof oil, brushed on after cleaning the feet, will make the hoofs look good and also protect them from cracking and splitting.

BASIC HEALTH CARE

The basic health needs of the horse are simple, and are the same as for every animal, including ourselves: enough food and drink, shelter, warmth, exercise and companionship.

That a healthy horse must have enough food is obvious, but "enough" is the operative word. Too much food and the horse will become fat; too little and it will be out of condition. It should be well covered, neither thin nor fat. It is as bad for the horse's health as it is for our own to be grossly overweight.

The health of the horse depends as much on the quality of the food and the cleanliness with which it is presented, as on the quantity. Horses, being grazing herbivores, are not scavengers (unlike many carnivores). Unless they are literally starving, they will not eat dirt, and they should not be asked to feed from dirty feed boxes or other receptacles. These should be kept scrupulously clean, because leftovers not cleaned out will rot or ferment.

Of particular importance to the health of the horse is that it should be kept free from worms. It should be dosed at least four times a year, and your vet will advise you about which wormer to use and how often.

Equally important is the care of your horse's teeth. Horses grind up their food with their molars, their back teeth. With wear these can become uneven and sharp, sometimes so sharp that they cut the insides of the cheeks when the horse chews. To prevent this, the teeth need rasping (floating) to

file down the sharp edges. This is not as horrific a performance as it might sound, because horses' teeth aren't as sensitive as ours. Most horses will benefit from having their teeth floated about once a year.

As well as regular worming and tooth floating, it is advisable (and necessary if the horse is to go to shows or competitions) that it be given regular injections and boosters to protect it from flu and tetanus. When the vet comes to give these, suggest that he also checks the horse's teeth, but warn him beforehand so that he brings his rasp.

In winter, nature provides all horses with thicker, denser coats which, if they were neither working nor clipped, would probably keep them warm enough when in stalls or shelters. Native ponies, given enough food, can live out happily in their winter coats. But working horses, because they use a lot of energy and are groomed and fully or partially clipped, will not keep warm in a stall, however deeply bedded, without being rugged.

Fully clipped horses will need an underblanket as well as a rug in winter. What other clips (or unclipped working horses) will need will depend on the climate and the individual horse. Some, like people, feel the cold more than others. The ears are a good guide: cold ears, cold horse; warm ears, warm horse. If the ears, and the horse, are cold, don't try to warm it by simply shutting the top of the stable door; put another rug on it.

Fresh air is essential to a horse's health, but if a horse comes in wet and cold, as well as drying off its body and putting a rug over it, dry off and warm its ears, rubbing them with a soft towel or rub rag. As with humans, it is sudden changes of temperature, or standing around getting cold after sweating or being soaked, that causes colds and chills. There will also therefore be times in summer when the horse will need drying off and rugging, for instance after strenuous exercise, or being shampooed before a show, or just getting drenched in a sudden downpour.

None of this means that horses are delicate creatures. Far from it — they are pretty tough constitutionally. To keep a horse in good health, it is only sensible to take as much care of its body temperature as you do of your own, putting on more clothes in winter and a sweater in summer if you've taken hard physical exercise. The horse's normal temperature should be between 100 and 101 degrees Fahrenheit (37.8 to 38.4 degrees Celsius).

The healthy horse should be alert, obviously interested in what's going on, eyes bright, eager for food and eating with relish, coat glossy and lying flat. The membranes of the nostrils, the insides of the eyelids, and the gums, should be a pale pink. Droppings should fall in firmly formed shapes and urine should be clear, pale yellow and not too strong smelling. With the first spring grass, droppings will be-

To keep your horse free from worms, it should be wormed at least four times a year.

come looser and somewhat green in color. If they become very loose, mix some dry bran with the horse's feeds.

Signs of ill health include the horse standing (in its stall or pasture) with its head down and hindquarters tucked under; dull eyes; and the coat not lying flat, and appearing dry rather than glossy. The droppings of a sick horse may be either very hard (a sign of constipation) or very loose (diarrhea), and the urine perhaps thick and strong smelling. As it is always better to be safe than sorry, if a horse shows any of these symptoms, consult your veterinarian. Meantime, if it is indoors, make sure it is warm enough; if it is out, bring it in, rug it, put down a bed and leave it with water.

In the old days of the cavalry, the men were enjoined always to see to their horses' welfare before their own. This is a good precept to follow if we are to keep our horses healthy and in good heart, our companions as well as our willing servants.

However, even the best-kept horses will from time to time need treatment for minor ailments and injuries. For example, azoturia is not common, but it can occur if a fit horse is given a day's rest in its stall without its energy food being reduced. Exercise the next day can bring on a sudden stiffness, almost a paralysis, of the

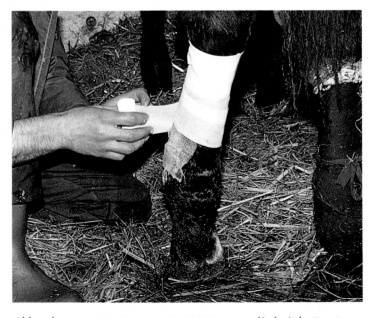

Although you can treat many minor injuries yourself, don't hesitate to call the vet if you aren't sure what to do.

hindquarters. It is probably similar to acute muscular cramp in humans. If it happens any distance away, the horse will have to be sent home. Keep the hindquarters warm and rugged, and give the horse a bran mash and no concentrates until the condition has worn off. Its old name is "Monday morning disease," from the days when horses were worked hard all week and were rested on Sundays.

Colic is not a "minor" ailment, but you should know what to do until the vet arrives. It is acute indigestion, which is more serious in horses than in humans as horses cannot vomit to clear their stomachs. The colicky horse will be in obvious pain, looking around at its stomach and sometimes kicking at it, lying down, rolling then getting up again, and sometimes sweating.

Unless the stall is big enough to allow the horse to lie and roll freely, rug it and keep it walking about. The activity of walking may cause it to pass wind, which

may help ease the pain. Never trifle with colic; always call the vet.

Horses can get ordinary head colds, like humans. Keep the nostrils wiped out with a weak solution of disinfectant. Don't turn the horse out with others or ride it while it has a runny nose, but hand walk it, rugged if the weather is cold or wet. Keep its haynet and feed bowl separate from those of other horses, and if there is also a cough, call the vet.

Cuts and scratches should be cleaned with either a mild disinfectant or salt and water, sponged until the bleeding stops and then dusted with antiseptic powder. A deep cut may need stitching by the vet. Meantime, clean as above, then put a gauze dressing under a bandage to protect the wound until the vet arrives.

Blunt-ended scissors will be useful for cutting away the hair from either side of a cut to stop hair healing in the wound. Any wound that has caused arterial

bleeding needs veterinary attention, and a tourniquet applied above it.

An infected puncture wound will need the poison, which causes the heat and swelling, drawn out of it. This is where a kaolin poultice or one of the many commercial poultices come in; how to use the latter is explained on the package. For kaolin, heat the paste, spread thickly over a dressing and place it over the puncture. Put some aluminum foil or plastic over the dressing to keep the heat in, and then bandage. Repeat this daily until there is no pus on the dressing when you remove it.

Mud cracks are caused by mud or dirt adhering to the skin and clogging the pores. When grooming, feel with your fingers for rough granulations around the pasterns and heels. If there are any, try working them gently away and smear the area with Vaseline (petroleum jelly) or zinc and castor oil ointment, or a commercial preparation. If horses are working, or turned out, in heavy, muddy ground, it is always sensible to protect their pasterns with one of the above three remedies. If untreated, mud cracks can cause lameness.

If a horse goes suddenly lame on a ride, get off and lift the foot on the lame side. It may have picked up a stone; if so, remove the stone and the horse will go sound. If there is no stone, walk the horse home and when you get there hose the leg or, if there is no hose available, sponge it with cold water and apply a kaolin poultice overnight. Repeat the hosing and poulticing next day, when the lameness may have decreased. If it hasn't, get veterinary advice, and when you get it, take it. For whatever time you are told to rest the horse, don't start riding it sooner because you think it seems all right. Incidentally, when bandaging an injured leg, always bandage the opposite, good one, as well, as it will be taking extra weight in saving the lame one.

If your horse gets an inflamed or "weepy" eye, bathe it gently with a very soft sponge, lukewarm water and only a drop of disinfectant, then squeeze a little eye ointment into the corner nearest the frontal bone.

Saddle sores and girth galls (abrasions) are really signs of bad management. The former are caused by ill-fitting saddles, the latter either by hard, dirty girths or by the skin and hair being pinched under the girth. Always, after tightening girths, either pull each foreleg forward, or run your hand down the inside of the girth

FIRST AID BOX

A first aid box or chest should be kept in the tack room, clearly labeled so that it can easily be found.

A basic kit should contain:
- a veterinary thermometer (at least 5 inches long)
- caustic powder
- a jar or tube of antibiotic ointment
- a jar or tube of antiseptic ointment
- Vaseline (petroleum jelly)
- kaolin poultice
- colic medicine
- Epsom salts
- iodine
- rubbing alcohol or witch hazel
- mild disinfectant
- sharp, blunt-ended scissors
- small surgical dish
- small, soft plastic sponges
- pieces of clean linen or cotton (for pads)
- 2 bandages (2½" wide)
- sterile gauze dressings
- roll of cotton
- adhesive tape
- a piece of rubber for use as a tourniquet

on both sides, to make sure the skin and hair are free.

Treat both types of sores by sponging them with salt and water, and resting the horse until the sores have healed (though you still can ride bareback if you like).

Sores can be prevented by using well-fitting saddles and clean girths, and by always drying and brushing off saddle patches, and where girths lie, after riding. Dried sweat can also cause galls, especially when horses or ponies are ridden in their winter coats. A diluted salt solution sponged over saddle patches and behind the elbows will help harden the skin of horses that have not been worked for a time.

Summer can be a miserable time for a horse. It becomes the focus of attention of hordes of biting insects, some of which, such as botflies, can cause parasitic infestation. To spare your horse this suffering, ask your vet to recommend a good insect repellant and begin using it, following the manufacturer's instructions, before the insects have become numerous.

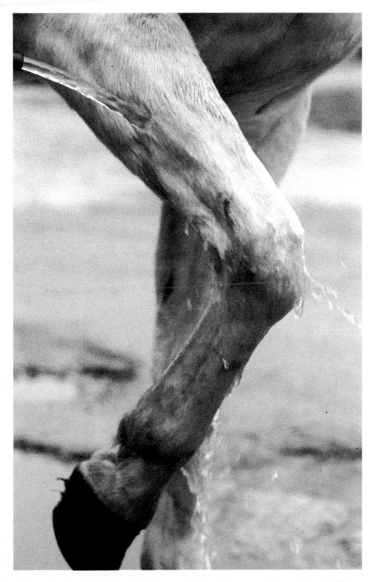

A cut leg should be hosed down and then the wound cleaned carefully with a mild disinfectant or salt and water.

BREEDING

Before you decide to put your mare in foal, please think of the future. Have you the facilities, the time and the money to look after the foal until it is old enough to be broken: for three years at least? Or, if you plan to sell it, are you prepared to ensure that it goes to a good home?

In short, are you prepared to accept responsibility for the equine life you are calling into being? Foals should not be bred irresponsibly, or indiscriminately; every one, whether horse or pony, should be capable of maturing into a useful adult. It is up to us to breed only from mares with good conformation and action, and to choose for them stallions we believe will allow them to produce foals able, when adult, to play useful parts in the equestrian world.

Genetically, a foal takes half its genes from the dam, half from the sire. It follows that however good, and expensive, a stallion may be, he cannot be expected to produce a wonder foal from a poor-quality mare. In breeding, although the female is not "more deadly than the male," she is equally as important. Only from a good mare, of whatever breed or type, are you likely to get a foal that will repay the trouble and expense of raising it.

The age of the mare is not so important, because mares are capable of breeding throughout their lives. It is sensible, however, not to put a mare in foal before she is four or five, when she will be more or less mature, nor to wait

too long, until her late teens, for instance.

What kind of foal do you want your mare to have? Bigger than she, or smaller, or lighter, or with more substance, or about the same? If she is a pony, with a pedigree and "papers," you can put her to a stallion of the same breed, although if you want something a little bigger you could use a small Thoroughbred or an Arab. It is worth knowing that the four largest British "native" ponies — Connemaras, Dales, Fells and Highlands — will produce excellent, versatile riding horses if crossed with the Thoroughbred or the Arab.

Be selective in your choice of stallion. Go to see several before you decide, and be sure you like the way the stud is run, because your mare will be spending some weeks there. The usual procedure is for the mare to go to the stud when she is about to come into season, to stay for three weeks after service, and for another three if she fails to hold to the first service.

Be sure you know exactly what her keep will cost and also, if she does not produce a foal, if the stallion fee includes a "no foal, free return" clause. When you collect her, ask the stud to give you a service certificate, because you will need this if the foal qualifies for any breed registration.

Mares carry their foals for an average of 333 days; colts for 334, fillies for 332, with a possible variation of 9 or 10 days either way. Colts are usually, but not

always, carried longer than fillies. For the first half of her pregnancy (five to five and a half months) a mare can be ridden and fed more or less normally, although preferably not ridden in competitive events involving stress.

After that, the foal, quickening and growing very fast, makes more demands on the mare; about one seventh of what she eats daily goes to its development. During this time she is best out at pasture – either all the time if the grass and the weather are good, or brought in at night, when she can have as much good hay as she will eat. Whatever her working food ration was, she is better now with

If a mare is in season she will stand quietly when a stallion is brought to her. If she is not, she will act aggressively.

either good-quality oats mixed with a little bran, or fed one of the brands of pelleted feeds that have vitamins and minerals added.

At all times she should have plenty of water, and access to a salt and mineral lick. Two or three weeks before foaling, decrease the proportion of concentrate feeds because her stomach is increasingly cramped by the pressure of the foal and too much food at any one time causes discomfort. If she is a "maiden mare," it is advisable,

THE BIRTH
The four pictures on the right show the main stages in the birth of a foal. In the first, the mare is standing and the water bag is beginning to appear. Next, the mare is now lying down and the emerging foal has broken through the water bag. In the third picture the foal is almost completely free, and in the final picture it is on its feet, being licked by its mother to warm and dry it. This licking is instinctive, but should the mare fail to do it the foal should be gently but thoroughly rubbed down with a soft towel.

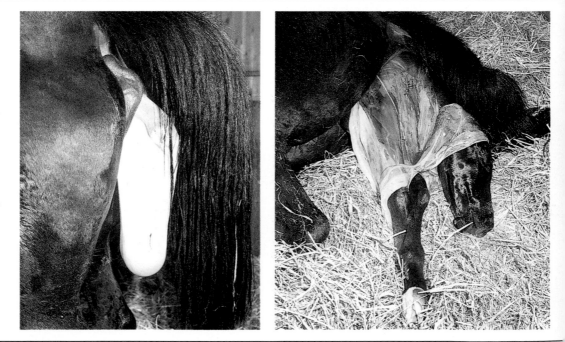

when grooming her, to handle her udder; some maidens are so ticklish there that they resent the foal's attempts to nurse.

Shortly before foaling, her nipples will "wax up" and her udder begin to fill. This varies from mare to mare. Some mares have milk dripping from their udders before the foal is born; some only produce a full udder after the birth. Externally, the muscles and sinews on either side of her tail will relax and sink, so that she appears hollow flanked.

The majority of mares foal easily, and fairly quickly. If foaling indoors, the box should be big enough, previously disinfected,

A Thoroughbred mare late in her pregnancy (left), and the "waxing" which appeared on her nipples (below) as her udder began to fill with milk shortly before her foal was born.

and deeply bedded with clean fresh straw.

Ponies that live out will foal happily out of doors (usually at night). It is important then to check the field for the afterbirth, which should be expelled not more than six hours after foaling. Although most mares do foal without trouble, it is well to advise your veterinarian promptly when foaling seems imminent so that help will be available if necessary.

This help will be essential if you find that the unborn foal is in the breech position, with the hindlegs emerging first instead of the forelegs. This situation will make the birth very difficult, because the foal's hindquarters will have to be forced out before the comparatively narrow head and shoulders (which in a normal birth ease the way for the hindquarters to pass through) can emerge.

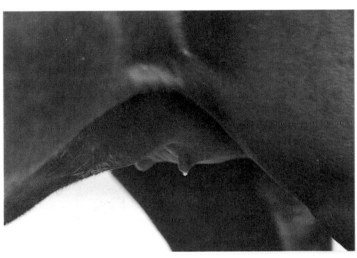

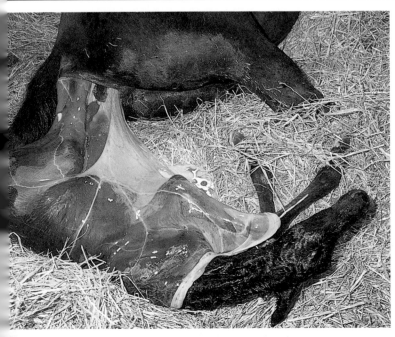

FOAL CARE

Foals that have been well handled from birth grow up with a confidence in humans that will stand them, and their owners, in good stead as they become bigger and stronger and progress from their initial handling to more complicated lessons; they will also have learned the habit of obedience.

The mare, once the foal is born and she is on her feet, will lick the little animal all over, rubbing it with her muzzle so that no part of it is untended. This is her instinctive way of not only drying, but also warming, the foal, because the difference in temperature between the womb and the outside world is very great. If she does not lick her foal, it should be dried and gently massaged with a soft towel.

Soon it will try, awkwardly, to stand up, and look for the mare's udder. If it has trouble finding it, you must help and guide it, for it must have that first milk, the colostrum, which will empty its bowels and clear its intestines of the matter with which those of all newborn mammals are filled.

Give the mare a warm feed such as a bran mash or some warmed bruised oats. Rub her down if she has sweated a lot and then, provided the foal has found the milk bar, leave them alone. But keep a check on them; within six hours the mare should have expelled the afterbirth. If she has, remove it, making sure it is complete, and remove all soiled bedding and replace with fresh. If she hasn't expelled the afterbirth, call your veterinarian immediately.

Ponies that foal outdoors will normally see to the drying, warming and suckling of their foals themselves, but you should check carefully in the pasture for the afterbirth.

On the second day after foaling, if the weather is warm and dry, mare and foal can go out, but on no account should they go out in cold, wet weather. Very young foals are susceptible to chills, which can turn into pneumonia. At first, you should let the foal just follow the dam, but after about a week you should introduce the foal to handling (see page 116). For mares that have foaled out, reverse the proceedings, bringing them in for a time each day so that the foal gets haltered and handled.

About nine days after giving birth, the mare will come into season, which will cause the foal to scour (have diarrhea); sponge its dock and buttocks if they become dirty. If scouring contin-

ues after the mare's period is over, consult the vet. Ask him also when, and with what, the foal should be wormed.

Warmblood foals may be fed concentrates to supplement their diets (see page 116), but until weaning, all that a pony foal needs apart from milk is grass and small shares of the mare's feeds. Don't give foals tidbits because that will encourage them to nip, which colt foals are more apt to do than fillies. If a foal does nip, don't shout at it or hit it; a smart tap on the nose, and "No" said very firmly, will soon teach it not to. As soon as a foal has teeth enough,

however, you can offer it slices of carrot from your hand.

It is not wise to wean foals until they are five months old, and six months is more usual. The least traumatic way is probably to separate mare and foal completely and keep them out of sight and hearing of one another for at least four weeks. The foal, of course, needs a companion, either another foal or, perhaps, an elderly gelding who can act as an "uncle" to the foal. When she is no longer being suckled, the mare's milk will gradually dry up. Don't try to milk her.

All weanlings, of whatever

ABOVE Plenty of exercise is essential to the proper development of a foal.
RIGHT After being separated from its mother, a foal needs a companion such as another foal.

breed, should be kept in at nights during the first winter of their lives. Two will happily share a stall, in which they should have plenty of good hay, a mineral lick, and water in heavy buckets difficult to overturn.

The amount of food that weanlings get should be roughly 1 pound for every month of their lives, up to a maximum of 8

Foals should not be weaned until they are at least five months old; six months is preferable.

pounds, given in two daily feeds. This can be either bruised oats mixed with bran or a hay mix chaff, or pellets. They should be wormed before you start bringing them in for the winter nights, so consult your veterinarian.

They should also continue with their leading lessons, and begin to learn "stable manners" and some of the words they will need to know all their lives, such as "stand" and "move over." Be patient with them; like children, they can't learn too many things at once.

Nothing is more enchanting than to have a mare and foal in your paddock and to watch over the development of the foal, nor more rewarding than to know you are giving a young equine a good start in life by having gained its trust and willing obedience.

BREEDS

The evolution of the horse began in the Eocene ("dawn") epoch some 40 to 60 million years ago with a small, multitoed creature, about the size of a fox or medium-sized dog, which scientists named Eohippus (the "Dawn Horse"). From this unlikely prototype it was possible to trace a progression on the American continent which culminated, about a million years ago, in *Equus caballus*, the forebear of the modern horse.

By the end of the last Ice Age, when the horse had become extinct in the Americas, three distinct "primitive" horses had emerged, from which it is thought the present domestic stock descends. These three were the Asiatic Wild Horse, known as *Equus przewalskii* Poliakov, after Nikolai Przewalski, the Polish colonel who discovered a wild herd in Mongolia in 1881; the Tarpan or plateau horse of Eastern Europe and the Ukrainian steppe lands (*Equus przewalskii gmelini* Antonius) and a very heavy, slow-moving horse, *Equus przewalskii* Silvaticus, which inhabited the wet marshlands of northern Europe. It is sometimes called the Forest Horse (Silvaticus) or the Diluvian Horse, since it became extinct in its primitive form during the Diluvial (postglacial) period.

In the most general terms it is held that the population of light horses descends from Asiatic and Tarpan stock, while the Forest Horse, possibly a deviant of the Asiatic, is at the root of the heavy breeds.

The hippologists Speed, Ebhardt and Skorkowski extended that basic premise and their researches led them to suppose that in the period immediately before domestication there existed four subspecies. They termed these Pony Types 1 and 2 and Horse Types 3 and 4.

Pony Type 1 lived in northwest Europe and was an exceptionally hardy specimen standing about 12 to 12.2 hands. The nearest modern equine to this ancient horse is the Exmoor pony, who retains a number of the prehistoric characteristics in the jaw formation, particularly, and in the "toad" eye and "ice fan" tail.

Pony Type 2, a bigger and coarser type about 14 to 14.2 hands, inhabited northern Eurasia and like Type 1 was exceptionally hardy. Of the modern breeds the Highland Pony would be nearest to this type.

Horse Type 3 was an even bigger specimen, probably standing upwards of 14.3 hands. In appearance it was long, narrow in the body, goose-rumped and long-eared. Its homeland was in Central Asia and its modern equivalent is the golden Akhal-Teké of Turkmenistan, a breed of great endurance and resistant to conditions of excessive heat.

Horse Type 4 was smaller and is possibly of even more importance. It was a more refined type with a high-set tail and a concave rather than a convex profile of the head. It is suggested that this was the prototype of the Arabian, the horse that has to be regarded as the progenitor of the modern breeds.

Its habitat was in Western Asia and it may have resembled the recently rediscovered Caspian Pony of Iran. (Although the Caspian is termed a pony on account of its size and many modern Arabians are less than 15 hands — the usually accepted division between horse and pony — both have *horse* characteristics and the latter is always described in that way.)

"Breeds" or groups of horse sharing similar characteristics of height, color, conformation and so on existed before the intervention of man, their development and characteristics being governed by the environment in which they lived.

The environmental factors encompass climate, soil conditions, the type of terrain and the availability of food. Consequently, animals inhabiting mountain areas, where food is scarce and the climatic conditions are severe, are small in stature. They become highly efficient converters of food; they grow heavy coats as a protection against the weather and they develop remarkable qualities of hardiness and constitutional toughness in the battle for survival.

Their feet are of dense horn to cope with rocky ground underfoot and their action is that best suited to the broken terrain. Mountain ponies are exceptionally sure-footed and in movement bend the knee to avoid stumbling over tussocks, rock outcrops and so on.

Conversely, horses bred in hot, desert conditions adapt to the needs of their particular environment. Those animals bred in ideal climatic conditions where food is plentiful grow larger, although they will be less hardy than the mountain- or desert-bred equine.

Today, and particularly since the advent of stud books and breed societies, the word *breed* has taken on an additional meaning. In fact, with the exception of the Thoroughbred, whose General Stud Book Vol. 1 was published in 1808, the stud books of most of the world's established breeds are no more than 100 years old and some are less than that.

A modern breed can be defined as a group of horses, selectively bred over a period of time sufficient to ensure the production of consistent stock, that share common characteristics of conformation, action, height and color. They must, however, be the progeny of "purebred" parents whose pedigrees are recorded in the stud book of the breed society. Such progeny are then themselves eligible for entry.

There are probably upwards of 150 established and recognized breeds but, of course, there are a great many horses and ponies deriving from specific breeds which are not purebred. In time it is hoped that these partbreds will themselves be included in some sort of register; until then they are classed as "types" on account of their lack of conformational consistency, fixed characteristics and background documentation.

A hunter is a type, so is a hack and a cob and there is no such thing as a *breed* of polo pony. In fact, even the British Riding Pony, that unique and near perfectly proportioned aristocrat of the show ring, is not a breed as such, although its carefully documented background makes it more deserving of the title than many others claiming that distinction.

CHOOSING A HORSE

Your choice of horse depends upon a number of interdependent factors. Principal among these are the price you can afford to pay, your own ability and experience, the purpose for which you want the horse, and the facilities you have available for keeping the animal, which include having enough money to cover feed, shoeing, veterinary bills and so on. Thereafter, and all else being equal, you may take account of your personal preferences relating to the height, color, sex or even breeding of the horse.

Compromises may be made in most of these respects, but the one area in which there can be no question of compromise is the soundness of the prospective purchase. In pragmatic terms, soundness entails the fitness of the horse to stand up to a sustained workload over extended periods. Horses that for any reason are likely to be unsound, and therefore unserviceable, when put to work are always expensive in the long run, however low the purchase price.

The price of a sound riding horse will depend on its age, its potential, and its appearance and conformation. Other criteria will apply if the horse is required specifically for breeding.

In the most general terms, a horse may be said to increase in value up to the age of seven or eight years and to decrease thereafter, but there are all sorts of exceptions to prove that rule. For instance, a ten-year-old, or even a horse older than that, which has a good performance record may fetch a much higher price than a six-year-old with no competitive experience.

The six-year-old, on the other hand, may have the potential to be very good indeed. Assessment in this respect depends upon the horse's conformation, the quality and gymnastic promise of its movement, its temperament (so far as that can be gauged) and, very importantly, its genetic background.

There is, of course, no guarantee implicit in the records of the parents, but a horse bred from a line of sound, proven performers, whose near relatives also have good records, has to be a better proposition than one produced from lines without those distinctions.

Horses of exceptional conformation and movement which are also outstanding in appearance and presence will obviously attract a higher price. Similarly, a really good middleweight horse (one capable of carrying up to 200 pounds) will be more valuable because of his greater versatility than one which is hard-pressed to carry 170 pounds.

Conformation is concerned with the symmetrical proportion of the horse's component parts and their perfection (see Points of the Horse, page 40). Good conformation results in good balance and, in theory and often in practice also, to enhanced performance levels. It will also contribute materially to a longer working life.

Critical to the choice of a horse is the riding ability of the person who is going to ride him. A very good, experienced rider who is able to bring along a young, green horse or to take on a potentially good one who may be a little difficult temperamentally (and many of the best performers have their little idiosyncrasies) has a wider range of choice than the less expert, who may be better off with a made (and therefore more expensive) horse.

For example, a good choice for a ten- or twelve-year old child who has never ridden before would be an experienced, and not too lively, pony or small horse. Even then, price alone is no assurance that the purchase will be satisfactory. A horse or pony that has done well for one rider may come nowhere near to attaining the same level of performance with another who is less competent or sympathetic.

Closely connected with ability and ambition is the purpose for which the horse is needed. This obviously must influence the choice and it will also affect the price. If you want nothing more than a quiet, comfortable horse to ride along bridle paths and untrafficked roads there should be little difficulty in obtaining something suitable. It becomes more of a problem and more expensive as the level of performance expected of the horse increases.

The larger of the pony breeds, such as Welsh or Connemaras, are good prospects for lightweight adults who want to hack and perhaps compete at club level. For serious eventing, however, the horse must have a fairly large proportion of Thoroughbred blood if he is to have the speed, courage and mental capacity for that demanding sport. A threequarterbred horse with some pony blood in his background is a good mix and that sort of combination should also be a good show jumping prospect.

Increasingly, of course, the Continental warmbloods (half-breds in the main) are very successful in show jumping, and they dominate the dressage arenas for which their even temperaments, less fiery and independent than that of the Thoroughbred, make them most suitable. Notable among them are the big, powerful Hanoverians, the more refined Trakehners and the versatile Dutch Warmbloods,

CHOOSING A HORSE

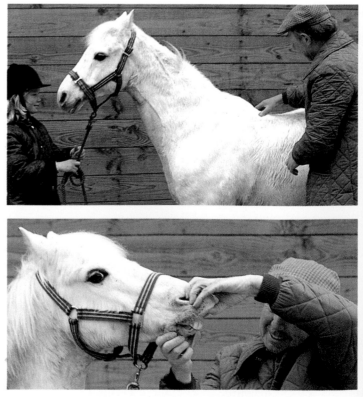

When you're buying a horse or pony, always have it examined by a vet before you commit yourself to the purchase. The vet will check the animal's pulse and breathing, and then examine it from head to toe, looking for signs of injury or sickness and any weakness in its bones, joints and muscles.

The Arab is probably the most beautiful breed in the world.

the Danish sport horses and the near *beau ideal* of the competition horse, the tough and versatile Selle Français.

For endurance riding the Quarter Horse is a good choice, although many people feel that nothing can really approach the Arab horse and his near derivatives. Tough and enduring, these horses have remarkable stamina and are very rarely sick, sorry or unsound.

They would not, however, be the ideal choice for jumping or cross country work although, as always, there will be the occasional exceptions. (In Britain, Arab horses are able to race on the flat under Jockey Club rules at meetings organized by the Arab Horse Society.)

For driving and general harness work the choice is wide. There are Cleveland Bays, Welsh Cobs, Hungarians, Lipizzaners, Oldenburgs, Gelderlanders, Holsteiners, Friesians and many other suitable breeds.

The final and, for many people, the controlling factor in choosing a horse is the facilities which are available. Thoroughbreds, who will rarely winter out well, or horses in continual work, will need to be stabled and fed a diet of concentrates and hay. Other considerations include the labor involved in caring for them and the extra cost of clothing for clipped horses, as well, of course, as the necessity of giving them adequate daily exercise.

Ponies, their crosses and equivalents are far more easily kept. They need a paddock of adequate size — not less than 1 to $1\frac{1}{2}$ acres per pony — and they will need supplementary feeding on a modest scale, but they live very well without a stable and all the extra work and cost that that inevitably entails.

If money is not a factor, horses can be boarded and then someone else does the work for you, but that is, of course, an expensive way of keeping them.

Color is hardly a matter of great importance since it is said, very rightly, that "good horses are never a bad color." It is advisable, however, to avoid pale colors since they usually indicate lack of a sound constitution.

The sex may be a matter of more importance. Some mares can be a little unpredictable and touchy when they are in season, and this could cause problems in a horse used primarily for competition.

POINTS TO CHECK	GOOD	BAD
Head	Teeth sound and meet properly. Nostrils clear. No signs of scars from wind operations	Teeth sharp, broken or missing or unevenly worn by cribbing. Cuts or ulcers in mouth
Breathing	Regular with no wheezing	Breathing shallow, difficult or irregular
Back	No sign of damage or injury	Misaligned vertebrae. Signs of galling or previous injury
Legs	Good bone, no scarring. Good joint action	Restricted or painful joint movement
Feet	Sound, well shaped. Hoofs properly trimmed and shod	Uneven wear of shoes. Defects in hoof wall. Signs of previous problems such as laminitis.
Action	Supple, strong and well coordinated	Signs of lameness. Difficulty in backing due to previous back injury
Temperament	Calm, confident and trusting. Easily handled	Nervous, highly strung, aggressive
Conformation	Standing square with good top line. Well proportioned	Stands awkwardly. Signs of disproportion

● Remember horses are usually measured in hands. One hand is 4 inches.

COLOR & MARKINGS

Horses are described by their coat color, and in stud books, registers and passports further specific identification is made by the white marks appearing on the body, principally on the head and lower legs.

The origin of the coat color lies in the 39 individual genes, the possible combinations being very numerous. In some breeds, color is of particular importance and breeders of such horses as Palominos, Appaloosas, Pintos and Albinos pay great attention to color when planning matings. Armed with a knowledge of simple genetics, based on the Mendelian laws of hereditary characteristics (the word "gene" was first used by the Austrian biologist/monk Gregor Mendel, 1822–84), breeding for color is no more difficult than breeding for any other characteristic.

The accepted basic colors are black, brown, bay and chestnut, doubtful cases being decided by examination of the hair color on the muzzle, and there is an established nomenclature to describe coat patterns. For instance, *whole-* or *solid-colored* describes a coat which contains no hair of a different color anywhere on the body.

Part-colored (or, in Britain, just "colored") refers to a coat with patches of different color, like the *skew-* and *piebalds*. *Flecked* is when the coat has small irregular groups of white hair. *Fleabitten* is the word given to the brown specks which develop with age on the coats of gray horses. *Gray-ticked* is the name for a coat in which a small number of gray hairs appear throughout.

whole/solid

colored/part colored

flecked

fleabitten

gray-ticked

LEG MARKINGS

stocking   sock   pastern

heel   coronet   ermine mark

Leg markings A stocking is a white area between the coronet and the knee or hock; a sock extends only to the cannon.

BODY MARKINGS

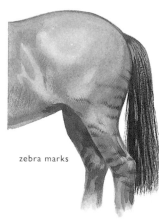

flesh marks

Flesh marks
Flesh marks are areas of unpigmented hair and skin.

FACE MARKINGS

blaze   star   stripe   star/stripe   white face

Zebra marks Bars or zebra marks on the legs are a throwback to the camouflage of early horses.

zebra marks

MUZZLE MARKINGS
Muzzle marks include snips, white muzzles and lip marks.

snip

white muzzle

lip marks

black

brown

black-brown

bay

bay-brown

chestnut

cream

dun

gray

blue roan

red roan

strawberry roan

piebald

skewbald

odd-colored

palomino

liver chestnut

dapple gray

fleabitten gray

tobiano

COLORS

Black The color occurs when black pigment is present throughout. White may be present in the markings.

Brown There is a mixture of black and brown pigment in the coat.

Black-brown Black is predominant but the muzzle, and sometimes the flanks, are brown.

Bay-brown Predominant coloring brown. Bay muzzle, black legs, mane and tail.

Bay The color varies from dull, reddish brown to a golden shade that is nearly chestnut.

Chestnut A gold color ranging through a number of shadings. A **liver chestnut** describes a coat the color of raw liver.

Cream The color is the result of an unpigmented skin. The iris is similarly deficient and the eye looks to be pink or blue as a result.

Dun This is a "primitive" coloring characteristic of the wild horse. It can be either yellow dun or blue, the skin being black in the latter instance with the body color being an evenly distributed dilution of the same color. The yellow dun shows a pronounced diffusion of yellow pigment in the hair. The reddish-yellow coloring with darker mane and tail which sometimes occurs is often referred to as a **Claybank dun**.

Gray A varied mixture of black and white hairs on a black skin.

Roan There are three divisions. **Blue roan** is when there is a percentage of white hair, giving the blue effect, on a black or brown body. **Red roan** is the result of a bay or bay-brown body color mixed with white hairs. **Strawberry roan** is a chestnut body color with an admixture of white hairs.

Piebald A term referring to a coat made up of large, irregular patches of black and white.

Skewbald This term describes a similar coat made up of white patches and any other color except black.

Odd-colored A coat of more than two colors.

Palomino A gold coat with white mane and tail.

Appaloosa The distinctive coloring of horses of the Appaloosa breed.

Albino An all-white animal, usually pink-eyed. It is the result of a congenital absence of skin pigment.

Certain color definitions are unique to the United States and include the following:

Buckskin A dark cream color described as being "a shade lighter or darker than a pumpkin."

Calico A name for a part-colored horse.

Pinto This covers all kinds of part-colored horses. In the West and Southwest, a part-colored horse is called *tobiano*. In South America *overo* is the word used to describe a dark body color with white patches or "lightning streaks."

Sorrel A chestnut-red-brown coloring which may be somewhere between bright bay and yellow chestnut, in which case the mane and tail are either white or reddish; or it can be a lighter shade of chestnut. It can also be applied to a red roan.

EXMOOR, DARTMOOR & NEW FOREST

The Exmoor, Dartmoor and New Forest ponies are the three breeds of British native pony which originated in southern England. They are all excellent ponies for children, and the larger Exmoor and New Forest ponies make good family ponies.

EXMOOR PONY

The Exmoor pony has from time immemorial inhabited the wild moorlands of southwest England, from which it takes its name. Without doubt, it is the oldest of the British native pony breeds and there is evidence of its use with chariots in the Bronze Age. There is also a strong connection with Pony Type 1 of the predomestication period, mentioned in the introduction to this section, which is sometimes referred to as the Celtic pony. Fossilized remains of this early equine, which were found in Alaska, reveal unique characteristics that still persist in the Exmoor.

The jaw formation, for instance, is the same and it is quite different from that of any other pony.

Only three herds now run on the Moor, although Exmoors are bred on a very small scale elsewhere in Britain. About 50 foals a year are registered with the Exmoor Pony Society in Britain and are branded with a star on the near shoulder, the herd brand being put on the quarter.

There is a basic uniformity of type among the Moor herds;

DARTMOOR PONIES

Exmoors are easily recognizable, for example, by the "toad" eye, "ice fan" tail and the flecked coloring around the muzzle, eye and flanks. There are, however, two distinct types, the Acland (the famous Anchor herd) and the Withypool, which is a little larger, is darker and has a somewhat straighter head profile.

EXMOOR PONIES

The height does not exceed 12.3 hands and the permitted colors for purebred are bay, brown or dun with black points. There are no white markings.

The Exmoor is robust, naturally hardy and very strong and at one time carried full-grown men hunting. It is still a great hunting pony for children and small adults and

DARTMOOR PONY Dartmoors are versatile ponies which can be ridden or driven. Their low, free action gives a comfortable ride.

HORSE	ORIGIN	HEIGHT	COLOR	CONFORMATION	FEATURES
Exmoor	England	up to 12.3 hands	bay, brown or dun	robust, hardy and strong	children's riding and harness pony
Dartmoor	England	up to 12.2 hands	bay, black or brown	compact and elegant	excellent riding pony for children
New Forest	England	12 to 14.2 hands	any except cream, pie- or skewbald	strong and agile, powerful quarters	good family and competition pony

NEW FOREST PONY The first known records of the New Forest ponies date from the reign of King Canute, who was king of England from 1016 to 1035.

EXMOOR PONY HEAD The head of the Exmoor pony has a wide forehead and an unusual flecked coloring around the muzzle and prominent "toad" eyes.

goes well in harness. Used as a first or second cross with the Thoroughbred, it makes an excellent hunter. Although the Exmoor is recognized as being a "rare breed" its survival does not seem to be in doubt within the foreseeable future.

EXMOOR PONY Exmoors have probably been in use since the Bronze Age (which in Britain lasted from about 2000 to 500 BC), when they are thought to have been used to pull chariots.

Hands			
18			
16			
14			
12			
10			
8			
6			
4			
2			
Exmoor Pony	Dartmoor Pony	New Forest Pony	

DARTMOOR PONY

Neighbor of the Exmoor is the popular Dartmoor pony, another equine of ancient origin first mentioned early in the 11th century and which for some 400 years was used to carry tin off the Cornish moors. Few Dartmoors are bred on the Moor today, but there are numerous studs throughout Britain and the United States.

The greatest influence on the breed was the stallion Leat, foaled in 1918 and a son of the purebred Arabian Dwarka. The modern Dartmoor is an excellent and elegant children's riding pony with a good low riding action and an exceptional temperament. The breed crosses well with either Thoroughbred or Arab, and purebreds are frequently seen in harness. The ponies do not exceed 12.2 hands and are usually bay, black or brown.

NEW FOREST PONY

The New Forest Pony originated in that area of southern England which was once a Royal hunting ground maintained for the preservation of deer. The Commoners of the Forest still exercise their Right of Common Pasture to run ponies there, but increasingly the modern New Forest pony is the product of private studs situated not only in the area but also farther away.

Because the Forest was on the way to Winchester, once the English capital, the opportunities to cross domestic stock with the wild ponies was always an easy option. In more recent times, particularly during the 19th century, efforts were made to check the degeneration of the Forest stock by introducing a variety of outcrosses. These included Welsh, Thoroughbred, Arab, Fell, Hackney and even Dartmoor, Exmoor and Highland. All of them play a part in the background of the Forester, and as a result, there is an inevitable variation in type.

Nonetheless, the present day New Forest is a resounding commercial success and in great demand as an all-round family and competition pony in Britain and elsewhere.

Its size (the upper height limit is 14.2 hands) gives it a greater versatility than the smaller natives and the pony is renowned for good riding action and a remarkably even temperament. There are smaller New Forest ponies, although very rarely below 12 hands, and the best of these often display more quality than their larger relatives.

The official standard of the New Forest Pony Society, the publishers of the New Forest Stud book in Britain, allows the ponies to be of any color except piebald, skewbald or cream, but bays, browns and chestnuts predominate.

NEW FOREST PONIES

WELSH PONIES & COBS

Each of the four Welsh breeds is ideal for both riding and for harness work. All of them – including the diminutive Welsh Mountain Pony – are well able to carry adults, although the Welsh Pony (Section B) is often bred specifically as a child's pony.

SECTION TYPES

The largest and most influential of the British native pony societies is the Welsh Pony and Cob Society. It was formed in 1901 (in 1907 a similar organization was founded in this country) and Volume 1 of the Stud Book was published in the same year. There are four sections to the Book plus another one for partbreds. Section A is devoted to the Welsh Mountain Pony, the foundation of the Welsh breeds, which does not exceed 12 hands, Section B is for the Welsh pony of riding type with a height limit of 13.2, and Sections C and D cover the Welsh Cobs. The first of these is for the Welsh Pony of Cob type, again with a height limit of 13.2, and the latter is for the larger Welsh Cob, which is usually between 14.2 and 15.2 hands but can be even bigger.

In the United States, the designations Welsh Pony and Welsh Mountain Pony are used interchangeably. Here they are categorized as Section A (not exceeding 12.2 hands) and Section B (not exceeding 14.2 hands). A further category, Section C, or Pony of Cob Type, which is not recognized in the United States, refers to a Welsh Pony that may have a strain of Cob blood.

MOUNTAIN PONY

The Mountain Pony provides the pattern for the Welsh breeds and is basic to them. From this most beautiful of the world's ponies the Section B and the Cobs are largely derived. The origin of the ponies cannot, however, be established with any certainty. Among the first references to Welsh ponies and cobs is that appearing in the laws of Hywel Dda, ruler of Deheubarth, which were written in AD 930. But there were ponies running in the mountains of Wales long before the Christian era and probably from the beginnings of the equine race in its recognizable form.

There have been infusions of Eastern, Thoroughbred and Hackney blood (of the old, original roadster type) from time to time in the breed's long history and, indeed, the patriarchal Dyoll Starlight, founding father of the "improved" breed (the watershed between the "old" and "improved" type being the establishment of the Stud Book), was out of the mare Moonlight who was believed to be a descendant of the Crawshay Bailey Arab, a stallion turned out on the Brecon Beacons in the 1850s. Since the formation of the Stud Book, however, the refinements in appearance and conformation have been the result of careful selection within the breed itself.

The Mountain Pony exhibits quite unmistakable characteristics. The small head, tapering to the muzzle, with its small pointed ears and dominated by the large bold eye, is particularly noticeable, while the action is no less so. The Mountain Pony moves with immense power, flexing the hocks under the body and using the foreleg from the shoulder with some knee action.

WELSH PONY

The Welsh Pony, Section B, is a larger, finer, edition of the Section A, the modern pony being described specifically as a riding pony with less knee action than

MOUNTAIN PONY The beautiful Welsh Mountain Pony is intelligent, tough and good natured. It is used both for riding and in harness.

COB TYPE PONY

MOUNTAIN PONY

WELSH PONY The Section B Welsh Pony is bred primarily for riding, but it will also perform very well when used in harness.

the Section A. In that role it has become extremely popular as a child's mount, both in the show ring and for all other purposes. It is an excellent jumper and like all the Welsh breeds goes well in harness.

The predominant influence is, of course, the Mountain Pony, but also at the root of the modern Section B is the stallion Tan-y-Bwlch Berwyn, foaled in 1924. He was by Sahara, described as a Barb but very Arabian in appearance. The Welsh Pony may be any solid color, but piebald or skewbald are not permitted.

PONY OF COB TYPE

The Welsh Pony of Cob type was originally the "farm pony" which was able to do every sort of job from hauling to shepherding sheep. It is, indeed, the stronger counterpart of the Mountain Pony and many of the best have been produced by Section A ponies bred to small cob mares. Sure-footed, strong, active and very hardy, it makes a wonderful all-round family pony suitable for

Hands

| 18 |
| 16 |
| 14 |
| 12 |
| 10 |
| 8 |
| 6 |
| 4 |
| 2 |

Welsh pony   Cob Type Pony   Welsh Cob

*PONY OF COB TYPE
The Welsh Pony of Cob Type is a sturdy, sure-footed animal that makes an ideal family pony.*

WELSH COB The largest of the Welsh breeds, the Welsh Cob is a strong, fast horse with great stamina.

FEET The Welsh Cob has well-shaped feet with round, dense hoofs which help it to work well over rough ground. There is also some silky feathering over the heels.

WELSH COB

WELSH PONY

HORSE	ORIGIN	HEIGHT	COLOR	CONFORMATION	FEATURES
Mountain Pony	Wales	12 hands	any except piebald or skewbald	all the Welsh breeds have well-shaped heads, long necks and powerful quarters	all the Welsh breeds are excellent for riding and harness work. the Welsh Pony is ideal for children
Welsh Pony	Wales	13.2 hands	any solid color		
Pony of Cob Type	Wales	13.2 hands	as Mountain Pony		
Welsh Cob	Wales	14.2 to 15.2 hands	as Mountain Pony		

general riding, jumping, hunting, trekking, pack and light draft work. It is also an excellent driving and harness racing pony.

The Section C Pony can be any color except piebald or skewbald. The head is of good quality and ponylike, with bold eyes spaced well apart, and set on a long neck and strong shoulders. The back is muscular and strong and the body is deep, with powerful hindquarters and strong legs with good bone.

WELSH COB

The larger Section D Cob is just as versatile and in harness is a phenomenal performer with exceptional powers of endurance. Additionally, it is an excellent mount under saddle and a good jumper. Crossed with the Thoroughbred, the result is a hunter, competition horse or driving horse of the finest quality.

In days gone by in Britain, the Welsh Cobs, which were essential to the life of the farming community, were in much demand for military use. They hauled guns and supporting transport and were ridden by mounted infantry. Up to World War II and after,

there was a thriving trade in cobs between Wales and the English cities, particularly London, where thousands were used for light delivery purposes.

The heartland of Welsh Cob breeding was always Cardiganshire and it remains so today, the "Cardi" men claiming with justification and a fierce pride that their Cobs are the world's best animals for riding and driving.

They are also very popular at shows (especially in their native Wales), where they are shown in hand to demonstrate the spectacular and high-stepping trot for which they are renowned. The action is notably free, with the knee well bent and the foreleg

extended far forward and straight from the shoulder.

In conformation, the Welsh Cob is a larger version of the Welsh Pony of Cob Type, and it may also be of any color except piebald or skewbald. Like the Section C pony, it has a good head and a long neck, which is usually well crested in mature stallions.

The shoulders are strong and laid back, the quarters are lengthy and powerful and the tail is well set. The hind legs should not be too bent, and the hocks should not be behind an imaginary line drawn from the point of the quarter to the fetlock joint. The hocks are large and flat, and the feet well shaped with dense hoofs.

FELL, DALES & CONNEMARA

The Fell and Dales ponies both originated in England, the Fell in the northwest and the Dales in the northeast. The Connemara is Ireland's only native pony, an ancient breed whose outstanding qualities have made it popular all over the world.

FELL PONY

The Fell pony is closely related to the Dales but is lighter in build. It does not exceed 14 hands and usually has a good riding shoulder, which makes it a suitable cross with the Thoroughbred, the resulting progeny being ideal hunters, strong, sensible and sure-footed. In its own right it is a good all-round riding pony for the family and like the Dales it is much used for trekking in Britain. Both ponies are noted for the soundness of their constitution and their ability to work and thrive on limited rations. The Fell breed description states uncompromisingly that they "should be constitutionally as hard as iron."

In earlier days the Fell was used as a pack animal to cart lead over the rough and demanding terrain between the mines and the Tyneside docks, as well as taking its turn on the farm. The ponies, working in trains of twenty or so under the charge of a single mounted man, could average 240 miles per week, carrying loads of 224 pounds each.

Although there is plenty of evidence to show the influence of the Friesian on the breed, it is probable that the Fell pony also owes much to the old, and now extinct, Galloway from which it gets its good feet of characteristic hard blue horn. The Fell colors are black, brown, bay and gray with a minimum of white markings.

One of the most famous of Fell stallions was Lingcropper, who was widely used in the fells during the 18th century. He was found on Stainmore (then a part of Westmorland) saddled and bridled, but there was no sign of his rider. This was during the Jacobite risings and that may account for the latter's absence.

DALES PONY

The Fell and Dales ponies are similar in many respects, the two benefiting from infusions of Friesian blood first introduced during the Roman occupation of Britain. The origin of the Dales Pony is on the eastern side of the Pennines, while the homeland of the Fell is on the northern edges and in Cumbria's Lake District.

Of the two the Dales (14 to 14.2 hands) is the larger and is sometimes described as a heavy horse in miniature. Capable of carrying a 225-pound man or pulling a ton of weight, the Dales was once used as a harness and pack pony, carrying lead and coal from the mines and also working underground. The ponies were also used extensively for every sort of work on the hilly farms.

Today the Dales is popular in Britain as a trekking pony, for which its sure-footedness and stamina make it particularly suitable. Increasingly, too, it is used as a harness pony, for it has always been noted as a brilliant trotter. In the 19th century the breed was much influenced by the notable Welsh Cob trotting stallion, Comet, and all modern Dales trace back to this sire. The usual color for the Dales Pony is black but bay, brown and occasionally gray are also found.

The Dales has a small, neat head set on a longish neck and deep, sloping shoulders. The girth is also deep, and the back is short and strong. The quarters are muscular and powerful, and although the legs are short they are strong with good bone.

CONNEMARA

The Connemara, although bred extensively in Europe and America, belongs to Ireland and takes its name from the rugged Connemara country on the western seaboard.

For centuries the ponies of Connemara were an essential element in this harsh and inhospitable area, being used as farm and pack ponies in every possible circumstance and subsisting on minimal feed. Against this background of bog and moor studded with rocky outcrops, the Connemara pony developed remarkable qualities of hardiness, sagacity and agility.

Its history goes back to the 6th century, when the Celts were raiding and trading actively on the west coast of Ireland. They introduced horses of Oriental type that would have been crossed with the indigenous stock, the latter then being similar to the ponies of Norway, Iceland and the Shetlands.

During the 19th century, Welsh Cobs were introduced with the object of improving the breed and a little later, and less successfully, Hackneys and Clydesdales and some Thoroughbred blood. It was not until 1923 that the Connemara Pony Breeders' Society was formed, and three years later it published the first Stud Book, restricting registration to

FELL PONY The Fell pony is one of the toughest of pony breeds. It is excellent as an all-around family pony and popular for trekking and driving.

FELL PONY

DALES PONY

seventy-five mares and six stallions that were considered to be of suitable type. The two most successful stallions were probably Rebel, foaled in 1922, and Golden Gleam, who was born a decade later.

Of all the native ponies the Connemara is probably the most versatile. Standing around 13 to 14.2 hands it is small enough to be ridden by a child and is well able to carry a small adult. A real riding pony, the Connemara is intelligent, very sure-footed and tractable. It excels as a hunting pony

and is a natural, athletic jumper.

The American Connemara Pony Society was founded in 1956 because of the increasing numbers of the breed in this country. Today, only about 15 percent of the ACPS registrations are of imported stock, in contrast to the nearly 70 percent which were imports at the time of the society's founding.

CONNEMARA PONY The Connemara is a native of western Ireland, taking its name from the rugged Connemara area of County Galway. Intelligent, sure-footed and athletic, it is an ideal competition pony.

CONNEMARA PONIES

DALES PONY

DALES PONY The Dales Pony is more heavily built than its close relative the Fell and it can carry or pull heavier loads. It is increasingly being used as a harness pony.

HORSE	ORIGIN	HEIGHT	COLOR	CONFORMATION	FEATURES
Fell Pony	England	14 hands	black, brown, bay or gray	muscular and strong	good riding and driving pony
Dales Pony	England	14 to 14.2 hands	black, bay, brown or gray	muscular and strong	good riding and driving pony
Connemara Pony	Ireland	13 to 14.2 hands	gray, black, brown, dun	strong, beautiful and intelligent	superb riding and jumping pony

HIGHLAND & SHETLAND

Highlands and Shetlands are strong, versatile ponies that have been in use for centuries in their native Scotland. The Highland is a fine all-round pony, and the tiny Shetland is a useful mount for very small children and like its cousin the American Shetland is a very good harness pony.

HIGHLAND PONY

Scotland's Highland Pony is usually described as being the modern breed nearest in character to the primitive Pony Type 2 referred to in the introduction to this breed section.

Without doubt, the breed is very old and it is possible that its descent can be connected with the North European Horse. The famous cave drawings at Lascaux, France, that are thought to be 15,000 to 20,000 years old, depict horses which are very similar in color (particularly the variations of dun) and conformation to some of the modern Highlands. They show, too, the barred or "zebra" leg markings that still occur on the Highland pony. (Colors in the modern Highland include all shades of dun, gray, some bays and the occasional liver chestnut with silver mane and tail. Dorsal stripes are usual.)

Up to relatively recent times there appeared to be two distinct types of Highland pony, the Mainland and the lighter Western Isles type, which had pronounced and superior riding characteristics. Today, however, no distinction is made between the two.

Over the years much use has been made of outside blood. Percheron and Clydesdale crosses were used with some regularity and in the 16th century the Mainland Highlands were much improved by French horses sent to James IV of Scotland by the French king, Louis XII. The greatest influence, however, was the use of Oriental blood and certainly the Dukes of Atholl, who for centuries bred the Highland selectively, used Oriental horses as early as the 1500s. The first recorded stallion bred by the Dukes of Atholl was, in fact, a piebald named Morelle who was foaled in 1853. His son Glen Tilt and grandson Glengarry I made significant contributions to the breed but probably the most fam-

ous of the Atholl Stud stallions was the great Herd Laddie. He was the sire of King George V's famous shooting pony Jock.

The Highland is a big-bodied, strong pony not over 14.2 hands and was used for every sort of agricultural purpose on the farms.

Because of their strength, placid temperament and sure-footedness Highlands make ideal hunting ponies and are used to carry the heavy carcass of the dead stag down from the hill. Today, they also work in the forestry plantations in Scotland and on the grouse moors, and they are popular as trekking ponies and for general riding and driving. The Highland is also good foundation stock for the breeding of hunters and competition horses when crossed with the Thoroughbred.

SHETLAND PONY

The other Scottish pony, the Shetland, is the ultimate *multum in parvo* of the equine race with a strength out of all proportion to its diminutive size. The average height is 40 inches at the withers, Shetlands by tradition being measured in inches instead of hands (the medieval measurement of a "hand" — the width of a man's hand — equals 4 inches). The foundation color is black but bays, browns, chestnuts and part-col-

HIGHLAND PONIES

HIGHLAND PONY The strong, well-built Highland is still used as a working pony in its native Scotland, as well as being a popular all-around pony there and elsewhere.

HORSE	ORIGIN	HEIGHT	COLOR	CONFORMATION	FEATURES
Highland Pony	Scotland	14.2 hands	dun, gray, bay, chestnut	compact and big bodied	good all-around pony
Shetland Pony	Scotland	40 inches	various, but usually black	short but very strong	good children's pony
American Shetland	USA	11 to 12.2 hands	various	fine and elegant	excellent riding and harness pony

Hands

18			
16			
14			
12			
10			
8			
6			
4			
2			

Highland Pony   American Shetland Pony   Shetland Pony

ored individuals are also found.

Because of the isolation of its geographical position, the Shetland is probably the purest of the native breeds, and it is the scarcity of forage on the islands that has ensured the maintenance of its exceptionally small size. Its origins are not entirely clear, but it is thought that the ponies may have come over from Scandinavia before the Bronze Age. The earliest traces of the ponies on the islands of Shetland and Orkney are dated as being of that period, which was more than 2500 years ago.

On the Islands the Shetlands were used on the farms for plowing, general farm work and as pack animals to haul the seaweed and peat. In the 1840s, when legislation prohibited the use of women and children to pull the coal cars in the mines, Shetlands were supplied in large numbers to the Durham coalfields, which led to the production of a miniature draft-type animal.

The type and character was fixed and reestablished largely through the agency of the Londonderry Stud in Bressay, Scotland, in about 1870. Most of the present-day quality stock can be traced to the famous Londonderry sires, in particular Jack and his sons, Lord of the Isles (exported to America) and Laird of Noss and Odin.

The Shetland is independent and intelligent and, properly treated, makes a good mount for young children and a useful harness pony. In general it does not cross satisfactorily. Nonetheless it is at the base of the American Shetland, the Pony of the Americas — the result of a Shetland stallion bred to an Appaloosa mare — and the pygmy pony, the Falabella.

AMERICAN SHETLAND

The American Shetland is the result of crossings between the finer types of Island Shetland with Hackney blood topped off with an admixture of Arab and small Thoroughbred. The result is a brilliant, extravagantly-moving miniature harness horse, spirited, intelligent and very spectacular. It is claimed that this new "breed" retains the native hardiness, constitution and frugality, but this is both arguable and unlikely. The pony can be any color but the height limit is 12.2.

AMERICAN SHETLAND PONY

AMERICAN SHETLAND The result of crossing the Shetland with other breeds, the American Shetland is larger and finer than the British. It is used both for riding and in harness.

SHETLAND The tiny Shetland is a strong, hardy pony which makes an ideal first mount for young children.

SHETLAND PONIES

MUSTANG, PONY OF THE AMERICAS & CHINCOTEAGUE

The origins of the legendary Mustang and of the Chincoteague Pony can be traced back to the horses brought to the New World by the early Spanish settlers, but the Pony of the Americas is one of the world's newest breeds, dating back only to the 1950s.

MUSTANG

The American Mustang, descendant of the horses that were brought to the New World by the 16th century conquistadors and that either escaped or were turned loose, still exists in small numbers in the feral state, but a greater number are preserved on ranches. Once they were the utility range horses of America and to some degree they are still used in rodeos. But although they are in theory and law a protected species, the Mustangs are now in serious decline and are often the subject of indiscriminate slaughter, like the Brumbies of Australia.

They were never a fixed breed, but rather a scrub type of lightweight horse varying considerably in conformation and height, the average being about 15 hands or less. Nonetheless, they formed the basis of many other breeds, and they were the ponies used by the Indians of the Plains.

The Mustang was originally a mixture of Andalusian and Barb blood, which developed into the Chickasaw horse and the Cayuse Indian pony. These both had admixtures of Appaloosa, Paint and possibly French Norman blood derived from the imports made by early settlers. In fact, the wild Mustang was only known by that name in Texas and New Mexico. Farther north they were called Broncos and even farther north they were called Cayuse. In the states of Wyoming and Montana they were usually known as either Texas ponies, Broncos or just Broncs.

PONY OF THE AMERICAS

The Pony of the Americas is one of the world's most recently established breeds. The breed was founded in 1956 by Leslie Broomhower of Iowa, who two years previously had crossed a Shetland pony stallion with an Appaloosa mare to create a miniature spotted horse suitable for young people in terms of size, temperament and performance.

The first Pony of the Americas was foaled in 1954 and was known as Black Hand 1. Since then the breed has been much improved.

There are now well in excess of 1500 ponies registered and the breed standard, which is exhaustive in comparison to that of many of the older established breeds, calls for a conformation that incorporates the best points of the Quarter Horse and the Arabian while displaying the Appaloosa coloring and principal characteristics.

The ponies vary in height between 11.2 and 13.2 hands and the following colors are accepted: *Leopard:* a basic white body color with dark spots over the whole

MUSTANG

MUSTANG The Mustang, whose ancestors were brought to North America by the Spanish, is a good light saddle horse once it has been broken and domesticated.

HORSE	ORIGIN	HEIGHT	COLOR	CONFORMATION	FEATURES
Mustang	USA	14.2 hands	various	small, robust, lightweight	good light saddle horse
Pony of the Americas	USA	11.2 to 13.2 hands	according to breed standards	sturdy and muscular	attractive all-round children's pony
Chincoteague	USA	12 hands	various	small and horselike	of limited use

CHINCOTEAGUE *The Chincoteague is found on two small islands off the coast of Virginia.*

CHINCOTEAGUE

EYE SCLERA Like the Appaloosa, the Pony of the Americas has a white ring (sclera) around each eye.

PONY OF THE AMERICAS

PONY OF THE AMERICAS The first Pony of the Americas – Black Hand 1 – was foaled in 1954, the result of crossing a Shetland stallion with an Appaloosa mare.

body and neck; *Snowflake:* a basic dark body color with a white blanket over the croup, hindquarters, loins and back or parts of those areas; *Frost:* a dark body color with "frost" type white markings "sprinkled" over all or part of the coat; *Marbleized Roan:* a roan body color (including the neck) with a mixture of light and dark hairs (the light color predominating) forming "varnish marks"; and *White:* white but with black spots on the quarters and/or body or on parts of the body, such as the back, loins, croup or quarters.

CHINCOTEAGUE

The ponies of Virginia's Chincoteague and Assateague islands have been there since the arrival of the conquistadors. Essentially they are degenerate, scrub stock of no commercial value. The 100 to 200 ponies concerned average about 12 hands and are poor physical specimens, due to inbreeding, with a predominance of colored coat patterns.

These islands are the responsibility of the Chincoteague Volunteer Fire Department. Once a year, the ponies are herded off Assateague and made to swim the narrow channel separating that island from Chincoteague. At Chincoteague the ponies are driven into pens to facilitate the sale of the colts. The money raised goes toward feeding the rest of the herd in their sandy marshland habitat.

In recent years there has been conflict between the interests of the Fire Department and the Federal Fish and Wildlife Service,

Hands			
18			
16			
14			
12			
10			
8			
6			
4			
2			
	Mustang	Chincoteague	Pony of the Americas

introduced to Assateague in 1943.

The latter, in an attempt to control the movement of the ponies, restricted the herds to a low, marshy area of the 9000-acre island. This limited the already-sparse grazing and prevented the animals from reaching the sea where they go in order to escape the virulent summer mosquitoes. In 1962, as a result of their confinement and exceptionally high flood tides, many drowned.

A number of children's books written by Marguerite Henry about the Chincoteague pony Misty probably accounts for their hold on the American imagination.

SABLE ISLAND, AUSTRALIAN & TIMOR

The Sable Island Pony is numerically a very small breed, most of whose members live in small, half-wild herds on their native island in the northwest Atlantic. The Australian and Timor ponies, though differing widely in type and refinement, are numerous and fully domesticated.

SABLE ISLAND PONY

Sable Island, first named Santa Cruz by the Spanish in the 16th century, is a barren island resembling a large sandbank, the vegetation being confined largely to the coarse sand grasses. It lies some 100 miles from Nova Scotia, Canada, in the Atlantic Ocean and is about 30 miles long and one mile wide.

Herds of half-wild ponies have lived on the island from the 16th century, when they were taken there in the hope of a settlement being established. As early as 1518, Baron de Lery attempted to found a small colony on Sable (sand) Island and took both cattle and some horses there. It is possible that toward the end of the century (1580s) the Portuguese may also have put ponies on the island in an attempt to create a colony.

However, there is written evidence that in 1739 the only animals on Sable Island were foxes, although the Boston Huguenot who "took possession" of the island at that date states later that "now there are ... between 20 and 30 horses . . ." Today, there are perhaps 300 ponies surviving on the rough herbage.

They are hardy animals by reason of their environment and are said to be docile if caught and trained early enough. The height of the ponies is around 14 hands, and the colors are usually chestnut, bay, brown, black or gray. As might be expected, the conformation is no more than moderate.

AUSTRALIAN PONY

The Australian Pony resembles the Welsh Mountain Pony, which was largely instrumental in producing this quality children's riding pony.

The first recorded pony arrived in Sydney, Australia, in 1803, but it was not until 1920, when the influence of imported Welsh ponies was being felt increasingly, that the Australian Pony emerged as a definite type.

Shetland blood has gone into the make-up of the pony as well as that of other British imports, including the Hackney and, more importantly, the Arab and the Thoroughbred.

An Australian Pony Stud Book Society was formed in 1929 with the declared object of encouraging the production of a home-produced child's riding pony of quality, and a Register was introduced within which there are sections for the contributing breeds, such as the Shetlands, Welsh (both Section A and B), the Connemara and the Hackney pony.

The ponies, varying in height from 12 to 14 hands, have good overall conformation and are strong, compact sorts with marked Welsh character. The movement is that of a good quality riding pony but obviously

SABLE ISLAND PONIES

SABLE ISLAND PONY The Sable Island is a tough, hardy pony which lives wild in small herds on the Atlantic island from which it takes its name. Once broken, it is a useful saddle and harness pony.

HORSE	ORIGIN	HEIGHT	COLOR	CONFORMATION	FEATURES
Sable Island	Canada	14 hands	various, but mostly chestnut	largish head, short body	light riding and harness pony
Australian Pony	Australia	12 to 14 hands	various, but mostly gray	compact and strong	good quality children's pony
Timor Pony	Indonesia	12 hands	various	sturdy and agile	good riding and harness pony

with a little inherited knee action. Gray is the most common color, as might be expected with so strong a Welsh influence.

The Australian Pony is numerous and well established but is not found outside Australia.

TIMOR PONY

The Indonesian islands all produce their own pony types, which are named after the islands on which they are to be found. There are Bali ponies; the Sumba and Sumbawa, which dance to the rhythm of the tom-tom with bells attached to their knees; the Sandalwood, the most valuable of the Indonesian breeds, which with the wood of that name is Sumba's

biggest export; the Java pony, used extensively in the heavy two-wheeled *sado*; and the Batak and Gayoe ponies of Sumatra.

Smallest of them all is the Timor (about 12 hands) from the most southerly of the Indonesian islands and the one closest to Australia. They have been exported to both that country and New Zealand and are held in good repute, being strong, agile, greatly enduring and very willing. Indeed, on Timor itself they are the mount of the local "cowboys" who, like their American counterparts, use the lasso to catch their stock. They are also employed widely in harness and as riding ponies.

They come in a variety of

colors and mention is made of a particular chocolate coat pattern, cream-spotted and with a cream colored mane and tail.

The origin of the Indonesian ponies, on which the economy of the islands largely depends, is not established beyond doubt but there are obvious similarities to the Mongolian, which would

have come to the islands with the ancient Chinese, while both the Portuguese and the Dutch imported ponies to the islands. It is interesting to note that Indonesian ponies wear a bitless bridle identical to that used in Asia 4000 years ago.

Improvements have been made by the importation of Arab horses, and the establishment of permanent studs, but there is little of the Arab influence evident in the Timor.

AUSTRALIAN PONIES

TIMOR PONY

TIMOR PONY Originating on the Indonesian island of Timor, this pony has been exported to both Australia and New Zealand.

AUSTRALIAN PONY Based on Welsh Mountain Pony, Arab and other blood, the Australian Pony emerged as a breed in its own right in the 1920s and it is now a popular child's riding pony.

HAFLINGER, FJORD & ICELANDIC

Having developed in areas where the terrain is rough and the climate severe, the Haflinger, Fjord and Icelandic ponies are tough, hardy and versatile breeds. Much admired in their native countries, where they have proved invaluable as working animals for centuries, these attractive, intelligent ponies are becoming increasingly popular elsewhere.

HAFLINGER

One of Europe's most attractive ponies is the golden Haflinger of the Austrian Tyrol. The ponies are now bred in many parts of the world, but their original home is in the area of the village of Hafling, near Meran in the Etschlander mountains, where Haflingers have been bred and raised for centuries.

The Haflinger is raised on mountain pasture (a practice known as *alpung* – alping) and is not used until it is four. Probably as a result, the breed is noted for its longevity; many of the ponies are still able to work at the advanced age of 40.

Haflingers are docile, strongly built, very tough and capable of much work without needing much food. These characteristics, together with their sure-footedness, make them the ideal choice for all sorts of agricultural and forestry work and as pack ponies for carrying loads over the mountain tracks. In this last context much use has been made of the breed as a military animal. Increasingly, however, the modern Haflinger is in demand as a riding pony.

The original descent of the Haflinger is possibly from the coldblooded Alpine Heavy Horse, but the greatest single influence is that of the Arabian sire El Bedavi through his halfbred grandson El Bedavi XXII. The latter was bred at the Austro-Hungarian Stud at Radantz and is responsible for four of the five main Haflinger bloodlines, the fifth being that of 40 Willy, a grandson of 252/233 Hafling. As a result of careful inbreeding, an unmistakable type has been produced and there is a notable similarity between the ponies.

The Haflinger, either chestnut with flaxen mane and tail or a golden palomino, stands at about 13.3 hands. The head is small but elegant and similar to that of an Arab, narrowing to a delicate muzzle. The back is broad and strong, the hindquarters are rounded and powerful and the legs short but sturdy.

The brand of the Austrian Haflinger is that country's native flower, the edelweiss, with a letter H in the center.

FJORD PONY

A particularly distinctive and interesting breed is Norway's Fjord, found all over Scandinavia. There are two types, the better known Westland, probably the original one, and the later *doele-hest*, or valley horse.

The ancient breed has inhabited Norway in much the same form since prehistoric times, and there is much evidence of its existence in engravings and rock carvings.

The Fjord was the horse of the Vikings, who as well as breeding them for working purposes used them in the sport of horse-fighting, when two horses were matched against each other to fight to the death.

The Fjord is a very recognizable descendant of the primitive Mongolian Wild Horse, and although now more refined in appearance, retains many of the latter's characteristics. The predominantly dun coloring with the accompanying dorsal stripe and zebra bar markings on the legs is typical, as is the erect mane with its black center, which is cut in the traditional crescent shape.

These charming ponies, standing 13 to 14 hands, are enormously strong and hardy, often taking the place of a tractor on the remote mountain farms where terrain is rough and climatic conditions severe. They are economical to keep and are noted for their longevity. The Fjord is an excellent performer in every type of harness and is a riding pony of boundless stamina.

HAFLINGER

HAFLINGER The Haflinger is one of the most attractive of pony breeds, as well as being strong, tough and nimble.

ICELANDIC PONY

The ponies of Iceland, usually known as horses, have much in common with the Norwegian ponies and like them were much used in the bloodthirsty sport of horsefighting. They are not indigenous to the country, having been brought to Iceland along with other domestic stock by the Norwegian settlers of the 9th century. Later, crossings were made with ponies imported in open boats from the Norse colonies in Scotland, Iceland and the Isle of Man. Connoisseurs of the breed still claim to distinguish four strains and there is one type, the Faxafloi, bred in the southwest, that bears a discernible resemblance to the Exmoor.

HORSE	ORIGIN	HEIGHT	COLOR	CONFORMATION	FEATURES
Haflinger	Austria	13.3 hands	palomino or chestnut	sturdy; deep body and short legs	sure-footed riding and harness pony
Fjord Pony	Norway	13 to 14 hands	various shades of dun	sturdy and muscular	excellent all-rounder with good stamina
Icelandic Pony	Iceland	13.2 hands	various	short and stocky	excellent riding and pack pony

ICELANDIC PONY The Icelandic pony is an agile, hardy little riding horse, kind, docile and intelligent.

ICELANDIC PONY

FJORD PONY

FJORD PONY The mane of the Norwegian Fjord Pony is traditionally cut to stand erect and show the tips of its dark center hairs.

The isolation of the breed's habitat and the severity of the terrain and climate have developed a characteristic agility and hardiness in these little horses, which do not exceed 13.2 hands in height. They are also noted for a highly developed homing instinct. Nine hundred years or so ago an attempt was made to upgrade the Icelandic stock by using Oriental blood. It was a disastrous failure and since then the breed has been kept pure and breeding, a well-developed industry, is controlled by the laws of the Althing, the world's oldest parliament.

Indeed, the Icelandic horse holds a very special place in the affections of the Icelanders. There are, for instance, over forty riding clubs in Iceland, forming a National Association, and shows, race meetings, dressage and cross country events are held frequently.

Much emphasis is placed on the gaits of the Icelandic horse. These are the walk (*fetgangur*) used by pack animals; trot (*brokk*) for crossing rough country; gallop (*stokk*); and the two specialized gaits, the pace (*skeid*), a lateral gait which covers short distances at speed and which is a much prized attribute, and the unique running walk, the *tølt*, used again for covering broken ground comfortably, sure-footedly and with expedition.

The variety of colors in the breed is a matter of pride with Icelanders and the range is very great. There are no less than fifteen basic color types and combinations, including several kinds of piebald.

THE ARAB

The most prepotent of all equines, the purest in terms of blood, and the one horse whose influence is evident in almost all modern breeds and types is the Arabian. It is rightly termed the fountainhead of the world's breeds and is arguably the most beautiful, certainly in the best of the modern specimens.

THE ARAB

The origin of the Arab is not easily established and is often obscured by myth and legend. There is, however, little doubt that an advanced equine race deriving, it is postulated, from the primitive Tarpan and thereafter from what the learned hippologists termed Horse Type 4 (see the introduction to this section), inhabited what we call Arabia thousands of years ago when that area was largely green and fertile.

Ancient Egyptian monuments dated at around 1300 BC depict a very pronounced Arabian type of horse; a statuette of about 2000 BC quite clearly represents what we would recognize as an Arabian and the rock carvings in the Nejd and on the Yemen plateaus provide additional evidence. The Arab people kept few, if any, written records but one historian, El Kelbi (AD 786), traced the pedigree of the Arabian to the wild horses of the Yemen that were captured by Bax, the great-great-great grandson of Noah. El Kelbi based his pedigrees on the stallion Hoshaba and the mare Baz, but clearly total reliance cannot be placed on his less than authenticated account. Nonetheless, it does confirm the great antiquity of this breed.

The Emir Abd-el-Kadr, writing to the French General Daumas, divided the history of the Arabian horse into four eras: Adam to Ishmael, the son of Abraham, that "fierce man" and first ancestor of the desert Bedouin, who was reputed to be the first ever to ride a desert horse; Ishmael to Solomon; Solomon to Mohammed; and then from the Prophet onward.

Ishmael, the outcast, who was to become the personification of the desert Bedouin, began that special relationship between the Bedu and the desert-bred horse, the mares and foals being tended as members of the family.

Solomon has to be the great horse-dealer of antiquity, keeping, in defiance of Judaic law, as many as 5,200 horses in his stables. But it is to Mohammed, the Prophet of Islam, that the spread of the superlative Arabian blood and its subsequent influence on the world's horse population is largely due.

Mohammed, appreciating the value of swift-moving mounted warriors in his prosecution of *Jihad*, the Holy War which was to bring the world to the acceptance and worship of the One True God, incorporated the care, breeding and management of the horse as an article of faith within the traditions of Islam. The result was to preserve the fixed type and character and the particular purity of line brought about by careful inbreeding within the tribes. The system, long practiced, the environment and the absence of outside blood produced horses of unbelievable stamina blessed with soundness, conformational strength, courage and speed, which was passed on when the Arab was crossed with other breeds.

After the Prophet's death in AD 632 the tribes burst out of their desert lands to conquer the whole of the Middle East. They were masters of Central Asia early in the 8th century, had by then begun their long occupation of the Iberian Peninsula and were only stopped from sweeping through Europe by their defeat at Poitiers, in AD 732, by Charles Martel and the Frankish knights.

Inevitably, the incomparable Arab horses were brought into contact with those of the conquered countries. The climax of the Arabian influence came in the 17th and 18th centuries when imported Arab horses began the process that was to result in the production of the world's superhorse, the English Thoroughbred.

A number of main strains and many substrains are recognized in the Arabian horse which derive from the stock bred by particular tribes. But although there are minor differences in type, the appearance of the purebred Arab is unique and quite unmistakable. Indeed, the formation of the back and quarters which culminate in the wonderfully high tail carriage is due to the difference in the number of ribs and lumbar bones between the Arab and other horses. The former has seventeen ribs, five lumbar bones and sixteen tail vertebrae in comparison with the eighteen–six–eighteen arrangement of other breeds.

It is held that the ideal height for the breed is between 14 and 15 hands, but much larger specimens are also to be found.

The purebred Arabian is bred extensively in all horse-raising countries, the United States, with an annual foal crop exceeding 10,000, having the largest Arab horse population. Each country has its own breed society that acknowledges the World Arab Horse Organization.

THE ARAB

THE ARAB The Arab is the oldest and one of the most beautiful purebred horses in the world. Its origins are unclear, but it has probably existed as a breed for several thousand years. It has had enormous influence on almost all modern breeds and types, and today is bred all over the world.

Hands

18
16
14
12
10
8
6
4
2

Arab

THE SPREAD OF THE ARAB
The Arab is thought to have originated thousands of years ago in the Arabian peninsula. From there it spread into North Africa and Asia Minor, but the greatest impetus to its wider distribution was its use by the followers of the Prophet Mohammed, who in the space of less than 200 years established an empire stretching from Central Asia, through the Middle East, North Africa and southern Europe, to Portugal.

→ Arab Conquests AD632–827

HORSE	ORIGIN	HEIGHT	COLOR	CONFORMATION	FEATURES
Arab	Arabia	14 to 15 hands or more	bay, brown, black, chestnut, gray	short head with a characteristic "dished" profile; broad chest, short back and muscular quarters	a beautiful riding horse; not as fast as a Thoroughbred, but has much greater stamina which makes it an ideal endurance riding horse

THOROUGHBRED

In comparison with many of the world's horse breeds the Thoroughbred is a relatively recent "invention." Nonetheless, it represents man's greatest achievement in the field of selective breeding and its influence on other breeds is equal to that of its progenitor, the Arab horse, which it far surpasses in terms of performance ability, although not perhaps in terms of soundness, constitutional strength and temperament.

THE THOROUGHBRED

This superb horse owes its existence to three Arabian horses (variously and loosely called Turk, Barb or Oriental) imported to Britain in the late 17th and early 18th centuries.

The first of the trio was the Byerley Turk, a horse captured by Captain Robert Byerley at the Battle of Buda and ridden by him, when he commanded the 6th Dragoon Guards, at the Battle of the Boyne in 1690. The horse then stood at stud in County Durham and later in Yorkshire. Through his son, Jigg, and his grandson Tartar he was the ancestor of Herod, founder of the Thorough-bred line that bears his name. Herod is one of the most important sires in the Thoroughbred history and his progeny won over one thousand races.

The Darley Arabian came from the Arab racing strain Munaghi and was bred by the Anazeh tribe living on the edges of the Syrian desert.

Thomas Darley, then British Consul in Aleppo, bought him in 1704 from the less than honorable Sheik Mirza for three hundred sovereigns and he later stood at Darley's home, Aldby Park, in East Yorkshire. He became the sire of the first great racehorse, Flying Childers, when mated to Betty Leedes, the daughter of the Leedes Arabian, and also of Bartlett's Childers, out of the same dam. Bartlett's sired Squirt, the sire of Marske, who in turn produced one of the greatest horses of all time, the legendary Eclipse. The modern lines of St Simon, Gainsborough and Blandford all trace back to the Darley Arabian.

Third of the founding fathers was the Godolphin Arabian, foaled in Yemen in 1704. This horse, if the records are to be believed, had something of a checkered history. He was exported to Tunis via Syria and was given to the French King Louis XIV by the Bey of Tunis. The story goes that his sojourn in France ended up with his drawing

PROFILE *The Thoroughbred has a refined, intelligent-looking head and an elegant neck. The profile is not noticeably concave, like that of the Arab, and the muzzle is not as small.*

Arab

Thoroughbred

a Parisian cart. Be that as it may, he was bought by Edward Coke of Derbyshire in 1729, and after his death in 1733 passed into the ownership of Lord Godolphin who used the horse as a "teaser" at his Gog Magog stud near Cambridge. It is said that he fought and beat the stud stallion for the favors of the mare Roxana. She produced Cade, foaled in 1734, who was the sire of Matchem, founder of the third of the male lines of the modern Thoroughbred.

The three foundation lines directly attributable to the trio of imported Arabians are, therefore, Herod, Eclipse and Matchem. The fourth is that of Herod's son Highflyer.

Of course, there were other Oriental horses concerned with the evolution of the Thoroughbred, as well as the all-important female foundation stock. There was, for instance, the Leedes Arabian, sire of Betty Leedes, who appears in more Thoroughbred pedigrees than any other horse, and Alcock's Arabian, to whom every gray Thoroughbred traces back.

As well as those two there were D'Arcy's Chestnut and White

Arabians, the enigmatically named Unknown Arabian and the Helmsley and the Lister Turk. They all figure prominently and Lady Wentworth, arch-publicist of the Arabian and a formidable scholar despite some fallacious historical assumptions, calculated that Bahram, the English Triple Crown winner of 1935 (the 2000 Guineas, the Derby and the St Leger), contained tens and sometimes hundreds of thousands of crosses of each of those sires.

The Thoroughbred would not, however, have been possible without the existence of a suitable female foundation. Ever since two Oriental horses, the mare Truncifice and the stallion Arundel, raced at the Court of King Edgar in the 10th century, and even for long before that, there was in Britain a tradition of "running horses," many having some Oriental connection, though not necessarily Arab. The English kings maintained Royal Studs. Henry VIII founded his Royal Paddocks at Hampton Court and his daughter Elizabeth I had a stud in Tutbury, Stafford-

Hands

shire. King James I, the ill-fated Charles I, and Charles II all encouraged racing at Newmarket, the latter establishing firmly the "Sport of Kings."

It is a mare by the Unknown Arabian, the more prosaically named Old Bald Peg, who is accounted a pervasive influence in

the evolution of the early Thoroughbreds. Repeat crosses to her appear 367,162 times in the pedigree of Big Game, 233,579 in that of Sun Chariot, and numbers of similar magnitude are present in the pedigrees of the race horses Hyperion, Fairway and Windsor Lad.

THOROUGHBRED The long, strong legs and powerful, muscular quarters, plus tremendous courage and stamina, help make the Thoroughbred the world's supreme racehorse. It also performs well in many other equestrian sports, such as show jumping and eventing.

HORSE	ORIGIN	HEIGHT	COLOR	CONFORMATION	FEATURES
Thoroughbred	England	14.2 to 17.2 hands, average around 16 hands	most solid colors, but usually bay, brown, black or chestnut	refined head, elegant neck, sloped shoulders, deep body, short back and powerful quarters	the fastest of all horses. Primarily a racehorse, but also does well in most other types of equestrian sport

ANGLO-ARAB

In theory, the cross between Arabian and Thoroughbred should produce the near-perfect riding horse for purposes outside racing, the progeny combining the best of both worlds, inheriting the speed and courage of the Thoroughbred and the temperament, constitutional soundness and stamina of the Arab. In an imperfect world that does not always occur, but the combination of blood in varying degrees does nonetheless produce some excellent all-round horses and some outstandingly good ones, particularly among those of French origin.

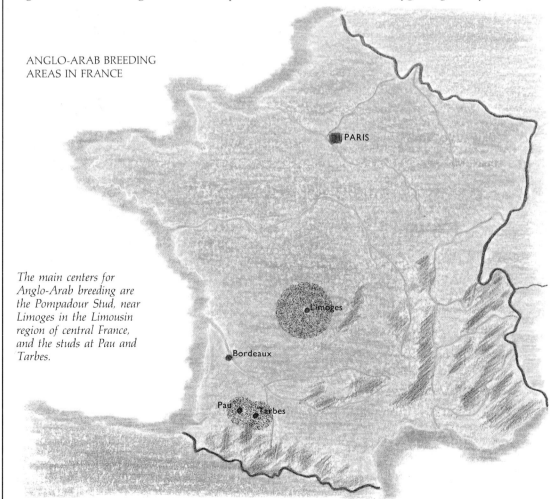

Hands
18
16
14
12
10
8
6
4
2

Anglo-Arab

ANGLO-ARAB

Although in Britain the Anglo-Arab is acknowledged as a breed in its own right, no type standard has been formulated and there is some variation in appearance according to the percentage of Arab and Thoroughbred blood within a particular individual.

The British definition is that the Anglo-Arab is an animal with no strain of blood in its pedigree other than Arab and Thoroughbred. It may be the product of an Arab sire and Thoroughbred dam or the other way around, or any further crosses of this blood. There is no fixed percentage one way or the other.

For an animal to be eligible for registration in the Anglo-Arab Stud Book, the Thoroughbred element in the pedigree has to be registered in the General Stud Book, and the Arab in the Arab Horse Stud Book.

The usually accepted practice in the breeding of Anglo-Arabs is to put an Arab stallion to a Thoroughbred mare. The resultant progeny may then very well exceed both parents in size. It has been found to be less satisfactory to breed the Thoroughbred stallion to an Arab mare, for in most instances the progeny is smaller and not so suitable for the competitive disciplines.

British Anglo-Arabs are increasing in number and there have been some notable performers among them. The best are horses of scope and size combined with substantial bone and great elegance. However, there are insufficient numbers as yet to have made any major impact, and while a type seems to be emerging it can hardly be described as being fixed.

In France, which may be regarded as being the home of the Anglo-Arab, the breed, allowing for type variations between the breeding areas, has been firmly established for over a century and has long since made its mark as a competition and riding horse of the highest class. Like the Thoroughbred, the French Anglo-Arab is officially recognized as a means of upgrading more plebeian stock and plays a significant part in the breeding of the all-round sports horse, the Selle Français.

From the days of the Moorish (Arab) occupation of the Iberian Peninsula and even before that, Oriental horses were brought into southwestern France and introduced to the native stock. Later, these horses, already carrying Oriental blood, were crossed with Arab, English strains and, most particularly, with Anglo-Arabs, to produce a halfbred horse called the Tarbais or the *demi-sang du Midi* (the halfblood of the southwest). This, together with breeds like the Limousin, the warhorse of the 18th century which was so highly regarded in Napoleonic times, provided a wonderfully secure base for the further development of the French Anglo-Arab.

Credit for the establishment of the breed belongs in no small way to the director of the National Studs, E. Gayot, who was at Pompadour in 1836 and began the systematic selective breeding of the Anglo-Arab.

As a base Gayot used three Thoroughbred mares, the Arab stallion Massoud and Aslan, described as a Turk but probably in this instance the nomenclature can be taken as being synonymous with Arab. A system of alternate crossing was employed to avoid the predominance of any one breed and to ensure the maintenance of the Arab character.

Today, all Anglo-Arabs in France are entered in a single Stud Book, whereas prior to World War II they were divided into purebred Anglo-Arab (50 percent of each breed) and halfbreds. The present requirement for the Anglo-Arab is that it must retain a minimum of 25 percent Arab blood.

Anglo-Arab stallions are kept at the National Studs at Pompadour, in Limousin, and especially at Tarbes and Pau. Special races

ANGLO-ARAB BREEDING AREAS IN FRANCE

The main centers for Anglo-Arab breeding are the Pompadour Stud, near Limoges in the Limousin region of central France, and the studs at Pau and Tarbes.

PARIS

Limoges

Bordeaux

Pau Tarbes

ANGLO-ARAB The Anglo-Arab, produced by crossing Arabs with Thoroughbreds, is bred in many countries but the best are usually those of French origin.

ANGLO-ARAB

are run for Anglo-Arabs, in the southwest particularly, and all types of the breed are good, natural jumpers. Up to World War II, French cavalry were mounted largely on these active, hardy and temperate horses.

The French version may not always be as elegant as, for instance, its English counterpart, but the French system has produced the world's finest Anglo-Arab.

HORSE	ORIGIN	HEIGHT	COLOR	CONFORMATION	FEATURES
Anglo-Arab	France	15.3 to 16.1 hands	most solid colors	large and elegant with a deep body, powerful quarters and substantial bone	athletic and often spirited, it is a first class riding horse which excels in all types of sport from racing to dressage

BARB & SELLE FRANÇAIS

The Barb is an ancient breed from northwest Africa, where it is still bred in large numbers. It played a significant part in the development of many other breeds, including the Thoroughbred and others, such as the Limousin and Anglo-Norman, which form the basis of the Selle Français.

SELLE FRANÇAIS

Unlike the uncertain history of the Barb, the carefully regulated breeding that has resulted in the Selle Français has been documented in detail.

The *Cheval de Selle Français* (French Saddle Horse) is an amalgam of several breeds and the term, first used in December 1958, describes halfbreds produced with the primary objective of use as competition horses. Before that date all riding horses other than Thoroughbreds, Arabs and Anglo-Arabs were called halfbreds.

The Selle Français can trace its development from the 19th century importations of English Thoroughbred and halfbred stallions, which were crossed with local mares. In Normandy two crossbreds of significance evolved, the Anglo-Norman and the fast harness horse, the French Trotter. The former (at one time clearly divided into a riding horse type and a draft cob) was in a sense the prototype for the Selle Français and the latter's Stud Book is, in fact, a continuation of the old Anglo-Norman one.

The French Trotter is also an offshoot of the Anglo-Norman, developed in the 19th century from Norfolk Trotter (Roadster) blood. Other provincial types emerged in the western and central districts, notably the Vendéen, Angevin and Charo-llais, the latter a workmanlike hunter type produced from Thoroughbred and Anglo-Norman crosses.

With Government aid, and the existence of established national studs, it has been possible to produce a specially-bred competition horse that on its record (a succession of Olympic medal winners) is as successful as any in the world.

The principal area of specialization is in the production of show jumpers, the stallion Galoubet being an outstanding example. Galoubet, arguably among the greatest jumpers of the century, combined top-class trotting blood on the side of his dam, Viti, with that of his Selle Français sire, Almé, whose background was largely Thoroughbred with an overtone of Anglo-Arab.

Secondly, Selle Français are bred to race under the appellation AQPSA (*autres que pur sang anglais* – other than Thoroughbred). Such horses race on the flat as three-year-olds and many of them go on to the sport of cross country racing, unique to France, and/or to horse trials.

Careful crossing of the base breeds continues to produce ever better standards of conformation and performance and partbred mares all go through a selection process before being admitted to the Stud Book.

Of the horses eligible to be called Selle Français, 33 percent are by Thoroughbreds; 20 percent by Anglo-Arabs; 45 percent by

SELLE FRANÇAIS

SELLE FRANÇAIS The Selle Français is the result of an amalgamation of the Anglo-Norman with several other regional French breeds.

registered Selle Français stallions, as in the case of Galoubet; and 2 percent by French Trotters.

Other acceptable crosses are Thoroughbred × French Trotter; Arab or Anglo-Arab × French Trotter and Thoroughbred × Anglo-Arab.

BARB

The Barb of northwest Africa, unlike its neighbor the Arab, with which it has been crossed certainly since the Muslim conquests of the 7th century and probably before that date, is by no means a beautiful horse nor a particularly temperate one. It is nonetheless tough, enduring, handy and fast over short distances, and big enough, between 14.2 and 15.2 hands, to be a practical choice for a

HORSE	ORIGIN	HEIGHT	COLOR	CONFORMATION	FEATURES
Barb	Northwest Africa	14.2 to 15.2 hands	bay, brown, black, chestnut, gray	long head, sloping quarters	good riding horse, but temperamental
Selle Français	France	15.3 to 16.2 hands	any solid color, but usually chestnut	fine head, long neck, deep chest and powerful quarters	bred for competition and for racing, and also all-around riding

Barb

Arab

Arab

Arab

Barb

Hands
18
16
14
12
10
8
6
4
2

Selle Français

Barb

BARB

HEADS AND TAILS The Barb and the Arab have much in common, but there are also some important differences. Compared with the Arab, the Barb has a longer head and a broader muzzle, and its hindquarters are much more sloped with the tail set quite a bit lower.

BARB The Barb is a good all-around riding horse but it has a tendency to be quick-tempered. It is strong and tough with great stamina, capable of running at high speed over short distances, and able to carry a lot of weight for a horse of its size.

variety of purposes. More importantly, it comes under that blanket description "Oriental" and has had a greater influence than is sometimes recognized. In influence it is often held second only to the Arab prior to the emergence of the Thoroughbred in 18th century England.

Thousands of Berbers served in the Muslim armies which occupied Spain and Portugal. They took with them their Barbs and began a traffic in the North Afri-

can horses which lasted for centuries.

Barbs were certainly imported to England for the Royal Studs of the Tudors, and there are numerous references to Barbary horses in the time of the Plantagenets and before. Barb blood was certainly in those "running horses" which formed the basis of the early Thoroughbred, and these horses of the Barbary Coast were to be found elsewhere in Europe also.

Barb stock was regularly imported into Marseilles from Morocco. There was certainly a Barb residue left in France following the Muslims' historic defeat at Poitiers, and there is quite enough evidence to show the breed's influence in the Limousin, while it is possible that it may also have had something to do with the white horses of the Camargue.

The breed originated in the fertile coastal area of northwest Africa, a horse-breeding area since

ancient times. It could be that this edge of Africa was one region in which the effects of the Ice Age were not felt and as a consequence the horses survived, but that is only conjecture and there is no certainty about the beginning of this important breed.

The Barb is still found and bred in present-day Algeria, Morocco and Tunisia and was the traditional mount of the famous Spahis, Algerian horsemen serving with the French Army.

CLEVELAND BAY, SADDLEBRED & QUARTER HORSE

The Cleveland Bay is primarily a carriage horse, unlike the American Saddlebred and Quarter Horse, which excel as riding horses. The Saddlebred, with its spectacular gaits, is a star of the show ring, while the Quarter Horse's speed and agility make it unequalled as a cattle horse and a superb race horse.

CLEVELAND BAY

The Cleveland Bay is as indisputably English as the other members of this trio are American, and is the oldest breed of the three by several centuries.

The origin of these big, bay horses with their black points is in the Cleveland area of northeast Yorkshire, from which they take their name. They were bred as long ago as medieval times as pack horses (hence the tendency toward a somewhat longer back than usual in the earlier specimens), for riding and driving purposes and for working the heavy clay land in an agricultural role.

They were much used by the travelling salesmen of the day, the *chapmen*, and so they became known as Chapman horses. The modern Cleveland Bay is an amalgam of the Chapman horse and the Andalusian and Barb stallions which were available to Yorkshire breeders during the 17th century.

In the Elizabethan era, when people began to travel by coach, the Cleveland was much esteemed as a harness horse because of its great strength and tractive power.

By the 19th century, the im-

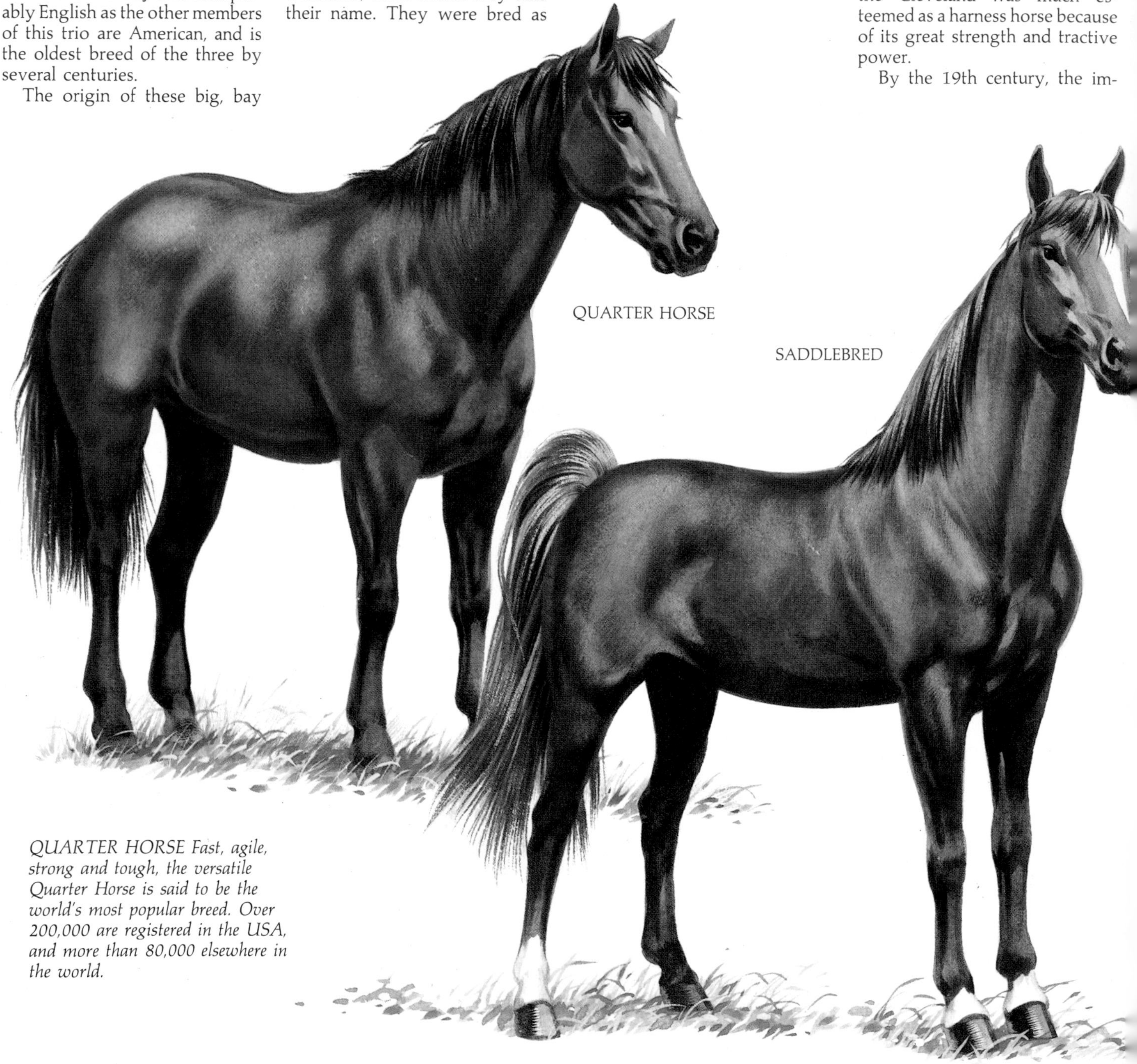

QUARTER HORSE

SADDLEBRED

QUARTER HORSE Fast, agile, strong and tough, the versatile Quarter Horse is said to be the world's most popular breed. Over 200,000 are registered in the USA, and more than 80,000 elsewhere in the world.

HORSE	ORIGIN	HEIGHT	COLOR	CONFORMATION	FEATURES
Cleveland Bay	England	16 to 16.2 hands	bay	deep girth, powerful quarters	good all-round riding and harness horse
Saddlebred	USA	15 to 16 hands	bay, chestnut brown, gray	powerful legs and quarters	saddle/light harness horse; unique gaits
Quarter Horse	USA	14.3 to 16 hands or more	any solid color, usually chestnut	strong shoulders, powerful quarters	excellent cattle, race and pleasure horse

SADDLEBRED Famous for its distinctive show ring gaits, the Saddlebred is also excellent as a general riding and harness horse and as a cattle horse.

Hands			
18			
16			
14			
12			
8			
4			
2			
Quarter Horse	Saddlebred	Cleveland bay	

provement in road surfaces called for a much faster horse, and to this end two notable stallions were introduced to the breed. They were Manica and Jalap (often called Trotting Jalap), the first a son of the Darley Arabian and the latter a grandson of the Godolphin. Both had a significant influence on the breed, but on the whole such infusions were not encouraged.

The Cleveland was at the root of the Yorkshire Coach Horse, possibly the most popular harness horse of the 19th century. Now extinct, this elegant and powerful horse was the result of

Thoroughbred/Cleveland crossings and was as a consequence faster than the true Cleveland.

During the 19th century, the Cleveland was exported extensively all over the world and became a considerable influence in the development of many European breeds.

After World War II, the breed went into decline, and in 1962 only four mature stallions remained in Britain. Its revival as a carriage horse and as a cross for the production of top-class jumpers and hunters was due largely to Queen Elizabeth II, whose stallion

CLEVELAND BAY The large, handsome Cleveland Bay, nearly extinct in the 1960s, has since been revived and is now a popular driving and competition horse.

CLEVELAND BAY

Mulgrave Supreme proved to be a remarkable rejuvenating influence.

AMERICAN SADDLEBRED

The American Saddlebred was developed when the Cleveland was already a long-established breed, but it evolved into a distinctive and fixed type with remarkable rapidity.

In its early form it was the creation of settlers in the South who wanted to breed an all-round horse, showy and spectacular in action but entirely practical for the variety of jobs for which it was needed. In those days it was a horse that could plow, carry a man comfortably and swiftly over rough going for the purpose of inspecting crops and could also take its turn as an elegant, fast carriage horse.

It was produced by selective crossbreeding of the Thoroughbred, the Morgan and the now extinct Narragansett Pacer, developed as a swift, easy-paced horse on the shores of Narragansett Bay, Rhode Island.

Initially, because of its close connections with Kentucky, the breed was known as the Kentucky Saddler, but it became the Saddlebred after the formation of the American Saddle Horse Breeders' Association in 1891.

The modern Saddlebred is an all-purpose riding horse and a show animal that also appears in harness classes. It is good with cattle and is said to jump well.

It is notable, of course, for its action, developed in order to cross terrain of varying types. It is shown as a three-gaited saddle horse in a slow, flat-footed springy walk, in a high action trot and a slow, smooth canter. In addition to the three basic paces, the five-gaited Saddlebred performs the slow gait and the rack.

The slow gait is a high-stepping four-beat pace, slow and contained, while the enormously exciting rack is described as "a flashy, fast, four-beat gait free

from any lateral motion or pacing."

QUARTER HORSE

The Quarter Horse is said to be the most popular horse in the world, and certainly it has the largest breed registry of all.

It derives from the horses brought to the New World by the Spanish explorers of the 16th century, and it was developed in Virginia from crosses made with English horses taken there by the settlers of the 17th and 18th centuries.

American horses were essentially practical and in Virginia the circumstances produced a compact, hardy little horse (14.3 hands and up) that developed a remarkable instinct for working cattle, becoming the equine equivalent of the sheepdog, as well as for galloping over short distances at great speed.

The English settlers, with their sporting tradition, lost no time in organizing racing, but since there were no race tracks they improvised by putting on impromptu contests anywhere that three or four horses could race over distances of a few hundred yards. Very often the course was no more than the length of a village street.

These sprint races produced a breed particularly strong in the quarters and hind legs, that could jump off into a full-stretch gallop from a halt. The horses soon became known as Quarter Horses, not because of their conformation but for their ability to race over that part of a mile.

Today's Quarter Horse still excels as a cattle horse and is preeminent in the rodeo classes. The breed is also used for trail riding, hunting and the competitive disciplines but in relatively recent years there has been an incredible revival in the industry of Quarter Horse racing, the prize money to be won often exceeding that offered in much Thoroughbred flat racing.

MORGAN, STANDARDBRED & TENNESSEE WALKING HORSE

The Morgan, the Standardbred and the Tennessee Walking Horse are three of America's most famous breeds. The little Morgan is one of the world's most adaptable horses, the Standardbred is unequalled as a harness racer, and the Walking Horse is renowned for its distinctive gaits.

MORGAN

The American horse population is more colorful and varied than any other in the world, despite its comparatively short history. Among the American breeds are preserved those "exotic" paces which were once so highly prized in the Old World and are now scarcely recognized there. They are retained in the Saddlebred, the Walkers, the Foxtrotters and the world's supreme harness racing horse, the Standardbred. In South America there are the specialist riding horses, the Peruvian Paso and the Paso Fino. But for all its wealth and variety no horse measures up to the romance of the Morgan, the little horse that is part of the American legend.

The breed descends from one exceptional horse, first called Figure and then named after his second owner, who was the Vermont schoolmaster Justin Morgan. He was a "freak" horse and none ever exceeded him in his achievements, but as a sire he was extraordinarily prepotent and prolific.

He is thought to have been foaled around 1790 in West Springfield, Massachusetts, but he made his reputation in the area around Randolph, Vermont, and it is there at the Morgan Horse Farm of the University of Vermont that he has his permanent memorial.

The breeding of the little horse, who stood no more than 14 hands, is obscure. It is said that he was by a Thoroughbred called True Briton, but many authorities, including the late Pauline Taylor

of the famous Llanarth Stud in mid-Wales, have suggested that more likely he was by a Welsh Cob stallion of that name, and there is some evidence to support that premise. The name itself is traditional to the Welsh Cob, and in the 18th century there were cobs in that area as well as a strong Welsh colony. The appearance of the Morgan, even in today's refined form, certainly resembles the Welsh Cob more than anything else. Without doubt, certain infusions of Thoroughbred and Arab blood have been made, but the overriding impression is that of the Welsh Cob.

Justin Morgan himself was probably the most versatile horse in history. He was used in the most gruelling conditions at the plow, in harness and in clearing forests and hauling the heavy timber. He was matched inhumanely and repeatedly in every sort of contest, never being beaten in harness, under saddle or in the most severe of weight-pulling competitions.

STANDARDBRED

Just as much an all-American product is the Standardbred, the foremost of the world's harness racers. The origin of the breed is much concerned with the Thoroughbred, for at its root is the gray horse Messenger, included in Volume 1 of the GSB as the sire of Mambrino, out of an unnamed mare by Turf, who had crosses to all three of the founding Oriental sires.

Messenger stood in America

TENNESSEE WALKING HORSE

for 20 years, died in 1808 and was buried on Long Island. He never raced in harness, but there was in his background a genetic link to Old Shales, founder of the dynasty of Norfolk Trotter. Bred to a variety of mares and with admixtures of Morgan, Narragansett and Canadian Pacer blood, he was largely responsible for the formation of a breed nucleus. Most important of his descendants was Hambletonian, a colt foaled in 1849 who is regarded as the foundation sire of the modern Standardbred. Ninety percent of all Standardbreds descend from him and from 1851 to 1875 he sired no less than 1335 offspring.

The term "Standardbred" was introduced in 1879 and appears in Volume 4 of the American Trotting Register published three years later. The name derives from the early practice of establishing a speed standard as a requisite for entry into the Regis-

ter. The standard was set at 2:30 minutes for conventional trotters (described as "line-gaited" or "passing-gaited") over 1 mile and 2:25 for the faster pacers, who increased in numbers very rapidly.

Today, standard times have been reduced, and indeed the first under 2-minute mile, now commonplace, was trotted as early as 1897 by a horse called Star Pointer.

TENNESSEE WALKING HORSE

Like the Saddlebred, the spectacular Tennessee Walker traces back to the Narragansett Pacer, the breed evolving to meet the needs of plantation owners who wanted a stylish but practical work horse. The earlier representatives were often referred to as Southern Plan-

Tennessee Walking Horse   Morgan   Standardbred

Hands
18
16
14
12
10
8
6
4
2

TENNESSEE WALKING HORSE The Walker is noted for its gaits. The three basic gaits are the flat walk, the running walk and the rocking chair canter. Both walks are in four-time, the head nodding in time with the movement.

MORGAN The Morgan excels as a pleasure and show horse, whether in harness or under saddle, and is a great performer in the competitive disciplines such as show jumping.

MORGAN

STANDARDBRED

tation Walking Horses or Tennessee Pacers, and in the early days the Walker was often called the Turnrow Horse because of its ability to inspect the crops row by row without damaging the plants.

Numerous breeds contributed to this strain, but the foundation sire of the modern Walker is recognized as Black Allan (Allan F–1), a Standardbred foaled in 1886. As a harness racer he was a failure because of his peculiar walking pace, which became a unique characteristic of his descendants. More quality was introduced when the Saddlebred Giovanni went to stand in Wartrace, Tennessee, in 1914. The Tennessee Walking Horse Breeders' Association was formed in 1935 and the breed was recognized officially in 1947.

STANDARDBRED The Standardbred has a notably free and straight action at the trot.

HORSE	ORIGIN	HEIGHT	COLOR	CONFORMATION	FEATURES
Morgan	USA	14.1 to 15.2 hands	bay, brown, black, chestnut	compact and muscular	versatile riding and harness horse
Standardbred	USA	14 to 16 hands	bay, brown, black, chestnut	robust with short but strong legs	the world's premier harness racing horse
Tennessee Walking Horse	USA	15 to 16 hands	bay, black, roan, gray, chestnut	strong back, powerful quarters	fine all-around horse; distinctive gaits

PINTO, PALOMINO & APPALOOSA

Color is the common feature in this group of American horses. Indeed, the Pinto or Paint horse (*pinto* comes from the Spanish, meaning "spotted") and the Palomino are color types rather than breeds with fixed characteristics such as height or appearance. It is different in the case of the Appaloosa, which is an established breed of recognizable character and has, indeed, the third largest breed registry in the world.

PALOMINO

The Palomino coloring occurs in ancient depictions of horses in Europe and Asia and is found in many breeds throughout the world. The color was probably introduced to America in the early 16th century and it is only in the United States that the Palomino is given "breed" status; elsewhere it is regarded as a "color type."

The official breed description of the color, laid down by the Palomino Horse Association Inc., is this: '*body color* – near that of an untarnished gold coin. The color may vary lighter or darker but *must be natural*. They must have a full white mane and natural white tail. The eyes shall be dark or hazel and both the same color.'

Palominos, which in the United States may vary in height from 14.1 hands to a maximum of 16 hands, take part in all sorts of Western activities, including pleasure riding, rodeos and trail rides, and they are especially popular as parade horses. They are also to be seen competing in both show and jumping classes.

PINTO

The Pinto was a popular horse with the American Indian and it seems likely that horses of this coloring were early descendants of the 16th century Spanish horses. The Pinto Horse Association was founded in 1956 and recognizes four types and two color patterns. *Overo* describes a dark body color splashed with large, irregular patches of white. The color predominates in South America and the gene is recessive. *Tobiano*, on the other hand, is a dominant gene. The color is a basic white with large black or brown patches. The head and neck are usually dark and the legs white from the knee down. The color is found principally in the West and in the Southwest of the United States.

The types recognized by the Association are:

a) *Stock type*. Horses of predominantly Quarter Horse breeding and conformation, ponies "displaying conformation associated with the Quarter Horse and the original Shetland Pony."

b) *Hunter type*. Horse of predominantly Thoroughbred breeding, pony reflecting conformation associated with the Thoroughbred and the Connemara.

PINTO

PALOMINO

PALOMINO As it is a color type rather than a breed, a Palomino might be, for example, a Quarter Horse or a Saddlebred – it's the color that matters.

PINTO The tough, good-tempered Pinto is a fine all-around riding horse and also performs well in long-distance riding.

HORSE	ORIGIN	HEIGHT	COLOR	CONFORMATION	FEATURES
Palomino	USA	14.1 to 16 hands	golden with white mane and tail	according to breed	according to breed
Pinto	USA	various	dark/white patches, white/dark patches	according to type	all-around riding and show horse
Appaloosa	USA	14.2 to 15.2 hands	various different spotted patterns	compact with short back	excellent all-around saddle horse

c) *Pleasure type*. Horse predominantly Arabian or Morgan, pony reflecting Arabian, Morgan or Welsh Pony.

d) *Saddle type*. Horses reflecting characteristics of Saddlebred, Hackney or Tennessee Walking Horse, ponies combining the appearance of those horses with that of the *modern* (that is, American) Shetland.

APPALOOSA

The Appaloosa markings are even more ancient than the Palomino coloring, the spotted coat pattern appearing in the cave drawings of early man that can be dated as being 20,000 years old. The color appears throughout Europe and Asia, but the Appaloosa breed belongs to America. These spotted horses, from strains which came to America with the first imports of Spanish stock, were bred with strict selectivity by the Nez Percé Indians, whose lands were in the northeast of Oregon and the southeast corner of Washington, bordering the fertile Idaho countryside. They kept their horse herds in the sheltered canyons of the Snake, Clearwater and Palouse rivers and it is from the latter that the breed got its name.

In 1877 the US government attempted to remove the Indians from their traditional homelands and to put them on reservations. The Nez Percé resisted, but after an epic journey of 1800 miles to the Bear Pass Mountains in Montana, the tribe was forced to make its last stand against the US Army. It was defeated and the horse herds that had been bred with such care were slaughtered.

In 1938 the Appaloosa Horse

Club was formed with a few of the descendants of the Nez Percé horses. Today, the Club has the third largest registry in the world, with more than 65,000 horses.

The Appaloosa is distinctive for characteristics other than the coat pattern. The mane and tail are wispy and sparse; the eye is encircled with white sclera; the hooves are striped vertically black and white and the skin is mottled round the nostrils and genitalia.

There are five principal coat patterns; *Leopard*: white over loin and hips with dark spots; *Snowflake*: spotting all over the body but usually dominant over the hips; *Blanket*: either white or spotted; *Marbleized*: mottled all over the body; and *Frost*: white specks on a dark ground.

Leopard

White blanket

APPALOOSA

Spotted blanket

APPALOOSA Appaloosas, noted for their good temperament and innate hardiness, are popular in every sort of activity and are much used by Western riding enthusiasts.

MISSOURI FOXTROTTER, BRUMBY & AUSTRALIAN STOCK HORSE

The Missouri Foxtrotter, one of America's gaited horses, was developed from a number of other breeds during the early 19th century. The Brumby and the Australian Stock Horse also originated in the 19th century, but while the Stock Horse is still being improved, the Brumby is now a feral horse whose numbers are now few.

MISSOURI FOXTROTTER

One of the most interesting of the American gaited horses, and a prime example of the adaptive genius of the early settlers, is the Missouri Foxtrotter.

Some 160 years ago, European settlers migrated westward across the Mississippi River from the states of Kentucky, Tennessee and Virginia to found new communities in the Ozarks of Missouri. These people took with them Thoroughbred horses, plus the tough and versatile Morgans (by that time well established in Vermont) and what are usually referred to as Arabs, although it is more likely that they were Barb/Spanish type crosses.

In their new environment, the settlers needed a horse that could be ridden for long periods over rough ground without fatiguing itself or its rider. By skillful breeding they developed a new type of smooth-actioned horse that was fast, enduring and very sure-footed. The horse moved with a unique, characteristic gait which was called a "foxtrot." In general terms, the foxtrot entails the horse walking actively in front while trotting behind, the hind feet stepping down and sliding over the track of the forefeet. A distinctive up and down movement of the head is encouraged and the slightly elevated tail bobs in rhythm with the gait.

It is this sliding action, greatly reducing the jarring effect of the conventional trot, that makes the gait so comfortable to sit. It can be maintained over long distances without the horse tiring and at speeds of 5 mph to 8 mph and sometimes up to 10 mph.

There are many famous Foxtrotter lines. One of the earliest was the Bremmer, originating with a racehorse of that name owned by the Alsup family. The Kissees family established the Diamond and Fox strains and William Dunn was responsible for Old Skip, a most prepotent Foxtrotter sire whose background was primarily Morgan with a judicious dash of Thoroughbred.

Two other notable sires were the Saddlebreds Chief and Cotham Dare. Both Saddlebred and Tennessee Walking Horse blood have been used at times over the years to improve the appearance of the Foxtrotter.

BRUMBY

The Australian Brumby (the name comes from an Aborigine word meaning "wild") is descended from stock turned loose on the ranges during and after the Gold Rush of 1851. There was much indiscriminate breeding and the stock degenerated significantly as it multiplied. So numerous did the wild scrub herds become that by 1962 they were considered pests, and it was necessary for them to be culled extensively.

MISSOURI FOXTROTTER

MISSOURI FOXTROTTER At shows, the Foxtrotter is judged in three paces, the principal one being the foxtrot, which accounts for 40 percent of the points awarded. The others are the four-beat, overstriding walk, and the canter.

HORSE	ORIGIN	HEIGHT	COLOR	CONFORMATION	FEATURES
Missouri Foxtrotter	USA	14 to 16 hands	various	short back; legs taper distinctly	its gait makes it very comfortable to ride
Brumby	Australia	up to 15 hands	various	varies; usually of poor quality	a wild horse which is intractable if caught
Australian Stock Horse	Australia	14.2 to 16 hands	any solid color	like a more robust Thoroughbred	agile stock and competition horse

AUSTRALIAN STOCK HORSE

Like the Missouri Foxtrotter, the Australian Stock Horse was developed to suit the environment and the practical needs of people whose lifestyle was dependent upon the possession and use of horses. Although the Australian Stock Horse Society works to promote and standardize the Stock Horse, it is not yet regarded as a specific breed as such because of its variations in type and character.

It derives from another horse of mixed breeding, the deservedly famous Waler, which it has now superseded. Developed in New South Wales (hence the name "Waler"), from imports made from the Cape of Good Hope as early as 1798 and subsequently crossed with Thoroughbreds, the Waler was used extensively on cattle stations. It was also widely used as a troop horse for the Australian and Indian cavalries, both of which served with great distinction in Allenby's campaign against the Turks in Palestine in World War 1.

Since then, a number of other breeds have been introduced to create the present day Stock Horse. As well as Thoroughbred, there are Arab, Percheron and Quarter Horse influences and even a degree of pony blood.

The Australian Stock Horse is the biggest single group of horses

Missouri Foxtrotter   Australian Stock Horse   Brumby

in Australia and is employed for every sort of riding activity as well as being widely used on cattle stations.

At its best, the Stock Horse inclines toward the Thoroughbred in appearance. All of them seem to be tough sorts, sound and capable of great endurance, but there is no discernible set type.

BRUMBY

BRUMBY Because of extensive and often controversial culling, there are now only a few small herds of wild Brumbies surviving in the rugged Australian outback.

AUSTRALIAN STOCK HORSE

AUSTRALIAN STOCK HORSE The Australian Stock Horse was developed originally as a working horse for use on the vast cattle and sheep stations of Australia. It is still used as a stock horse, and for every kind of sport and pleasure riding.

CAMARGUE, FRENCH TROTTER & SALERNO

CAMARGUE The Camargue is the wild horse of the Camargue marshlands in southern France. It was officially recognized as a breed in 1968.

CAMARGUE

The Camargue Horse (or Camarguais), the French Trotter and the Salerno are all European breeds. The Camargue is used mainly for stock work and as a trekking horse, the French Trotter is a superb harness horse and the Salerno is an all-round saddle horse.

CAMARGUE

No one knows for sure where the gray horses of the Camargue came from, but for hundreds of years they have eked a living from the watery marshlands of the Rhône delta in southern France. The probable explanation is that the Camargue was indigenous to the area as long as 50,000 years ago. The cave paintings at Niaux and Lascaux, dated as being from 15,000 BC, depict horses of remarkably similar appearance, and then there are the horse skeletons of even greater antiquity unearthed at Solutré in southeast France in the 19th century. Mon-

gol horses, the mounts of the invading Vandals and Ostrogoths, must also have played a part, as well, much later in time, as Barbs and Spanish horses which came with the Moors from the Iberian Peninsula.

The traditional role of the breed is as the mount of the *gardiens* (the Camargue "cowboys") in their work with the cattle and the famous black bulls of the Camargue. Increasingly, however, as the area is being developed, the horses are used in the tourist industry for general riding and for carrying visitors on treks through the nature reserves, filled with bird and animal life,

which are now being established in the region.

The Camargue is always gray in color and is generally around 14 hands. It is not prepossessing in appearance, having a coarse, heavy head, a short neck and, more often than not, straight, upright shoulders. For all that, there is depth through the girth and good muscular development. The limbs are well-formed, as are the hard, sound feet.

The action is peculiar. The walk is long, high-stepping and very active; the trot by comparison is almost unnaturally stilted, but the gallop is extraordinarily free.

Fiery and courageous by nature, the Camargue is slow to mature, not being fully grown until the age of 5 to 7 years, but in compensation the breed is very long-lived. Their stamina is legendary and as might be expected they thrive on the poorest fare.

FRENCH TROTTER

In comparison the French Trotter is very much a newcomer to the scene, its development dating from the 19th century when the National Studs encouraged the import of English Thoroughbred and halfbred stallions and the incomparable Norfolk Roadsters.

Of particular note were the Roadster, Norfolk Phenomenon, the halfbred Young Rattler and the Thoroughbred, foaled in 1841, The Heir of Linne. These imports were crossed with the native mares to produce the powerful Anglo-Norman horse.

The five most important bloodlines which were established were those of Conquerant, Lavater, Normand, Phaeton and Fuchsia and the majority of today's French Trotters trace back to these prepotent sires. There have been outcrosses to both the Standard-

FRENCH TROTTER

FRENCH TROTTER The French Trotter is bred for stamina and speed. A superb trotter, it is also used for racing under saddle, has been used successfully as a sire of show jumpers and has been much concerned in the evolution of the Selle Français. Trotters unsuitable for racing are often used as hunters and general riding horses.

Camargue   French Trotter   Salerno

SALERNO The Italian Saddle Horse is often referred to as the Salerno, which was one of its foundation breeds.

SALERNO

bred and the Russian Orlov, but the breed has remained pure for very nearly 50 years to produce a finer type of horse standing at about 16.2 hands and inclining increasingly towards the Thoroughbred in appearance. It is now quite the equal of the Standardbred and often beats that superlative trotter.

Trotting in France, where some 6000 races are held annually, is just as popular as flat racing. Harness racing, of course, predominates but the French Trotter still races under saddle. It is believed that the more powerful type required to race under saddle has a particular value for stud purposes, and it is for this reason that valuable saddle races are held.

SALERNO

Today, the Italian Saddle Horse is frequently referred to as the Salerno, which was one of the foundation breeds of the Saddle Horse and was formerly the mount of the Italian cavalry. The heavier and once more common Maremmana, with which the Salerno shares some of its early ancestry, and which was also used for army purposes, has been absorbed and is no longer in evidence.

The horse originated in Mareninio and Salerno and evolved as a quality saddle horse at the stud farm of Persano, originally founded as a hunting lodge in the first half of the 18th century by Charles III, King of Naples and then of Spain. The foundation stock was Neapolitan, to which heavy infusions of Andalusian (Spanish) blood was added.

In more recent times the Salerno has been much improved by Thoroughbred and Arabian crosses. The modern specimen is a good sort of all-around horse, standing at about 16 hands and showing considerable quality as well as adequate substance. It is claimed that the breed has a particular aptitude for jumping.

HORSE	ORIGIN	HEIGHT	COLOR	CONFORMATION	FEATURES
Camargue (Camarguais)	France	about 14 hands	gray	robust; short back and quarters	wild bred; makes a good riding horse
French Trotter	France	16.2 hands	chestnut, bay, brown	similar to the Thoroughbred	superb harness racer; good saddle horse
Salerno	Italy	16 hands	most solid colors	elegant, well proportioned	popular riding and jumping horse

ANDALUSIAN, ALTÉR REAL & LUSITANO

Three related breeds of the Iberian Peninsula are the Andalusian, the Altér Real and the Lusitano. The Andalusian has played an important part in the development of many other breeds, both in Europe and in the Americas.

ANDALUSIAN

The Andalusian, the modern name for what in previous times was known universally as the Spanish horse, was pre-eminent in Europe from the 16th to the 18th century. It was the classical horse of the Renaissance period and the highly prized mount of military commanders and royalty. No one expressed the general admiration of his time for this spectacular horse more tellingly than William Cavendish, Duke of Newcastle and acknowledged as the sole English riding Master. Writing in the 17th century, Newcastle called the Andalusian ". . . the noblest horse in the world . . . fittest of all for a King in the Day of Triumph."

The Andalusian, bred principally in the sunbaked regions of Jerez de la Frontera, Cordoba and Seville, is the "third man" in the history of equine development and perhaps, when one considers the popular acclaim for the Arab and its descendant the Thoroughbred, is in danger of becoming the forgotten one.

The influence of the Andalusian was pervasive throughout 18th century Europe and it was much used in the development of a number of breeds. In Britain it had an influence upon the Cleveland and on the Continent it was closely concerned with the Holstein and Hanoverian, as well as the Württemburg, Oldenburg, Kladruber, Knabstrup, Nonius and Frederiksborg. Portugal's Altér Real and Lusitano are in the position of first cousins, while the Lipizzaner is virtually a direct descendant, the stud at Lipizza, near Trieste, being set up with nine stallions and twenty-four mares imported from Spain in the 16th century.

The Spanish Riding School in Vienna was so called because of the Spanish horses supplied originally by the stud at Lipizza, and to this day the principal strains of the School's Lipizzaners are strongly influenced by Spanish (or Andalusian) blood. In recent years, indeed, the School has purchased horses from the famous Terry stud at Jerez de la Frontera, a notable acquisition among these being the purebred Andalusian Honoroso VI.

The horse population of the Americas owes just as much to the Andalusian horse, which was taken to the New World, where the equine species had been extinct for some 8000 to 10,000 years, by the *Conquistadores* of the 16th century. Spanish blood is at the root of many of the American breeds and today's Pasos, Appaloosas, Pintos, Quarter Horses and Saddlebreds all owe something in varying degrees to the Spanish foundation stock.

Controversy surrounds the origin of the breed, but the most likely premise put forward is that the Andalusian is the result of crossing indigenous Spanish stock (which may, it is sometimes claimed, have been based on an unaffected pocket of ancient wild horses which escaped the traumas of the Ice Ages) with the Barb horses of the Muslim invaders who held sway in the Iberian Peninsula from AD 711–1492.

Most Spanish experts believe the Andalusian to be quite free of Arabian blood, even though it is known that the Emirs of Cordoba kept large numbers of Arab horses at the royal stables near the River Guadalquivir. However, the distinctive conformation and action of this 'noble' horse would seem to give the strongest support to the contention that little if any Arabian blood went into the makeup of the breed.

The Andalusian is by no means a big horse and rarely exceeds 15.2 hands, but he has enormous presence, spirit and fire. For all that, the breed, including the stallions, is exceptionally friendly and docile. A very agile horse with spectacular action, the Andalusian is particularly suited to the discipline of the *manège* and is still used by the *rejoneadores*, Spain's mounted bullfighters.

Today, the breed is enjoying a revival and pure Andalusians are in demand outside of Spain. That the breed has survived turbulent times in its own country is due largely to the devotion of the Carthusian monks of Jerez, who for centuries preserved the Spanish horse in its pure form.

ALTÉR REAL

Like the Andalusian, Portugal's Altér Real is particularly suited to the work of the *haute école* and it was for this purpose that the breed was first developed.

In 1748 the House of Braganza founded a stud farm at Vila de Portel in the Alentejo Province of Portugal, using as foundation stock some 300 Andalusian mares imported from Jerez. Some years later this stud was moved to Altér from which the breed takes its name (meaning "Royal Altér").

ANDALUSIAN The Andalusian is an athletic horse with great spirit, and is becoming much in demand as a riding and jumping horse.

ANDALUSIAN

Hands

18
16
14
12
1
8
6
4
2

Andalusian   Lusitano   Altér Real

The Stud was abolished in 1834, and after many vicissitudes, which included the unsuccessful introduction of Arabian, Hanoverian and Norman blood, it was taken over by the Portuguese Ministry of Economy in 1932, by which time a return had been made to the old Andalusian outcrosses and more Andalusian mares had been introduced.

The modern Altér, obviously owing much to the Andalusian, is a spirited, very active riding horse of about 15.2 hands, with a high, showy action. It is courageous but possibly more highly strung than its progenitor.

LUSITANO

The Lusitano is another Andalusian derivative, with a possible Arabian infusion, which is believed to have existed in Portugal for many hundreds of years. It was once much in demand as a cavalry horse but its agility and athleticism make it a particularly suitable mount for the Portuguese *rejoneadores*. Such horses are trained to the highest level of the *haute école* and are very valuable. A brilliant, courageous horse it is sometimes a little larger than the Andalusian (up to 16 hands) and may be speedier but it lacks the latter's presence.

LUSITANO MANE AND TAIL The mane and tail of the Lusitano have an abundance of hair, which is often wavy. The Lusitanos used by the Portuguese mounted bullfighters have their manes braided and tied with ribbons.

LUSITANO

ALTÉR REAL

ALTÉR REAL The Altér Real was developed in Portugal in the 18th century as a High School horse, using Andalusians imported from Jerez, in Spain, as foundation stock.

LUSITANO Like the Andalusian from which it is derived, the agile and courageous Lusitano of Portugal is used in the bullring.

HORSE	ORIGIN	HEIGHT	COLOR	CONFORMATION	FEATURES
Andalusian	Spain	15.2 hands	usually gray	deep body, muscular quarters	athletic horse with a spectacular action
Altér Real	Portugal	15.2 hands	bay, brown, gray	deep body, muscular quarters	popular general riding and High School horse
Lusitano	Portugal	up to 16 hands	usually gray	deep body, muscular quarters	athletic saddle horse; used in bullfighting

CRIOLLO, PERUVIAN PASO & PASO FINO

Descended from the Andalusian of Spain, the Criollo, Peruvian Paso and Paso Fino are three of South America's most important breeds. The Criollo is a tough, fast little horse, while the other two are best known for their elegant gaits.

CRIOLLO

One of the best known of the South American breeds is the Criollo, the native horse of the Argentine which, with slight variations, is also found in most of the other South American countries, most particularly Brazil, Peru and Venezuela.

Its origins can be traced back to the Andalusian, the first breed to be taken over to the South American continent by the 16th century Spanish conquistadors. It is probable that these Andalusians also carried Arab and Barb blood and certainly the toughness of these North African breeds is reflected in the Criollo.

It is famous, too, for its incredible stamina and longevity, and the harshness of its environment ensured that only the fittest survived. In spite of this, however, wild herds formed and multiplied to such an extent that within fifty years their descendants were numbered in thousands. The summer droughts and heat on the pampas, and the freezing winters in the rugged mountain passes, taught them to survive for long periods without food or water. In due course the gauchos, realizing their potential usefulness, adopted these tough, agile little horses as pack animals as well as riding them to round up their cattle on their vast *estancias*.

Standing from 13.2 to 15 hands, the Criollo is usually dun in color, often with a dorsal stripe and zebra markings on the legs, but it can also be piebald and skewbald and occasionally bay or brown. It is short and deep in the body, muscular and with plenty of bone and good, sound feet. Versatility and strength are the Criollo's special characteristics, combined with outstanding toughness and soundness.

Inspired by the popularity of polo throughout South America, the Argentinians created the ideal polo pony by using the Criollo with repeated infusions of Thoroughbred blood to add quality to the Criollo's renowned endurance.

PERUVIAN PASO

The influence of the Spanish Andalusian can be clearly seen in another of its descendants, the Peruvian Paso, a native (as its name implies) of Peru.

While the natural gaits of horses and ponies are the walk, trot, canter and gallop (and, in the case of the Icelandic pony, the *tølt*), both North and South America have developed, in addition, their own particular variations, and the Peruvian Paso is possibly the best known of the so called "paso" breeds — "paso" literally meaning "step" in Spanish.

The paso, the name of the pace, is similar to the lateral paces of the American Saddlebred and the Tennessee Walking Horse, but differs inasmuch as while the hind legs move forward well under the body in a straight line, almost gliding along the ground,

CRIOLLO

PERUVIAN PASO The Paso is very comfortable to ride because of its unusual gait. It also has great stamina, making it excellent for endurance riding.

CRIOLLO One of the world's hardiest horse breeds, the sturdy, intelligent Criollo of South America is used for general riding as well as for cattle and pack work.

HORSE	ORIGIN	HEIGHT	COLOR	CONFORMATION	FEATURES
Criollo	Argentina	13.2 to 15 hands	usually dun	compact and muscular	versatile riding, stock and pack horse
Peruvian Paso	Peru	14 to 15.2 hands	usually bay or chestnut	compact and muscular	fine riding horse; distinctive gaits
Paso Fino	Puerto Rico	14.3 hands	various	compact and muscular	fine riding horse; distinctive gaits

the forelegs swing out extravagantly from the shoulder, stretching right out in front with the knee well bent and arcing around in a dishing action. This easy gait, which is said to be extremely comfortable, has been developed over the last three hundred years to carry the Peruvian riders over some very rough and rocky terrain for long periods at a time, without tiring, at a steady 10 to 11 mph. It can, of course, trot, canter and gallop as well but rarely moves in anything other than the "paso."

The Peruvian Paso is small in stature, averaging 14 to 15.2 hands, with dense bone, sloping hindquarters and low set luxuriant tail. It is deep through the girth, strong and compact with very

hard, sound limbs and feet. Bays and chestnuts predominate but grays, blacks and palominos are also found. Piebalds and skewbalds, however, are rare. The temperament is kind and docile and it is extremely hardy, tough and sure-footed.

PASO FINO

Very similar to the Peruvian Paso in both appearance and gait, and hailing from the same part of the world, is the Paso Fino, whose homeland is Puerto Rico although it is also bred in Colombia, Peru and the Dominican Republic and is increasingly popular in the USA.

Showing a strong affinity to the Spanish Andalusian, it is

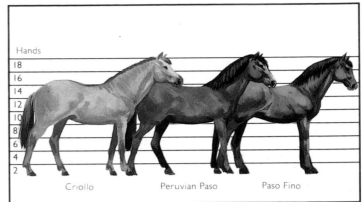

Hands			
Criollo	Peruvian Paso	Paso Fino	

chiefly noted for its lateral gait which differs from the usual because it is four distinctly separate steps, the hind foot of each lateral pair reaching the ground fractionally in front of the forefoot. This results in a very smooth and comfortable ride.

The Paso Fino has three speeds in this gait: the *paso fino* is the slowest and is a collected pace; the

paso corto is somewhat quicker, and the fastest speed in the lateral gait is the *paso largo*, which may be up to 16 mph.

Standing about 14.3 hands, the Paso Fino has a short back and powerful quarters, with short but strong legs that have good bone. It has great presence, and its comfortable ride makes it popular as a trail riding horse.

PASO FINO The little Paso Fino is very strong for a horse of its size, and like the Peruvian Paso it is a comfortable horse to ride.

PERUVIAN PASO

PASO FINO

LIPIZZANER, HANOVERIAN & HOLSTEIN

The Lipizzaner is famous around the world because it is the breed used by the Spanish Riding School of Vienna, the foremost exponent of the art of *haute école*, or High School riding. The Hanoverian and the Holstein, both German breeds, have gained well-deserved reputations as first-class competition horses.

LIPIZZANER

LIPIZZANER

Bred throughout Austria, Yugoslavia, Hungary, Czechoslovakia and Romania, the Lipizzaner is best known for its association with the Spanish Riding School of Vienna. It derives, as do so many of these European breeds, from the Andalusian and bears a strong resemblance to it. It takes its name, however, from the Stud at Lipizza, near Trieste, in the Karst country which is now part of Yugoslavia but was then in Austria when it was founded, in 1580, by the Archduke Charles II.

From the nucleus of twenty four mares and nine stallions with which the Stud began, plus occasional outcrosses, six strains developed and these were the foundation stock upon which the Lipizzaner breed is based. The six were: Pluto, a white pure Spanish stallion; Conversano, a black Neapolitan, and Neapolitano, a bay of the same breed; Favory, a dun from the Kladrub Stud in Bohemia; Siglavy, a white Arab; and Maestoso, a Spanish/Neapolitan cross.

Today, the Lipizzaners used in the Spanish School are bred at Piber, and at six months old the foals are branded with a "P" and the Austrian crown, together with an "L" for Lipizzaner and the initial letter of the sire's lineage, for instance "P" for Pluto.

All foals are born black or dark brown, the vast majority of them changing to white as they mature, although occasional bays are still produced.

Standing 15 to 15.2 hands, they are very compact and strong with short cannons, are deep through the girth and have an abundance of mane and tail. The neck is well crested and the head shows a straight or convex profile, while the quarters are particularly powerful and well muscled, a characteristic which is of assistance when performing the "airs above the ground" for which they are noted.

HANOVERIAN

One of the principal warmblood breeds of West Germany, the Hanoverian, was developed originally for use by the cavalry and as a carriage horse by George II, Elector of Hanover, in 1735. He established a stud at Celle, to the north of Hanover, and this remains the State Stud today.

Due to the Napoleonic Wars and the consequent reduction of stock at Celle, the English Thoroughbred was introduced to increase the numbers, but this infusion of Thoroughbred blood, when crossed with the stallions of mixed Neapolitan and Andalusian stock which had been used to establish the Stud, was found to produce a horse which was too light for the agricultural work required at that time.

However, as the need for "working" horses decreased and that for "riding" horses increased, Trakehners were introduced as were, more recently, Arabs and again Thoroughbreds with the object of refining the breed while

LIPIZZANER Famous as a High School horse, the Lipizzaner is also excellent in other roles. In Yugoslavia it is widely used in dressage, the Hungarians use it as the basis for fine driving horses, and crossbred Lipizzaners have proved ideal farm horses in Yugoslavia, Hungary and Romania.

still retaining the action and temperament of the original type.

The Hanoverian is now one of the most popular competition horses in the world, excelling at both show jumping and dressage, and indeed Hanoverians have produced world champions in both these disciplines, perhaps the most famous example of recent times being the show jumper Simona.

Hanoverians can be any solid color and vary in height from about 15.3 to 16.2 hands. They

are strong, bold, deep and muscular with sloping shoulders, powerful quarters and frequently a high set tail. The cannons are short, usually with at least 9 inches of bone, and the feet hard. The Hanoverian often has spectacular action and moves with long, ground-covering strides.

HOLSTEIN

Another of West Germany's warmbloods, and possibly the oldest because the breed was

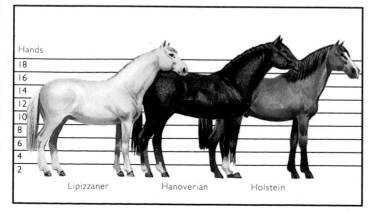

Hands
18
16
14
12
10
8
6
4
2

Lipizzaner Hanoverian Holstein

HANOVERIAN

HANOVERIAN The Hanoverian is a good general riding horse and superb in competition, both under saddle and in harness.

HOLSTEIN Noted for its intelligence and good temperament, the Holstein excels in eventing, show jumping, dressage and carriage driving.

HOLSTEIN

established as long ago as the 17th century, is the Holstein. The breed was developed from a mixture of the existing German horses with the addition of Spanish and Neapolitan blood, which resulted in big, strong, high-stepping horses with a look of the Andalusian about the head.

Later, during the 19th century, infusions of Thoroughbred and Cleveland Bay took place and a lighter, more active horse was produced, which was acclaimed as a tough but elegant carriage horse. Holsteins were introduced into Great Britain by George I, and they were used to pull coaches at the Royal Mews.

Further Thoroughbred blood was introduced to meet the demand for riding and competition horses, and a lighter type has resulted that has proved its worth in all competitive disciplines.

HORSE	ORIGIN	HEIGHT	COLOR	CONFORMATION	FEATURES
Lipizzaner	Austria	15 to 15.2 hands	gray, bay	compact and strong	famous High School horse
Hanoverian	Germany	15.3 to 16.2 hands	any solid color	muscular with powerful quarters	fine all-rounder and competition horse
Holstein	Germany	16 to 17 hands	any solid color	muscular with powerful quarters	one of the best competition horses

TRAKEHNER, OLDENBURG & WESTPHALIAN

The Trakehner, Oldenburg and Westphalian are popular German breeds that make excellent all-round riding horses and perform well in competitions, the Westphalian in particular having had great success as a jumper. The Trakehner is also one of the three foundation breeds of the modern German warmbloods, the other two being the Hanoverian and the Holstein.

TRAKEHNER

The third of West Germany's principal breeds of warmblood horses upon which regional variations and strains have been based is the Trakehner. It is also known as the East Prussian, since it has its origins in what was then East Prussia but is now Poland, and many are still bred throughout the latter country.

The Royal Trakehner Stud was established by King Friedrich Wilhelm I of Prussia in 1732. It was based on the native Prussian horses, but in the early 1800s infusions of both Thoroughbred and Arab blood were added to give quality and endurance, and an elegant carriage horse was the result.

World War II drastically depleted the stock of Trakehners, only twelve hundred out of the two and a half thousand Trakehners registered in the East Prussian Stud Book managing to reach what is now West Germany after a lengthy and difficult journey. Using these as the foundation stock, West German breeders preserved and increased the breed, which is now bred in many parts of Germany.

Standing 16 to 16.2 hands, Trakehners may be any solid color and have many of the Thoroughbred's characteristics, including refinement and elegance. The shoulder is well sloped, the neck long, the body close-coupled and the quarters well muscled and rounded. Cannons are short and the bone dense, and the movement is straight and free. Trakehners are noted for their stamina and endurance, and their temperament is notably tractable, making for an ideal quality riding horse which, in addition, tends to be a good jumper.

OLDENBURG

The biggest and heaviest of the German warmbloods is the Oldenburg, a breed which was based on the Friesian horse and established as long ago as the early 1600s. It was developed as a coach horse, being very strong and bold and showing a lot of knee action.

It has, however, had many infusions of outside blood, introduced with the object of adding quality, and the English Thoroughbred was also used to further upgrade the breed.

The beginning of the 19th century saw further infusions of Thoroughbred blood as well as Cleveland Bay, Hanoverian and Norman blood to produce a big, all-round horse suitable for agricultural work as well as haulage and general carriage work.

When mechanization replaced the need for horsepower on the land and the demand grew for a more all-purpose riding type, yet more Thoroughbred and Norman blood was introduced as well as, later, Hanoverian and Trakehner blood.

Today the Oldenburg is still a large individual, standing 16.2 to 17.2 hands with a large frame to match its size. It is very strong, and deep, with short legs for its size and plenty of bone. The shoulder is sloping, the head

TRAKEHNER

HORSE	ORIGIN	HEIGHT	COLOR	CONFORMATION	FEATURES
Trakehner	Germany	16.1 to 16.2 hands	any solid color	broad head, muscular quarters	good competition and general riding horse
Oldenburg	Germany	16 to 17.2 hands	usually brown, bay or black	large, muscular and very strong	good general riding and driving horse
Westphalian	Germany	15.3 to 16.3 hands	any solid color	substantial, well muscled horse	excellent riding and driving horse

TRAKEHNER The Trakehner or East Prussian has earned itself a high reputation as a competition horse, but it is also good for general riding.

*TRAKEHNER HEAD
The head of the
Trakehner is large but
fine and elegant. Seen
from the front, it is
noticeably broad between
the eyes and narrows
quite sharply to the
muzzle. In profile, the
head has a concave or
"dished" appearance
which is similar to that
of the head of an Arab.*

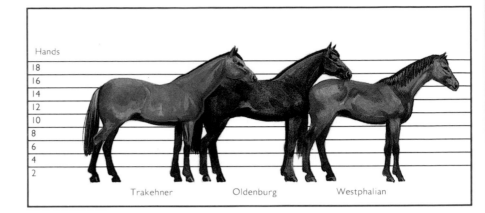

Hands

18
16
14
12
10
8
6
4
2

Trakehner   Oldenburg   Westphalian

*WESTPHALIAN Since the 1970s, the
Westphalian has been one of the world's
top competition breeds, especially in show
jumping.*

*OLDENBURG The large,
handsome Oldenburg, developed
originally as a coach horse, is
now a popular driving and
general riding horse.*

WESTPHALIAN

OLDENBURG

somewhat plain and the neck long, while the quarters are extremely powerful. The Oldenburg is noted for the early age at which it reaches maturity and its temperament is kind and bold. Any solid color may be found but brown, bay and black are the predominant colors.

WESTPHALIAN

All of the West German warmblood breeds are based on the Hanoverian, Holstein and Trakehner (or East Prussian), but slight variations have come about due to the environmental differences in each area. One of these, a virtual Hanoverian in all but name, is the Westphalian Horse of Westfalen.

It is bred principally at the stallion depot, the Landgestut, at Warendorf, which was founded in 1826, and is a good strong, medium-sized horse, resembling a good English middleweight hunter. A useful all-round riding horse, being tough and reliable, it has an even temperament and is ideally suited for the three disciplines of show jumping, dressage and eventing, having a particular talent for the former.

The stallion who has probably had the most influence on the Westphalian breed is Radetsky, born in 1951, by the Anglo-Arab Ramzes who came originally from Poland.

Standing 15.3 to 16.3 hands, any solid color may be found in the Westphalian. The shoulder is sloping and the withers tend to be high and pronounced, while the neck is long and fine and the head medium sized, clean cut and refined, with an intelligent expression and a large, bold eye. It is deep through the girth, strong and well muscled with powerful quarters and a well set on tail. The cannons are short with plenty of bone, the joints well formed and the feet clean and hard.

GELDERLAND, GRONINGEN & DUTCH WARMBLOOD

The Gelderland and the now near-extinct Groningen are native Dutch breeds which were used as the basis for a new breed – the Dutch Warmblood – which has been competing with great success in most equine sports since the 1970s.

GELDERLAND

The Gelderland region of the Netherlands is the homeland of the warmblooded horse of that name. Native mares from the province, which lies in the center of Holland, were bred to imported stallions from Britain, in particular the Norfolk Roadster and Hackney, as well as Arabs from Egypt and horses from Germany, Hungary, Poland, Russia and France. The result was a useful carriage horse that could double as a farm horse, being somewhat slow but steady and strong.

Over the years German Oldenburg blood was added as was East Friesian, and more recently there have been outcrosses to the Anglo-Norman. With these infusions the Gelderland has proved its worth under saddle and particularly in the sphere of show jumping.

A rather plain horse, it is nevertheless well made, having a good sloping shoulder, powerful hindquarters and a high head carriage with a rather Roman nose. It has a docile temperament and is a good mover. Standing 15.2 to 16 hands, it is usually gray or chestnut although skewbalds do occur.

GRONINGEN

A breed which almost no longer exists as such is the Groningen, which originated in the far north of the Netherlands. A big, heavy horse, it derived from a crossing of the German Oldenburg with the Friesian, and it bore a striking resemblance to the former being very strong, especially in the back and hindquarters and having plenty of bone. These characteristics made the Groningen ideal as a farm and draft horse, purposes for which it was primarily used, although with the advent of mechanization on farms its use there declined.

With this decline the Groningen was put to carriage work, an area in which it excelled due in no small part to its stylish action and endurance. It was also used as a heavyweight riding horse and being docile, obedient and willing it adapted well to this role too.

In height the Groningen stands around 15.2 to 16 hands.

DUTCH WARMBLOOD

The Dutch Warmblood has derived from a crossing between the virtually extinct Groningen and the warmblooded Gelderland,

GELDERLAND The Gelderland's quiet temperament and stylish action make it a first-class carriage horse.

GELDERLAND

HORSE	ORIGIN	HEIGHT	COLOR	CONFORMATION	FEATURES
Gelderland	Holland	15.2 to 16 hands	gray, chestnut, sometimes skewbald	strong shoulders and quarters	athletic riding and jumping horse
Groningen	Holland	15.2 to 16 hands	black, bay, dark brown	strong back, powerful quarters	good riding and harness horse
Dutch Warmblood	Holland	15.2 to 16 hands	any solid color	muscular horse with good bone	good all-around riding and harness horse

GRONINGEN The Groningen was almost extinct in the 1970s but is now being carefully preserved. Like the Gelderland, it was originally a farm horse and works well in harness.

combined with English Thoroughbred blood and warm-blooded horses from France and Germany.

With the decline of the horse as an agricultural animal and the simultaneous upsurge of interest in it for recreational purposes, the aim was to produce a useful all-round riding horse resembling a good middleweight hunter. This has been achieved to a very large degree, the strength and power of both Groningen and Gelderland being retained and offset by the quality and refinement of the Thoroughbred.

In conformation, the Dutch Warmblood is a well-proportioned animal having a good sloping shoulder with a well set on head and neck, ensuring that the horse is well balanced at all paces. Its withers tend to be pronounced,

the back shortish and strong and the hindquarters powerful and muscular. It is deep through the girth with strong loins, short cannons, plenty of bone, big, flat joints and good, sound, open feet.

Temperament and action are important, too, and willingness, reliability, intelligence, obedience and tractability are all desirable qualities. The action should be straight and true, the horse moving from the shoulder with long, ground-covering strides, and there should be very little knee action. In height the Dutch Warmblood varies between 15.2 and 16 hands and may be any color.

The Dutch Warmblood Stud Book – the *Warmbloed Paardenstamboed Nederland* – was formed in 1958 with the object of developing and promoting the breed.

To ensure that the high standards of the breed are maintained, only the best animals exhibiting correct conformation and action and a good even temperament are used for breeding purposes, both stallions and mares undergoing a strict selection procedure. Those not meeting the requirements are ineligible for entry into the Stud Book.

The success of the Dutch Warmblood has been such that the breed is now to be found competing very successfully in virtually all equine sports. One of the best-known horses of this

breed in recent years is Marius, the stallion who show jumped internationally with the late Caroline Bradley for a number of years. However, they perform equally well in the other disciplines of eventing and dressage, as well as performing light carriage duties and excelling in driving competitions.

Such is the popularity of the breed that they have been exported throughout Europe, particularly to Germany, Austria and Belgium, where they are being used to upgrade the existing stock.

GRONINGEN

DUTCH WARMBLOOD A relatively new breed, the Dutch Warmblood is a very successful competition horse.

DUTCH WARMBLOOD

SHIRE, CLYDESDALE & SUFFOLK PUNCH

The Shire, the Clydesdale and the Suffolk Punch are Britain's three heavy horse breeds. These big, powerful horses have for centuries been used in agriculture and for haulage, but today they are more often seen in the show ring than on the land.

SHIRE

A descendant of the Great Horse of medieval times, the Shire is one of the largest horses in the world, standing 17 to 18 hands and sometimes a little above. It was founded on the Old English Black and, as its name implies, came from the English Shire counties of Leicestershire, Staffordshire, Derbyshire, Warwickshire and Northamptonshire. The stallion who probably had the greatest influence on the breed in the early years was Packington Blind Horse, who stood at stud in Leicestershire in the late 1770s.

The Shire is a big-barrelled, powerful horse weighing a ton or more but very kind, docile and gentle in relation to its enormous size. The back is short, strong and muscular, the girth deep, the shoulder sloping, the chest wide and the quarters wide and well muscled. The head is rather fine in comparison with the body, the eyes large, the profile slightly Roman and the neck is fairly long and well set on. Legs are long with big flat knees and hocks and are set well under the body, and there is an abundance of fine, silky feather. Shires may be black, brown, bay or gray.

Today, Shires are still used in England on the farm as well as for hauling brewers' wagons. There has been a revival of interest in the Shire over the recent years and there are numerous show classes for them, the popular Shire Horse Show taking place annually in England. Shires have also been exported worldwide, principally to the United States, Canada, Australia and Russia. While never numerous in the US, in the Midwest Shires were bred to Standardbreds to produce a medium-sized farm work horse.

CLYDESDALE

Scotland's native heavy, the Clydesdale, comes from the Clyde valley in Lanarkshire and was founded on the native mares of the region crossed with Flanders stallions. During the 18th century, further infusions of Flanders blood were introduced and a useful draft horse, equally at home on the farm as doing road haulage work, was the result.

Standing 16.2 to 17 hands, the Clydesdale is a big, muscular horse with a longish neck, sloping shoulder, short, strong back and long and well-muscled thighs and quarters. Limbs are straight and well set under the body, thus encouraging the already naturally active movement for which the breed is noted. Feet are exceptionally good, being open and sound.

The Clydesdale Horse Society was formed in 1877, the first volume of the Stud Book listing a thousand registered stallions, and a year later a similar Society was formed in the United States. Although still to be seen performing haulage and farming duties it is now more frequently seen in the show ring, particularly at the Royal Highland, where many classes are held for the breed. Its popularity as an active draft horse

SUFFOLK PUNCH

HORSE	ORIGIN	HEIGHT	COLOR	CONFORMATION	FEATURES
Suffolk	England	16 to 16.3 hands	various shades of chestnut	big-bodied, compact, strong	farm, show and draft horse
Shire	England	17 to 18 hands	black, brown, bay or gray	massive, powerful and muscular	farm, show and draft horse
Clydesdale	Scotland	16.2 to 17 hands	bay, brown, gray, roan or black	large, powerful and muscular	farm, show and draft horse

SUFFOLK PUNCH *The Suffolk or Suffolk Punch is an intelligent, even-tempered horse with great pulling power. The breed is very pure, and probably dates back to at least the 16th century.*

has spread worldwide. Many Americans know the Clydesdale from the Budweiser commercials and from its appearances in parades.

SUFFOLK PUNCH

The Suffolk is the oldest and probably the purest of Britain's three native heavy horse breeds, and hails from East Anglia where it has worked the heavy clay soil of the area since the 16th century. All modern day Suffolks can be traced back to one horse, Crisp's Horse of Ufford, who was foaled in 1760.

Smallest of the heavies, the Suffolk ranges from 16 to 16.3 hands and weighs in the region of a ton. It is a big-bodied, compact horse, with a deep body, muscular shoulders and strong, powerful quarters. It stands on short legs that have plenty of bone and, unlike the other British heavy breeds, are almost totally devoid of feather.

The Suffolk is an active breed with straight, free action, and it is noted for its docile temperament, stamina, longevity and ability to

thrive on a minimum of feed. Suffolks are always chestnut in color, ranging from very dark to bright red, although seven shades are officially recognized, and white markings are frequently found on the large, broad face.

Today the Suffolk Punch, as it is sometimes known, can still be

found working the land in its native Suffolk as well as being used for haulage work over short distances.

The Suffolk Horse Society, founded in 1877, numbers many enthusiastic Suffolk owners among its ranks, and when not working, the Suffolk can be seen

in the show rings, particularly (as might be expected) in East Anglia.

Such is its popularity as an agricultural and draft horse, the Suffolk has been exported to many parts of the world, most notably to the United States and Australia as well as Africa, Pakistan and Russia.

SHIRE The massive, gentle Shire is one of the largest horses in the world.

SHIRE

CLYDESDALE The Clydesdale, the native heavy horse of Scotland, is a splendid workhorse and hugely popular in the show ring.

CLYDESDALE

IRISH DRAFT HORSE, PERCHERON & ARDENNAIS

These breeds all originated as draft and farm horses. The Ardennais (or Ardennes) is still widely used as a workhorse, but the Irish Draft and the Percheron are now more important as bases for halfbred riding horses.

IRISH DRAFT

There are no early stud books relating to the Irish Draft, so its origins are therefore somewhat obscure. However, it is thought that the breed developed from crossing the indigenous Irish mares with imported English Thoroughbreds. The indigenous stock probably, in turn, evolved from the Connemara pony, which had a good deal of Spanish and Arabian blood in its veins, and which, once away from its native western seaboard, had grown larger on the lusher grazing.

It was originally used in Ireland on the farm as an all-round workhorse, being strong and compact and standing on short legs, but mechanization gradually reduced its usefulness in this field. After a few years in the doldrums, however, there was a revival of interest in the breed when its potential as a base from which to breed halfbred hunters was realized, and the Irish Draft Horse Society was formed in 1976.

The Irish Draft has a small head, intelligent eye, deep chest, sloping shoulder, short back and strong loins and quarters with plenty of good flat bone and no feather on the legs. Standing 15 to 17 hands it is predominantly bay, brown, chestnut or gray. Its action is straight and the movement active, and it has good jumping ability. It is sensible, willing, kindly and has stamina, all of which are extremely desirable and useful qualities in a hunter.

PERCHERON

Originating in the Perche region of France, south of Normandy, the Percheron developed from a cross between Norman, German and Danish horses and Arabs, and owes much to the early influences of the latter. Other draft breeds were introduced over the years as was more Arab blood when Arab stallions from the Royal Stud at Le Pin were used to upgrade the the quality of the breed.

Primarily used in France for draft purposes, the Percheron was also used on the farm and as a carriage horse at the turn of the century, a period when it was enjoying a lot of recognition. Although a heavy horse noted for its stamina, endurance and longevity, the Percheron, due in no small measure to its Oriental ancestry, is more active and graceful than many of the world's heavies, and many have been exported, principally to the United States and Britain.

In Britain, where it has been bred mainly in East Anglia, more "fineness" has been bred into the horse and it has lost practically all the feather on its legs. Here, too, the mares are frequently and very successfully crossed with Thor-

IRISH DRAFT HORSE The Irish Draft is light and fast for a heavy horse, and has good jumping ability.

IRISH DRAFT HORSE

PERCHERON

HORSE	ORIGIN	HEIGHT	COLOR	CONFORMATION	FEATURES
Irish Draft	Ireland	15 to 17 hands	bay, brown, chestnut, gray	long body, powerful quarters	good riding, farm and competition horse
Percheron	France	16 to 17 hands	gray or black	wide body, strong quarters	farm, show and draft horse
Ardennais	France	15.2 to 15.3 hands	chestnut, roan, bay	compact, stocky and strong	excellent farm and draft horse

PERCHERON The Percheron is a handsome and popular heavy horse, used in agriculture and haulage and sometimes for carriage driving.

Hands

18
16
14
12
10
8
6
4
2

Irish Draft Horse   Percheron   Ardennais

ARDENNAIS The tough, hardy Ardennais takes its name from the Ardennes — the heavily forested plateau straddling the border between France and Belgium — where the breed originated.

ARDENNAIS

oughbred stallions to produce good heavyweight hunters with plenty of bone.

Standing 16 to 17 hands, the Percheron may be either gray or black and weighs about three-quarters of a ton. Its head is relatively fine, the neck arched, shoulders sloping and the chest deep and wide. It is deep through the girth with a short, strong back and the quarters tend to be sloping. Limbs are clean with big, flat joints and good, sound feet.

Today, the Percheron is used mainly as an agricultural horse and for haulage work, but it is also sometimes used for driving.

ARDENNAIS

The Ardennais, one of the four principal breeds of heavy horse to be found in France, is bred in the northeast of the country where it has performed draft duties since the Middle Ages. It is extremely strong, tough and hardy, qualities which found favor with the military when it was used as an artillery horse both during the French Revolution and World War I.

At the turn of the century, Percheron, Thoroughbred and Arab blood was introduced and over the years three separate types of Ardennais have developed. The French Ardennais is very similar in both appearance and temperament to the Belgian Ardennais, being short, thick set and very muscular and compact. The neck is crested, the head large with a straight profile and large eye, the chest deep and the back short and strong. Hindquarters are wide, rounded and well muscled while the loins and thighs are muscular.

In height the Ardennais is approximately 15 to 15.3 hands, and the predominant colors are chestnut, roan and bay, although grays and liver chestnuts are also found.

The Trait du Nord is a larger and heavier version of the Ardennais with a big, heavy head; it has Dutch and Belgian Draft blood, while the Auxois is again very similar.

The latter owes much to the old heavy horse of Burgundy which existed in medieval times, but the subsequent extensive crossing with Percheron, Boulonnais and particularly and more recently Ardennais has resulted in an Ardennais lookalike.

All three types are quiet, kind, willing, easy to handle and hard workers and are used in draft and on the farm.

ARDENNAIS

BOULONNAIS, BRETON & BRABANT

The Boulonnais and the Breton are both from northern France, and the Brabant is a native of nearby Belgium. They are good farm and draft horses, but many end up in the European meat markets.

BOULONNAIS

Very similar to the Percheron in appearance, the Boulonnais also owes much to its Oriental ancestors. It has been known in northern France since Roman times, when local stock was crossed with Arabs or those of Arab derivation, and in the time of the Crusades more Arab as well as Andalusian blood was infused into the breed.

At the beginning of the 17th century two types developed, one, the smaller version, averaging around 15.2 hands and the larger one 16 to 16.3 hands, although the smaller type, known as the Maréeur, has almost completely disappeared.

Predominantly gray in color, although blacks, chestnuts and bays can occasionally be found, the Boulonnais has a thick, arched neck and short, elegant head with large eyes and wide forehead. Shoulders are muscular with fairly prominent withers, the back is short and broad, the chest broad and the quarters round and muscular. Limbs are strong with short cannons and large joints without feathering.

Elegant and well proportioned, the Boulonnais is intelligent and gentle and may be seen performing general all-round draft duties on the farms of France. It may also be seen in harness on the roads, although unfortunately many are now finding their way to the meat market in France.

BRETON

From the northwest area of France, and particularly Brittany, comes another draft horse but one with a decided "pony" look about it. This is the Breton, which can be traced back to the Middle Ages and which has resulted over the years in the evolution of two different types.

The heavier type of draft Breton was produced by crossing the indigenous French mares with the Boulonnais, Ardennais and Percheron and a short, sturdy, very muscular horse with a big barrel and powerful quarters was produced. The head is short and wide with a rather dished face and there is an abundance of feather on the legs and plenty of bone. It is used principally for agricultural work and as a pack animal.

The Postier is the lighter type of Breton and has had infusions, during the 19th century, principally of Hackney and Norfolk Roadster blood. It is a smart, active little horse with an energetic trot, a trait acquired from its ancestors. It is used as a carriage horse and in draft, particularly working in the vineyards, and is good natured and willing.

In height the Postier averages 15 hands while the draft Breton is slightly larger. Red roan and chestnut are the predominant colors, although bays and grays are also found. The neck is short, strong and arched and the head is straighter and more square than the draft Breton. The shoulders are sloping and the body is short and broad with a lot of depth through the girth. Hindquarters are powerful and limbs short and strong with considerably less feather than the draft Breton.

Stud Books for the Breton have existed since the early 1900s, but since the 1920s one Stud Book has covered both types and is now closed. Increased popularity over recent years has led to the export of Bretons, particularly to North Africa and Japan and parts of Europe.

BRABANT

Also known as the Belgian Heavy Draft or the Flanders Horse, the Brabant is a native of the Brabant area of Belgium around Brussels, although it is found throughout Flanders, Anvers, Limburg, Hainaut, Liege, Namur and Luxembourg.

BOULONNAIS The Boulonnais is one of the most elegant heavy horses, due to past infusions of Arab and Andalusian blood.

BOULONNAIS

HORSE	ORIGIN	HEIGHT	COLOR	CONFORMATION	FEATURES
Boulonnais	France	15.2 to 16.3 hands	gray, black, chestnut, bay	broad, muscular and strong	good farm and draft horse
Breton	France	15 to 16 hands	roan, chestnut, bay or gray	powerful and thick set	good farm, draft and pack horse
Brabant	Belgium	16 to 16.3 hands	mostly red roan, some chestnut	muscular and very powerful	an ideal heavy draft horse

Strict selective breeding was practiced, and by the turn of the last century three types had developed: the Gros de la Dendre, which can be traced back to the stallion Orange I; Gris du Hainaut, founded by the stallion Bayard, a line producing gray, dun or roan horses; and the Colosses de la Mehaique, which traces back to the bay Jean I. All are very similar in conformation, the Gris du Hainaut being rather finer and more elegant than the other lines and the Colosses de la Mehaique being somewhat taller, although less muscular than the other lines and with exceptionally good hard bone.

Standing 16 to 16.3 hands, the Brabant is immensely powerful, strong and muscular with a short back and great depth through the girth. Legs are short with a great deal of feather and it has a very active walk. Its head is small and square, the neck is well muscled and arched and it is known for its willing temperament. It has been crossed with other European breeds and has influenced the Clydesdale and the Ardennais among others.

Hands
18
16
14
12
10
8
6
4
2

Boulonnais   Breton   Brabant

BRABANT The Brabant is a large, powerful horse with a calm temperament and a capacity for hard work that makes it a popular farm horse in its native Belgium. The breed is thriving there, and large numbers are exported.

BRABANT

BRETON

BRETON Like the Brabant, the energetic Breton is an excellent workhorse. The heavier type is used for farm and pack work, and the lighter type, the Postier, is used in vineyards and as a carriage and coach horse.

NORIKER, SCHLESWIG & RHINELAND HEAVY DRAFT

The Noriker, Schleswig and Rhineland Heavy Draft were developed in Germany for farm and draft work. The Rhineland, the newest of these breeds, is the most powerful of the three.

NORIKER

Bred throughout Bavaria, south Germany, where it is known as the South German Coldblood, and Austria, where there is also a spotted strain called the Pinzgauer, the Noriker has been developed in the Austrian Alps. It can, however, be traced back to the days of the Roman Empire, some two thousand years ago, but has probably evolved from the Haflinger, to whom it bears a striking resemblance, although from the 16th century onwards Spanish, Neapolitan and Burgundy blood has been infused to increase the size of the Noriker.

Bred in this harsh, mountainous area, the Noriker has become extremely hardy and sure-footed and is noted for its qualities of soundness and endurance; attributes which have made it a popular all-round workhorse for draft work and in agriculture.

Standing 16 to 17 hands, the Noriker is a rather plain horse with a heavy head and a straight profile and a relatively short neck. The back is short, the chest broad and deep and the quarters well-muscled and powerful. Legs are long and clean with big, flat joints, well-muscled "second" thighs and good sound feet. Predominantly bay, chestnut or brown in color, blacks and grays are also found, but white markings on the face and legs are not encouraged. The Noriker is known for its docile temperament and good action.

SCHLESWIG

The origin of the Schleswig is, as the name implies, the Schleswig–Holstein area of northern Germany, it being descended from the coldblooded Jutland horses of the west coast of Germany and of Denmark.

At one time used for draft work, it found particular favor with the transport companies for pulling buses and trolleys. In the 19th century Yorkshire Coach Horse blood was introduced, as was Thoroughbred blood, and although selective breeding started in 1860 (the Society of Schleswig Horse Breeding Clubs being formed in 1891) the breed was maintained by regular use of Danish stallions until 1938.

The result was a medium-sized, compact, cob-like draft horse with a placid temperament, who was, due to the influx of Thoroughbred blood, an active mover and a willing workhorse for farm and urban transport, although its rather poor quality, soft, flat feet proved detrimental to its otherwise all-round usefulness.

In an effort to counteract this deficiency, French stallions, namely Breton and Boulonnais, were used on the Schleswig, the Boulonnais having a particularly strong influence on the breed.

Standing 15.2 to 16 hands, the Schleswig is predominantly chestnut, although bays and grays are also found. It has a rather plain head with a convex profile, short, crested neck and powerful shoulders with well-muscled hindquarters. Deep through the girth, the body is somewhat long with a flat barrel and the legs are short with plenty of bone and a certain amount of feather.

RHINELAND HEAVY DRAFT

In the early part of this century the Rhineland Heavy Draft was the most popular working horse in Germany. It was developed in the

NORIKER

NORIKER The Noriker takes its name from the ancient Roman province of Noricum, most of which is now Austria. The Noriker is used for farm, pack and forestry work in Austria and Germany.

TAIL DOCKING Docking the tails of farm horses to stop them getting caught in machinery was once common, but is now illegal.

Noriker   Schleswig   Rhineland Heavy Draft

SCHLESWIG

SCHLESWIG The Schleswig is compact and cob-like in stature but its energetic and willing nature has made it popular as a farm horse in northern Germany.

RHINELAND HEAVY DRAFT

Rhineland in the latter part of the 19th century from the Belgian Draft Horse with infusions, at varying times, of the Suffolk and the Clydesdale, and after World War I it became a recognized breed, the Rheinisch–Deutsches (or Rhenish–German) horse.

The breed quickly spread to other parts of Germany, particularly Saxony and Westphalia, where it was used extensively in agriculture, although Shires, Clydesdales and Ardennais were also used for farm work.

Due principally to its early maturity, kind and willing temperament, great pulling power and the fact that it does exceedingly well on very little feed, the Rhineland became extremely popular as a general all-round farm horse and for use in heavy draft, and two types gradually emerged. Very similar in conformation, a heavier, bulkier horse was developed in the Westphalia area than that used elsewhere.

With the increase in mechanization, however, the heavier type began to decline, the lighter type taking the agricultural role throughout all regions, until following World War II the numbers of that type also began to drop, although they do still exist in a few areas.

Chestnut and roan are the favored colors and the general height ranges from 16 to 17 hands. Noted for its even temperament, the Rhineland Heavy Draft is a very powerful horse which stands on short legs and is capable of great traction. It has a short muscular neck, powerful shoulders, short back and powerful, sloping hindquarters. "Second" thighs and forearms are well muscled and the cannons short.

RHINELAND HEAVY DRAFT The Rhineland Heavy Draft was very popular in the first half of the 20th century, but since then its numbers have declined and there are now very few of them.

HORSE	ORIGIN	HEIGHT	COLOR	CONFORMATION	FEATURES
Noriker	Austria	16 to 17 hands	bay, chestnut, brown, black, gray	broad, deep body, powerful quarters	good all-round farm and draft horse
Schleswig	Germany	15.1 to 16 hands	usually chestnut, some bay or gray	long, deep body, powerful quarters	strong, energetic farm and draft horse
Rhineland Heavy Draft	Germany	16 to 17 hands	chestnut, roan	broad, deep body, powerful quarters	good farm and heavy draft horse

DUTCH DRAFT, FRIESIAN & JUTLAND

Of these three northern European breeds, the Dutch Draft and the Friesian originated in the Netherlands and the Jutland in Denmark. The Friesian and the Jutland are ancient breeds, but the Dutch Draft has a relatively recent history.

DUTCH DRAFT

Very similar in appearance to the heavy draft horse from Belgium, the Brabant, from which it is descended, the Dutch Draft is a real heavyweight with a massive frame that belies its very quiet and docile temperament. Of relatively recent origin, the Dutch Draft only really evolved following World War II when it was used extensively on the farmlands, both on the sandy soils of the coastal areas and on the heavier clay soils in other parts of the Netherlands.

The indigenous mares of the area were crossed initially with the Brabant and later with the Belgian Ardennais, and this useful heavy draft horse was the result.

Standing up to around 16.3 hands in height and predominantly chestnut, bay or gray in color with occasional blacks, the Dutch Draft is noted for its longevity and the early age at which it matures. It has great stamina and endurance and is a willing worker with a turn of speed and remarkably active paces for its great size and weight. It also does well on a minimum of feed.

The head is of medium size with a straight profile, the neck is short and well muscled and the shoulders very powerful. The body is short and wide with great depth through the girth, and the hindquarters are extremely powerful and rather sloping. Legs are short and strong with an abundance of feather and the feet are hard and sound.

Careful records of the Dutch Draft have been kept since the breed was founded and no horses with unknown pedigrees have been included in the Stud Book since 1925.

FRIESIAN

One of the oldest breeds in Europe, the Friesian originated in the Friesland area of the Netherlands. It can be traced back to the coldblooded heavy horses that survived the last Ice Age, and fossil remains of a coldblooded heavy horse bearing a resemblance to today's Friesian have been found in northern Holland.

During the 19th century, infusions of Oriental and Andalusian blood were added to the Friesian, resulting in a very much lighter horse. This horse's speed, kind disposition and high action at the trot made it successful in the trotting races that were becoming popular at the time, but it was unsuitable for farming, which had previously been its main use. As a result, its numbers declined and by 1913 there were only three Friesian stallions left.

However, it was saved from extinction by the addition of Oldenburg blood, which gave the breed its substance again, and during World War II it was able to play a vital part in agriculture. The Friesian is now exceedingly popular as an all-round workhorse and also for driving, a sport at which it excels.

Strong, muscular, energetic and with a very placid temperament, the Friesian is always black, white

DUTCH DRAFT

DUTCH DRAFT *The Dutch Draft breed was established in 1914 and developed specifically as a heavy farm horse.*

HORSE	ORIGIN	HEIGHT	COLOR	CONFORMATION	FEATURES
Dutch Draft	Holland	16.3 hands	chestnut, bay, gray, some black	broad, deep body, powerful quarters	strong, energetic farm and draft horse
Friesian	Holland	14.3 to 15.3 hands	black	strong, compact elegant	popular farm, draft and carriage horse
Jutland	Denmark	15 to 16 hands	usually chestnut	very deep body, muscular quarters	powerful farm and draft horse

markings being considered undesirable. Standing about 15 hands, the Friesian has a rather long, fine head with a high carriage. The neck is elegantly arched, the shoulders powerful and the body strong and compact. The hindquarters are strong and sloping, the legs are short and strong with a good amount of bone and feathering, and the feet are hard and sound.

Hands | Dutch Draft | Friesian | Jutland

JUTLAND

The Jutland has existed in the Jutland Peninsula of Denmark for a thousand years or more, and owes its origins to the warhorses of the Middle Ages who carried the armored knights into battle. Indeed, it was as warhorses that they became renowned, being massively built and with enormous depth through the girth. Later they were equally accomplished at general agricultural work, having great strength and endurance and being easily managed and versatile in draft work.

Today's Jutlands can be traced back to an English stallion, Oppenheim LXII, who was exported in the 1860s. It is possible that he was a Shire in view of the enormous frame, but more likely that he was a Suffolk, to which he bore a stronger resemblance. Infusions of the Yorkshire Coach Horse were also made at one time.

Like the Suffolk, and its other close relative the Schleswig, the Jutland is predominantly chestnut in color with a flaxen mane and tail and stands 15 to 16 hands. The head is rather plain but kind and the neck short and very muscular. Shoulders are strong and powerful, the back fairly short, the chest broad and the body exceptionally deep – approximately, in fact, as deep as its rather short, strong legs. It has plenty of bone and an abundance of fine, silky feather and is very kind and willing.

JUTLAND The Jutland is an ancient breed of heavy horse from the Jutland Peninsula of Denmark. Small numbers of these powerful, versatile horses are still used for farming and haulage work.

FRIESIAN The Friesian horses of Holland, which were revitalized by the addition of Oldenburg blood, are used for both riding and driving.

FRIESIAN

JUTLAND

TECHNIQUES

The techniques involved in driving and riding horses, and the training involved in preparing them for these purposes, have their origin early in the history of man's association with the horse.

Nomadic Aryan tribes inhabiting the steppe lands bordering the Caspian and Black Seas are generally credited with the domestication of horses toward the end of the Neolithic period, some five to six thousand years ago. Probably, these people were originally herders of reindeer, their movements being governed by the migratory character of those animals. Archaeological evidence suggests that reindeer were hauling sledges in northern Europe as early as 5000 BC and it is certain that their domestication precedes that of the horse by some two thousand years or even more. Furthermore, there is every reason to suppose that these reindeer people rode their animals as well as herding them and using them for draft.

They made the change to a horse culture as a result of a greater availability of these animals which were in every way a better proposition than reindeer, being non-migratory and better equipped to find food in difficult, snowbound conditions. When they did so it was not a matter of great difficulty to transpose the handling techniques learned with reindeer to the horse herds.

By the second millennium BC, Kassite and Elamite warriors mounted on rough, wiry ponies had penetrated into northwest Persia, the Hyksos were in Asia Minor and a pattern of armed mounted migrations had been established by the people of the Asiatic and Ukrainian steppes. Clearly, these horsemen, the predecessors of Parthians, Scythians and Mongols, had learned how to manage and control their mounts to considerable effect with a minimum of equipment.

Nonetheless, the greatest impact of the horse on the ancient world was initially made in conjunction with the chariot, which was ideal for use in the flat, open terrain of Syria, Egypt and the lands along the Tigris, Euphrates and Indus rivers when drawn by a team of three horses — horses that would hardly have been large enough to carry a heavily armored man in those conditions.

The Hittites used 3500 chariots when they defeated Rameses II of Egypt at Kadesh, in 1286 BC, and it was their chariot corps which gave rise to the first horse-training manual. It was written in about 1386 BC by Kikkuli the Mitannian and it covered equine management, conditioning and training in pretty comprehensive terms.

The chariot remained an essential element in the armies of the ancient world up to and beyond the Christian era, but as improved methods of feeding and selective breeding produced bigger horses, the accent was increasingly upon the use of cavalry and the systematic training of horse and rider became a matter of primary importance.

In the 4th century BC, the Greek general Xenophon (c. 430–355 BC) was writing training manuals like The Cavalry Commander and The Art of Horsemanship, which reveal a very deep knowledge of riding and training. Horses were trained in the basic paces, they were taught to strike off correctly at the canter, they learned movements like the demi-pirouette and they were taught to jump and cross rough country — and all without benefit of saddle.

Xenophon's works remain largely relevant to this day, and they formed the inspiration for the early Masters of the Renaissance period (1500–1600) who, by refining movements performed by the medieval knight in battle, created the foundations of "classical" riding.

In the 18th century, under the influence of François Robichon de la Guérinière, riding was to become a rational science based on the systematic training of horse and rider and the development of communication between the two dependent on the aids, the signals given made by the rider's limbs and body-weight. The Spanish Riding School in Vienna, founded in 1572, claims that it still, in the 20th century, preserves the principles of de la Guérinière in all their purity.

The methods of the later classical Masters influenced very largely the cavalry schools of Europe up to the turn of the century. Then, as the role of cavalry changed in the face of increasingly devastating firepower and the enclosure of the countryside with walls, hedges and so on, it was time for yet another revolution in equestrian thought and practice.

It was brought about by an Italian cavalry officer, Captain Federico Caprilli (1868–1907), who in the space of his short life altered the concept of active, outdoor riding. He schooled his horses and riders to acquire a natural balance over the country in which they were to operate. He discarded the collected movements of the manège and taught the "forward system" of riding which obliged his riders to shorten their leathers and sit forward (the so-called forward seat) both across country and over fences.

Caprilli's theories were not accepted in their entirety by later generations, but as a result of them the modern world sits forward over its fences, otherwise employing a blend of classicism with his innovative teaching in training and riding techniques.

A different and older school of riding and training was inherited by the Western horsemen of America. It derives from the practices of the 16th century conquistadors who, in turn, had learned from the Moors, whose 700-year occupation of the Iberian Peninsula did not come to an end until the 13th century.

The conquistadors reintroduced the horse to the American continent, in which it had been extinct since the Ice Age, and took with them their training techniques and equipment. Even today, the Western saddle resembles closely that of the Spanish knight and the method of bridling a horse through the hackamore system (jaquima, in Arabic hakma) continues virtually unaltered.

BASIC HORSE TRAINING

Although differing in detail, there is a basic agreement on the progression of training in Europe and its American counterpart in the modern Western pattern of schooling. Both seek to develop the natural powers of the horse by a progressive system of training, and then to develop them to the greatest advantage according to the purposes for which the horse seems best suited. Essentially, the training of the young horse is divided into four distinct sections, each having its own objectives.

The first period begins at birth and extends up to the age of three years. It is undemanding in terms of physical effort, and is really a time of acclimatization for the young horse during which, often following the example of its dam, it comes to accept humans and being handled by them. That is one objective; another, of course, is concerned with the physical development which is encouraged by supplementary feeding as well as having the freedom of good and ample pasture in company with companions of its own kind.

As a guide, a warmblood foal can be given a daily ration of 1 pound of concentrate feed for each month of its age, up to a maximum of 5 to 6 pounds according to its size (pony foals, until they are weaned, need only grass and a share of the dam's feeds). These feeds can comprise nuts, oats, a *very little* bran (a food high in phosphates which, if fed to excess, can cause a calcium deficiency), dried milk, cod-liver oil (to promote bone growth), and succulent appetizers like apples and carrots. It will also need as much clean, good-quality hay as it will eat during the winter months.

At the age of nine days the foal should be introduced to handling, and to this end the mare, and her foal, should be brought to the stable daily. At this point no attempt should be made to catch the foal, which will naturally follow its dam closely.

In a few days it should be possible to cradle the foal with one arm around its hindquarters and one around its chest, and to persuade it to follow as the dam is led around the stall. The secret lies in placing the mare against the wall with the foal at her near side

ABOVE The foal can be taught to lead from a soft rub rag, with the handler's right arm around its quarters to push it.

LEFT The foal should not be weaned until it is at least five months old; weaning at six months is preferable.

so that it gains confidence from the contact.

Thereafter, the foal can be taught to lead from a soft rub rag placed around its neck, the handler, meanwhile, putting his or her right arm around the hindquarters so that the foal is *pushed* forward rather than *pulled*.

When the foal can be led on a rub rag to and from the paddock, it is time to introduce a foal slip (a type of adjustable halter made from soft leather). This will be fitted in the stable, the foal being *pushed* forward into the open noseband.

The fitting of the slip and subsequently leading the foal from it is the first lesson in submission and is one of the most important in the horse's life. If it is accomplished tactfully, without the foal becoming frightened, it paves the way for future training; if not, and the animal is handled roughly, the bond of trust between human and animal is never formed and there is every chance of the foal becoming head shy.

As part of the youngster's

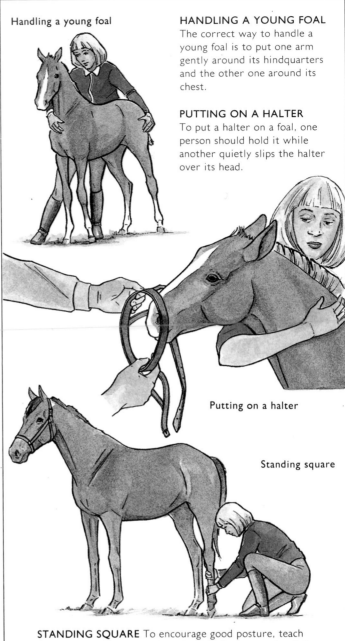

Handling a young foal

HANDLING A YOUNG FOAL
The correct way to handle a young foal is to put one arm gently around its hindquarters and the other one around its chest.

PUTTING ON A HALTER
To put a halter on a foal, one person should hold it while another quietly slips the halter over its head.

Putting on a halter

Standing square

STANDING SQUARE To encourage good posture, teach your foal to stand up straight. Arrange its legs so that it is standing square, and reward it for doing so.

training it may be taken to an *occasional* show with its mother. This involves entering a trailer or box, which will be quite easily accomplished if the foal, cradled in the arms of two helpers, is loaded first, when the mare will invariably follow to avoid separation.

As a yearling and a two-year-old the young horse has to be taught to lead in hand, another immensely important lesson since it inculcates the habit of moving freely forward. The horse should be led from both sides, with the handler at his shoulder holding a long whip in his unengaged hand so he can tap the horse's flank.

At two years old the horse should be taught to stand while being groomed, and he should by then have become well-used to having its feet handled and trimmed by the farrier.

In the April of its third year the horse enters into the second primary schooling period. This extends for some four months, after which the horse is allowed to run out (with, of course, ample supplementary feeding) so that its natural development can continue. It is brought back into work in the following April as a four-year-old for the third stage in its schooling.

The second stage, though short in duration, is nonetheless critical, for within this period the horse learns to carry a saddle and then a rider. The objectives to be achieved are these:

● The extension of handling techniques and discipline. The horse will, for instance, be shod in this period and will need to be confirmed in its stall and trailer drill.

● It has to be prepared physically to carry weight on its back. This is done by strengthening and suppling exercises on the lunge, combined with an appropriate feed ration of about 9 pounds of concentrates, given daily in three feeds, plus hay.

● It has to learn to work on the bit, if it was not made familiar with one as a two-year-old.

● It has to accept the rider on its back and learn how to carry his weight, since this involves the horse making continual adjustments to its own natural balance.

● It has to be taught the meaning of the aids applied by the rider.

The schooling begins when the horse is brought in and a stable routine is established. It is, however, advisable for it to be turned out in its paddock each day for a couple of hours, so that it has an opportunity to unwind.

In the first week or so it will be exercised in-hand, being led about the place and, if it is possible, through water and even over small ditches and banks. During this period it will also be shod for the first time.

BASIC HORSE TRAINING 2

Once the initial introduction to the new circumstances has been made the horse can begin to work on the lunge line for short periods each day. In simple terms, lungeing is about the horse circling the trainer, a lunge line running from the nose ring of the lunge cavesson to the trainer's hand, connecting the two.

Properly carried out by a skillful trainer who insists on active, regular paces at the walk and particularly at the trot, the exercise builds muscle correctly, improves the gaits and the balance and, since lungeing is carried out in both directions, it begins to supple the horse on both sides of the body.

Just as important are the mental benefits derived from lungeing. The horse learns to work in a state of calm, it learns obedience to the voice and the exercise encourages forward movement, which is as much a mental quality as a physical one and is the first essential in the riding horse.

Teaching the horse to work on the lunge line is not difficult if it has learned to walk in hand. It is only necessary for the trainer to step back and urge the horse forward with a slight movement of the whip. At the outset, however, it is helpful to have an assistant.

The lunge sessions are initially of short duration – no more than 20 minutes a day – but they can be increased as the horse becomes stronger and new exercises, including jumping, are introduced.

The next step is to work the horse with a bit in its mouth, fitted under the cavesson, and then to put side reins to the bit. This will involve the horse wearing a roller, to which the reins can be attached, and probably a crupper, which helps to keep the roller in place. The roller acts as an introduction to the saddle.

Side reins encourage the horse to drop its nose, they accustom it to a slight pressure on its mouth and they help in producing a nicely rounded form. They should not be adjusted tight – it is sufficient if they form just a slight curve between mouth and roller.

Other exercises which can be practiced on the lunge line (but without the side reins, which would restrict the extension of the head and neck) are the crossing of a grid of up to six thick rails or poles, laid on the ground at a trotting distance of from 4 to 5 feet (according to the horse's length of stride), and jumping over low fences. The grid is a strengthening exercise which encourages a rounded form and increases engagement of the hocks.

As a prelude to the horse being "backed" (carrying a rider) it has to be worked on the lunge line wearing a saddle with the irons secured to prevent their banging against its sides. Before the backing of the horse, however, and for some time after that has been accomplished, many trainers like to work the horse in long reins.

This involves the use of two reins, both, after first being put on the cavesson rings, being fitted directly to the bit rings. By gradual steps the inside rein passes through a ring on the roller to the trainer's hand. The outside rein passes through a corresponding ring and then around the quarters before returning to the hand.

The horse can now be driven forward from behind and it learns to make changes of direction in accordance with the light pressures on either side of the mouth, as well as to alter speed and pace, to halt and to rein back as the hands indicate.

Backing commences, after work when the horse is settled, with a light assistant lying across the horse's back while the trainer, with a bowl of oats, stands at the horse's head. When the horse submits to that, the assistant can slide the leg over and sit quietly in the saddle while the horse is led forward for a few strides by the trainer.

Quite soon, it will be possible for the trainer to lunge the horse at the walk and the trot with the rider in position. If the horse has already learned obedience to the voice, it is then a simple matter to transfer control to the rider and to teach the horse the meaning of the simple aids.

If, for instance, the rider squeezes with the legs as the trainer gives the command to walk, the horse quickly associates the squeeze with the order to walk. Similarly, a squeeze on the reins accompanied by the verbal command to halt will have the same result.

After a short period in which the young horse can be ridden within the schooling area independently of the lunge line, but still under the trainer's supervision, it can be taken out for a ride in company with an older, steady horse.

Every opportunity should be taken to ride the young horse in open country where undulating ground will cause it to adjust its balance continually, and where it is possible for it to be ridden over small natural obstacles such as logs, ditches, and streams.

No more should be asked of the three-year-old at this stage. By September it can be turned out and allowed to continue its natural development, but it must be fed well through the winter.

The third stage of training begins in the April of the horse's fourth year. The third-year training can be looked upon as "primary" schooling; the fourth year as a secondary education which produces an obedient, comfort-

By using long reins, the trainer can teach the horse to change direction or speed in response to light pressure on its mouth.

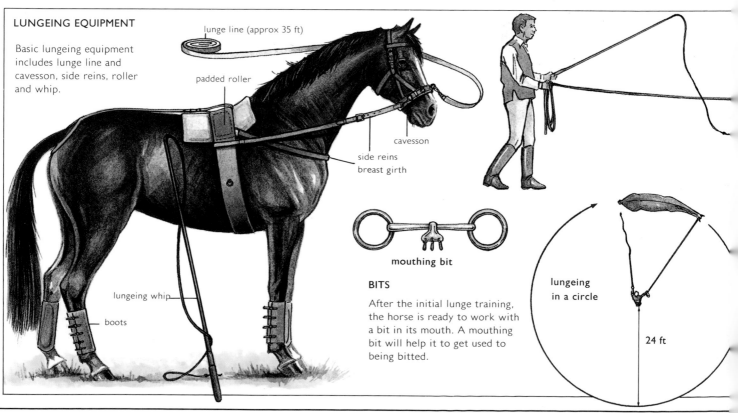

LUNGEING EQUIPMENT

Basic lungeing equipment includes lunge line and cavesson, side reins, roller and whip.

lunge line (approx 35 ft)

padded roller

cavesson

side reins
breast girth

lungeing whip

boots

mouthing bit

BITS

After the initial lunge training, the horse is ready to work with a bit in its mouth. A mouthing bit will help it to get used to being bitted.

lungeing
in a circle

24 ft

SEQUENCE OF TRAINING
Training a mature 3-year-old. Periods may vary according to individual horse's needs.
WEEKS 1–3 Walk in hand leading off cavesson; Introduce bit in stable
WEEK 3 Lunge off cavesson with bit in position
WEEK 4 Lungeing with roller and side reins
WEEK 5 Using long reins
WEEK 6 Introduce saddle:
● without stirrups
● with stirrups tied up
● with stirrups down but tied under belly
● with stirrups loose
WEEK 7 Lungeing/long reins with saddle
WEEK 8 Backing
WEEKS 9–12 Lungeing with rider. Introduce basic aids
WEEKS 12–14 (approx) Off lunge. Riding in enclosure. Leg and hand aids.
WEEKS 14 ONWARD (approx) Riding with older horses.

able all-round horse which can take part in competitive disciplines up to a middle level. For many horses, and for the majority of riders, this, in fact, will be the limit of their capabilities.

In this stage, the horse is further developed by progressive work on the flat which involves the accepted school figures, based largely on the circle. The transitions between the paces, and the variation within each pace, have to be refined and the balance improved until the horse works within an outline in which is on the bit or approaching that state. It carries its head high, flexing at the poll and in the lower jaw and with its face held on or near to the vertical.

The final stage of training is concerned with the especially talented horse, and can be likened to a college education in one of the specialist disciplines of jumping, eventing or dressage.

Although racehorses (who are bred to mature early) are raced at two, it will be counterproductive to expect the same of a riding horse in its sphere of activity.

The structure of the animal — bones, ligaments, tendons and muscles — is in the process of development and is subject to unacceptable strains, resulting in a shortened working life, if work is begun too early in the horse's life. The resulting wastage, and the incidence of chronic unsoundness in racehorses, is unacceptable and impractical in the riding horse.

LUNGEING
During lungeing, the horse is worked in both directions in a circle around the trainer.

LONG REINS
Long reins are fitted to the cavesson and bit rings and enable the horse to be driven forward from behind, so that it learns to respond to reins.

Long reins

Backing

BACKING
To 'back' the horse, the trainer stands at its head with a bowl of oats to divert its attention. Then a light assistant lies gently across the horse's back, and when it is used to that, the assistant can sit astride.

TACKING UP

One of the first and most basic aspects of horsemanship to learn is the correct way to tack up your horse. An experienced horseman will tack up very quickly, but if you are a beginner, do not confuse this with being in a hurry. Take the time to see that everything is done correctly and the horse is comfortable. Speed will come with practice.

If you have to catch your horse from its pasture, it is easier and safer to use a halter than a bridle. You will frequently see a person march up to a horse's head, the noseband of a halter held open in outstretched hands, as though expecting the horse to walk up and put its nose in it. A quiet and well-trained horse might oblige, but this is not the way to catch a nervous horse, one which is reluctant to be caught, or one you do not know.

When you approach a horse, for whatever reason, walk up to its shoulder. Its eyes are at the sides of its head and it can't see you if you stand directly in front of it, so don't be surprised, when you do so, if it steps back or at least turns its head sideways. When you are at its left shoulder, however, it's a simple matter to reach over its neck with your right hand, take

hold of the top strap, slip the halter over its nose and fasten it.

A halter should fit snugly, so that it cannot easily be rubbed off if the horse is turned out to pasture, but with the noseband slack enough that it can comfortably open its jaw, and high enough not to irritate the soft, sensitive part of its nose.

Most horses will be tacked up for riding in their stables and the saddle may be put on first, while the horse is tied up. Make sure that the stirrups are run up the leathers and the girth, if attached, is folded over the top of the saddle. The saddle pad or numnah, if you are using one, may be put on separately.

Place the saddle pad or saddle gently over the withers, then slide it back into position so that the coat hair lies flat and is not rubbed the wrong way. Take care not to bang the saddle down heavily on the horse's back. Attach any loops on the saddle pad to the girth straps and pull it well up into the channel of the saddle to avoid creating pressure on the horse's spine.

Fasten the girth *loosely*. Many horses are ticklish at the girth and may swing their heads around to bite, or raise a leg in irritation, so

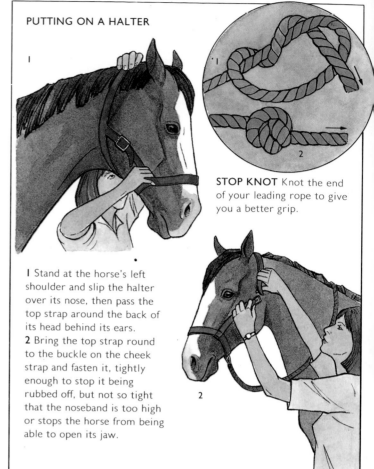

PUTTING ON A HALTER

STOP KNOT Knot the end of your leading rope to give you a better grip.

1 Stand at the horse's left shoulder and slip the halter over its nose, then pass the top strap around the back of its head behind its ears.
2 Bring the top strap round to the buckle on the cheek strap and fasten it, tightly enough to stop it being rubbed off, but not so tight that the noseband is too high or stops the horse from being able to open its jaw.

SADDLING UP

1 With the stirrups run up the leathers and the girth strap (if attached) folded over the top, place the saddle gently over the horse's withers.

2 Slide the saddle along into position so that the coat hair is not rubbed the wrong way.

3 Do up the girth loosely, and then tighten it in stages to give the horse a chance to get used to it. Never simply jerk it tight.

FITTING A BRIDLE

1 Holding the cheek piece and crownpiece in your right hand, slip the bit into place.
2 Position the crownpiece.

3 Do up the throatlatch, leaving a hand's width between the strap and the horse's jaw.
4 Fasten the noseband. Leave two fingers' width between it and the jaw.

REMOVING BRIDLE

To remove the bridle, undo the curb chain (if used), the noseband and the throatlatch, in that order. Slip the crownpiece off and lower the bridle, using your left hand to remove the bit.

LEFT Fasten the girth loosely at first, and then tighten it gradually so that the horse has a chance to get used to it.

until you know the horse well, proceed with caution. Always tighten the girth by degrees, to give the horse a chance to get used to it. If you suddenly jerk a tight hand around its middle, you cannot blame it if it objects.

As soon as you've finished riding, loosen the girth a couple of holes. To unsaddle, run up the stirrups, undo the girth and fold it over the top, then lift the saddle clear of the horse's back.

Whatever you are doing at a horse's head, be careful of its eyes and ears, avoid knocking its face and don't make sudden gestures or loud noises which might startle it. Horses soon object to careless treatment around their heads and can quickly make bridling an impossible task.

To put on the bridle, put the reins over the horse's head, laying them on its neck so that they are not dangling down at one side. (Once the halter is off, the reins can be used to hold the horse if necessary.)

Next, remove the halter and hang it up. Take the bridle cheek pieces in your right hand, passing your hand under the horse's chin, up the far side of its face and over the bridge of its nose. Take the bit in your left hand and ease it between its lips, at the same time encouraging it to open its mouth by sliding your finger on the offside, or your thumb on the near side, into the gap between its teeth. If it objects, you have your right hand over its nose to help control the position of its head. Once the bit is in its mouth, raise the bridle and use both hands to fit the head-piece carefully over its ears.

Do up the throatlatch, allowing a hand's width between the strap and the horse's jaw — a too-tight throatlatch restricts the horse's breathing. Next, fasten the noseband, allowing two fingers' width between the noseband and jaw, then fasten the curb chain, if you are using one, so that the links lie flat and the curb comes into action when the cheek pieces of the bit are at 45 degrees. Check that the mane is pulled out from under the crownpiece and browband, and that the bridle is straight with the browband and noseband level and comfortable. Ensure that the bit is correctly adjusted in the horse's mouth, neither too high nor too low. If you are using a snaffle, the lip corners should be wrinkled slightly.

A bridle must be taken off as carefully as it was put on. With the reins over the horse's neck, undo the curb chain (if present), noseband and throatlatch, always keeping to that order so that nothing is forgotten. Slide your right thumb under the crownpiece and take the bit in your left hand. Take the crownpiece forward over the horse's head and lower the bridle, keeping hold of the bit and restraining the horse's nose gently with your right hand, until it releases the bit.

If you let the bit slide out of its mouth quickly, it will bang against its teeth and upset it. This will lead to a dislike of having the bridle removed, with the horse pulling back.

As your riding progresses you will come to use other items of tack, such as martingales and protective boots. Fitting them is always a matter of common sense. For example, when putting on a martingale, put the neck strap over the horse's head before putting on the saddle. Then you can slip the girth through the loop of the martingale as you do it up, rather than having to undo it again. A little thought can save a lot of time and trouble.

MOUNTING AND DISMOUNTING

According to tradition, the left, or near, side of the horse is the correct side at which to mount and dismount. It is a convention which supposedly developed from the fact that a cavalry soldier, wearing a sword at his left side, had to mount from his horse's near side in order to keep the sword clear of the horse.

There are several ways of mounting a horse. You can mount from the ground, using the stirrup, in the conventional manner. Alternatively, you might be given a leg up, or use a mounting block, particularly if you are not so agile, or the horse is very tall. An athletic person, or anyone riding bareback, might vault onto the horse, while at the more formal end of the scale, there is a correct way for a helper (men are preferred) to 'put up' a woman riding sidesaddle.

There are a few points common to all methods of mounting which should become second nature to all riders. Firstly, the horse should be trained to stand still. This may take a little time and patience, but there is nothing more annoying than trying to mount a horse which is either dancing around or attempting to trot off.

Secondly, the rider must have consideration for the horse. If you grab the reins, jerking the horse in the mouth, then kick it in the ribs as you swing up, before banging down in the saddle, you can't expect the horse to appreciate the experience, or to stand still for you.

To mount a saddled horse in the conventional manner, first run down the stirrups and check that they are at approximately the right length. Tighten the girth (which should not have been done up too tightly when the horse was

Hold the horse's mane with your left hand to steady yourself, but don't pull on it.

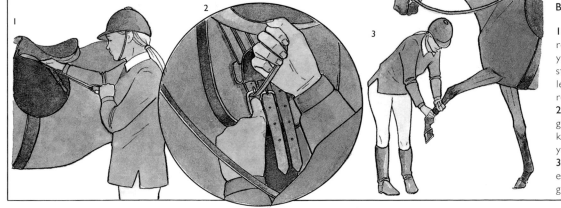

BEFORE MOUNTING

1 To get your stirrups at roughly the right length, put your knuckles against the stirrup bar and adjust the leather until the iron just reaches your armpit.
2 Remember to tighten the girth strap before you mount, keeping hold of the reins while you do so.
3 Draw each foreleg forward to ensure that the skin under the girth is not wrinkled.

MOUNTING – TRADITIONAL METHOD

I Turn the iron clockwise toward you, so your foot goes in the right way and the leather isn't twisted when you are mounted.

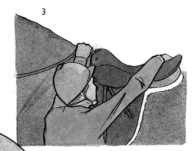

3

2 Lift your left foot and put it into the stirrup as far as the ball of the foot.

3 Hold the reins in your left hand and the pommel or waist of the saddle in your right, and then spring into the saddle. Pivot slightly as you leave the ground, and try not to dig your toe into the horse's ribs.

4 Straighten both knees and swing your right leg over, keeping it clear of the horse's back. Then settle gently into the saddle.

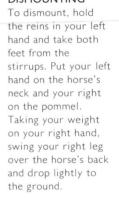

4

LEG UP METHOD

If someone is giving you a leg up, you stand facing the horse's side with the reins in your left hand and your right placed on the off side of the saddle skirt. Then you bend your left knee so that your helper can take a secure hold on your left leg and foot, and at the count of three you swing up, boosted by your helper.

right hand view

DISMOUNTING

To dismount, hold the reins in your left hand and take both feet from the stirrups. Put your left hand on the horse's neck and your right on the pommel. Taking your weight on your right hand, swing your right leg over the horse's back and drop lightly to the ground.

first saddled), making sure that it doesn't pinch the horse's skin. If the horse has sensitive skin, you can draw each foreleg forward in turn to ensure that the skin under the girth is stretched free of wrinkles before you mount.

Stand at the horse's shoulder, facing slightly toward the rear, and speak to it quietly so that it knows you are not going to do anything to hurt it. Gather up the reins, taking the buckle end in your right hand and drawing the reins through your left so that they are evenly taken up on both sides until you have a gentle contact, just sufficient to restrain the horse. If you take a too strong a contact, the horse will become restless and probably step backward or sideways.

Hold the reins in front of the withers in your left hand, with a piece of mane if it helps you to balance, but be careful not to pull on it as you mount. Using your right hand, turn the stirrup toward you from the back and, bending your right knee slightly to assist balance and make you more mobile, lift your left foot and place it in the stirrup as far as the ball of your foot. If you push your foot too far home, it may get caught should the horse move off before you mount, whereas if you just put the tip of your toe into the stirrup it will slip out when you put your weight on it.

As soon as your foot is in the stirrup, grasp either the pommel or the waist of the saddle on the far side with your right hand and spring up. Do not take hold of the cantle – putting your weight on it will twist the saddle tree, which will very probably result in a sore back for the horse.

Put as much spring into mounting as you can, so that your weight doesn't drag down on one side, and take care not to dig the horse's ribs with your toe as you pivot toward its side. Straighten both knees, swing your right leg clear of the horse's back and gently settle into the saddle, with your right hand helping to support your weight at the pommel so that you don't land with a bump. As soon as you are in the saddle, reward the horse with a pat.

Learn to find the right stirrup quickly and quietly with your foot, without fumbling or kicking at the horse's girth or shoulder. Switch the reins to your right hand and check the girth. Adjust your position, sit straight, take up the reins in both hands and you are ready to move off.

To give a leg up takes a little practice. The person mounting should stand facing the horse's side with the reins in the left hand and the whip, if carried, also in the left hand (transfer it to your right hand when you're mounted). The right hand is placed on the off side, at the skirt of the saddle. The left knee is bent and the lower leg raised. The helper stands square to the rider's left side and puts his left hand under the rider's knee, with his right hand under the left foot. At the count of three, the rider springs up and at the same time the helper boosts him straight upward from the knee. Care must be taken to be active enough, but not over energetic, or the rider may end up on the ground on the far side of the horse.

To dismount, take both feet from the stirrups and put reins and whip in your left hand (or your right hand, if you are dismounting on that side). With your left hand on the horse's neck and your right hand on the pommel, bend forward, swing your right leg backward and over the horse's back, making sure you do not touch his back with your foot. Land lightly, facing slightly forward and bending your knees as you land to absorb the impact. Take the reins over the horse's head and over your forearm to put up the stirrups and loosen the girth.

THE BASIC SEAT

A good seat is the fundamental basis of all good riding, yet it is frequently skimmed over quickly or even ignored by riding schools. A beginner might be forgiven for thinking that a good seat refers simply to the position in which he sits passively on the horse. This is far from the case. What the term actually covers is the rider's ability, during all phases of riding, to *maintain* a position that is both perfectly balanced and effective. Any thinking rider will soon realize that this requires fit, active muscles, great sensitivity and considerable practiced bodily coordination, none of which can be acquired overnight.

However eager you may be to get on with show jumping or cross country riding, there is no substitute for at least several months spent acquiring a good basic seat (also known as an "independent" seat). It will always stand you in good stead and those who do persevere and learn to ride well find that this aspect of riding is as rewarding, if not more so, than all the excitement of jumping.

Before you can begin to develop a good seat you must learn a correct basic position and your riding instructor should explain this to you as soon as you are first mounted on a horse.

The first and most essential aspect is the position of your seat in the saddle. It must be pushed well forward underneath you, so that your weight is evenly distributed down via your seat and your spine. The base of the spine, also known as the coccyx, is the third point of what is frequently referred to as the "triangular seat," the idea being that the seat bones and coccyx are the three points of balance. However, the coccyx does not actually reach the saddle.

Your seat should be open and relaxed, allowing as much close contact with the saddle as possible. Your hips must be upright and level, neither twisting to one side, nor collapsed on one side. These are very common faults in beginners, which instantly put the rider out of balance, with resultant loss of control.

Your back must be straight and upright, with the small of the back braced, to enable you to use seat and weight aids. However, your whole back must also remain flexible, in order to absorb and follow the movement of the horse.

Your head – a very heavy part of the body – must also be held up straight. You should be looking forward through the horse's ears, in the direction in which you are going. If your head tips forward – another very common fault – your balance is again immediately upset.

This may all sound complicated, and a correct position feels very strange at first, but riding does involve complex physical coordination, much of which does not come naturally to the human body and so requires considerable practice. Beginners must constantly correct an automatic tendency to tip forward (known as "sitting on the fork") while clutching at the reins for support. Another common fault is allowing the body to tip too far backward, with the shoulders becoming rounded and the back completely ineffective. You will undoubtedly discover the feeling of both these mistakes while you learn to maintain a correct seat, and to realize that it is only from such an initially balanced position that you can develop the ability to control your horse effectively.

The legs should extend fully downward. The best way to position them is first to draw the knees up toward the pommel of the saddle, push the seat well forward and then extend the legs downward again, letting them hang naturally through their own weight. The flat inner sides of the thighs should lie along the saddle and to achieve this they need to be turned slightly in from the hips, which also helps to open the seat. To find the correct position, especially for female riders, it might help to grasp the muscles at the backs of your thighs and pull them outwards, thus creating space for the flat inner sides of the thighs to lie on the saddle.

The knees also should be in contact with the saddle, never moving away and leaving a gap. The angle of the thighs at hip and knee must conform with the correct position of the upper body. If the stirrups are too short the knees will tend to be raised forward, tipping the rider's body back. Conversely, if they are too long and the legs too straight, the rider will be forced off balance in order to keep his stirrups. The correct length for general riding is to have the irons level with the ankle bones, when the legs are hanging straight down. The lower legs should hang close to the horse's sides at the girth and no part of the legs should grip the horse.

If the thighs are turned slightly inward, as mentioned above, it

The development of a good seat is an essential part of learning to ride properly.

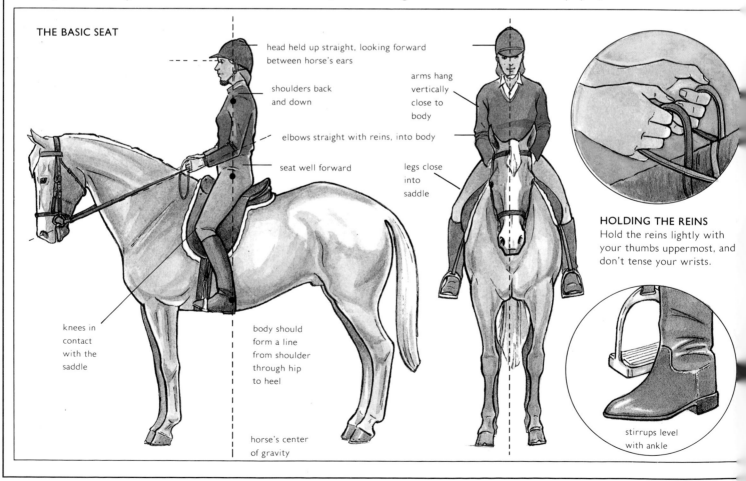

THE BASIC SEAT

head held up straight, looking forward between horse's ears

shoulders back and down

elbows straight with reins, into body

seat well forward

arms hang vertically close to body

legs close into saddle

knees in contact with the saddle

body should form a line from shoulder through hip to heel

horse's center of gravity

HOLDING THE REINS
Hold the reins lightly with your thumbs uppermost, and don't tense your wrists.

stirrups level with ankle

COMMON FAULTS

1 Riding with your head tipped forward will upset your balance. Hold your head up and look forward through the horse's ears.
2 If you have adjusted your stirrups too short, your knees will be raised and your body will lean back.

3 Sitting off balance is a common fault in beginners. They tend to lean forward and grip the reins tightly for support.
4 Another common fault in beginners is sitting with the body tipped too far back, which makes it very difficult to control the horse properly.

will be seen that the natural tendency of the toes to point outward will be corrected, bringing the feet parallel to the horse's sides. When the stirrups are taken, the feet should rest in them with the heels dropping slightly below the front of the foot.

The position of the arms begins at the shoulders, which must be back and down, with the shoulder blades flat and the chest open. They must not be held stiffly in place, but should be relaxed, flexible and kept parallel to the hips. The upper arms should hang vertically down, with the elbows bent and close to the body, but not held tensely in place. The forearms should be almost at right angles to the upper arms, and the hands and wrists should continue a straight line through the forearms to the reins and the bit.

The wrists must be kept elastic, not stiffened or tensely bent back, and the fingers should be closed on the reins, with the thumbs uppermost and pointing toward each other. The hands should be turned fractionally toward the body from underneath, so that the rider, on glancing down, can just see his fingernails.

USING THE AIDS

When you begin to ride, you will be taught the aids. These are the messages which the rider gives to the horse to encourage it to react in accordance with his wishes. At the most advanced level, the aids are given so precisely and harmoniously that they are invisible to the spectator. Few people attain this level of achievement and initially it is enough to concentrate on applying the aids in such a way as to obtain the correct response from the horse.

Beginners often have difficulty in discerning between a correct and an incorrect response. For example, if you want to turn left or right, the manner in which the horse turns is as important as whether or not it actually turns. If you achieve a turn incorrectly, the horse is not using its body in the most efficient way and, in time, the accumulation of wrong responses will make it impossible to progress further with your riding, for several reasons.

Firstly, your confused messages to the horse will bewilder it, and it will be unsure how to perform the movements you want. Secondly, incorrect training will unbalance the horse and lead to inappropriate muscle development and stiffness. Thirdly, if the horse is allowed to work inefficiently, it won't want to change to a better way of going and is likely to become evasive or simply disobedient. Inexperienced riders often blame these problems on the horse, when in fact the fault lies in their own lack of finesse.

The natural aids are the seat (or weight), the legs, the hands and the voice. The artificial aids are the whip and the spurs.

Seat (or weight) aids involve the use of the whole upper body and can only be used effectively when the rider is well balanced and positioned. They are fundamental to every request the rider makes of his horse and are reinforced by the supporting aids of legs and hands. On a young horse, whose muscles are still soft and developing to support the weight of the rider, the seat aids must be used with discretion, or the horse may hollow its back instead of rounding it, to avoid the pressure of the rider's seat. However, this need not concern the beginner and he should learn how to use his seat to create impulsion, that is, active forward movement.

Another important point to remember is that the aids must all be used together in a coordinated action, not one after the other as they come into your head. Obviously this again requires practice, and the beginner will frequently find himself remembering his hands but forgetting his legs, or losing his seat while using his legs,

The aids are your means of giving instructions to your horse when riding.

THE AIDS

LEGS
The legs are used when controlling forward movement. To get the horse moving or to speed up, you use your seat while pressing your calves in against the sides of the horse. Always release the pressure as soon as the horse responds.

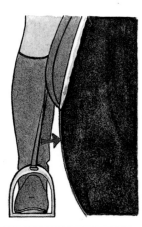

VOICE
The voice is useful for calming, soothing and encouraging (or if necessary reprimanding) a horse.

normal seat

giving with reins, stretch arms forward slightly

HANDS
The hands are always used together with the other aids, and you should learn to use them with sensitivity. To give with the reins, don't lean forward but simply stretch your arms slightly ahead of you.

SEAT
Seat (or weight) aids can only be effective when you are well balanced and positioned. To use the seat to get the horse moving or to speed up you lean slightly back from your normal seat position, bracing your back and pushing your seat bones down and forward. At the same time, you should apply the appropriate leg aid by briefly squeezing your calves against the horse's sides.

THE WHIP
Use the whip briefly but effectively behind your leg to reinforce a leg aid which has been ignored.

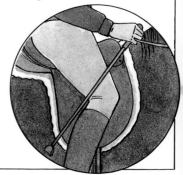

BASIC MANEUVERS

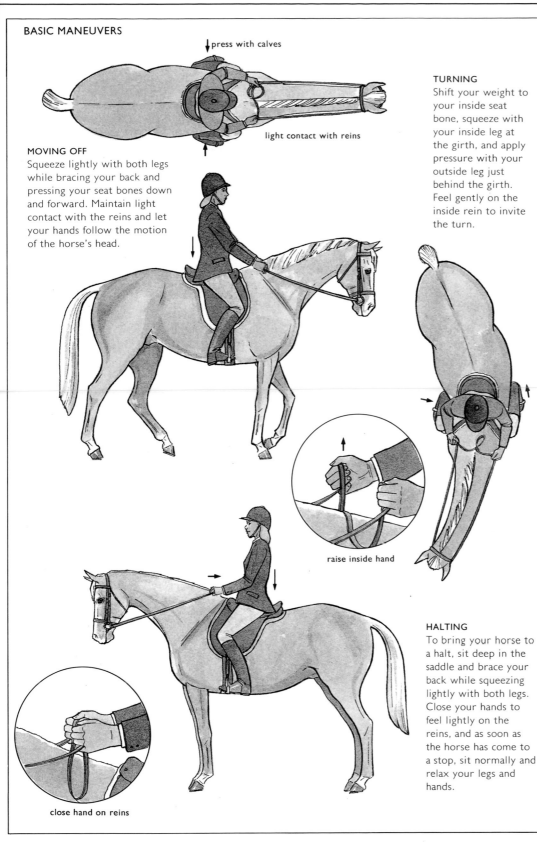

↓ press with calves

light contact with reins

MOVING OFF
Squeeze lightly with both legs while bracing your back and pressing your seat bones down and forward. Maintain light contact with the reins and let your hands follow the motion of the horse's head.

TURNING
Shift your weight to your inside seat bone, squeeze with your inside leg at the girth, and apply pressure with your outside leg just behind the girth. Feel gently on the inside rein to invite the turn.

raise inside hand

HALTING
To bring your horse to a halt, sit deep in the saddle and brace your back while squeezing lightly with both legs. Close your hands to feel lightly on the reins, and as soon as the horse has come to a stop, sit normally and relax your legs and hands.

close hand on reins

first he should concentrate on having the horse walking freely and rhythmically forward, while remaining straight.

To turn, the weight is transferred to the inside seat bone, the inside leg (the leg on the inside of the turn) is used at the girth, encouraging the horse to bend around it, and the outside leg controls the horse's quarters, moving back if necessary to prevent them swinging outwards. The inside hand is fractionally raised and the little finger turned in the direction of the rider's opposite hip, to invite the turn, while the outside hand controls speed and provides support to prevent the horse from "falling out through the shoulder."

The latter will happen if the inside hand asks too abruptly, or pulls backward. The rider should think of *pushing* the horse around the bend from the outside, rather than *pulling* it round from the inside. The turn should be smooth and fluid, with the horse's hind legs following the track of the forelegs.

The voice is most frequently used when training the horse from the ground, as a reinforcement to the lungeing rein and whip. However, it is useful in many aspects of riding, to calm and soothe, to encourage or to reprimand, and its use should not be neglected.

The artificial aids, the whip and spurs, are used to reinforce the natural aids, never to punish the horse.

The whip must be used quickly and effectively behind the rider's leg to reinforce a leg aid which has been ignored. The rider must be ready for the horse to respond sharply and must allow for the resultant forward movement. If he is unprepared and jerks the horse's mouth, the horse will become confused and unsure of what to do next.

The whip is carried in the inside hand, except when it is specifically required to reinforce an outside leg aid, so when you are doing school work with your horse, the whip should be changed over with each change of direction.

Spurs are for use by experienced riders who can fully control their leg aids. They should never be used as a matter of course, but are useful for horses who are slow to respond to the leg aids. They may have short or long necks but should be blunt, and are used by pressing the side against the horse's side, which is achieved by turning the toe fractionally outward. Care must be taken never to allow the back of the spur to dig into the horse's side.

or letting the horse escape "through the front door" while attempting to push it forward.

By bracing the back and pushing the seat bones down and forward, the rider encourages the horse to stride forward more actively. This seat aid is reinforced by the lower leg at the girth and the forward movement is "collected" into the rider's hands, via the bit and reins. The hands must "follow" the movement of the

horse's head and never be stiff or resistant. At the same time, tiny adjustments of give and take with the fingers must be made, in order to maintain the desired carriage and pace of the horse.

This is a brief description of the operation of the natural aids, which applies to all paces. Initially, however, the best way to acquire a good seat, and to learn the feeling of the seat aids, is by riding on the lunge line, without

stirrups and without the impediment of reins. Control of the horse is left to the trainer, allowing the rider to concentrate on his seat and position.

Off the lunge line, the rider will begin at the walk. He should correct his position and apply the seat aid to encourage the horse to move off, at the same time squeezing lightly with his lower leg just behind the girth and taking up a light contact with the reins. At

RIDING ON THE FLAT

Flatwork, as riding on the flat is called, is the essential basis of both riding and training the horse.

It is used in training the young horse, to strengthen and supple his muscles and to teach him to be obedient to the aids. For the older horse it is a useful reminder of his basic training. It also helps to make him supple and improves his carriage and way of going. For those who wish to progress beyond basic schooling into the higher realms of competitive dressage it is an aim in itself, while show jumpers and cross country riders use flatwork to school and improve their horses. In fact, many competitive jumpers do very little jumping at home.

For the beginner, which is our main concern here, it is the means his instructor employs to teach him how to communicate with his horse and ask him to submit to his requests. "Control" is too strong a word, as the horse is much stronger than the human and any attempt to force him to obey you will result in failure. Riding requires great tact and empathy with your mount.

The best place to tackle flatwork is in an enclosed school, where there are no distractions, but if you do not have the facilities, any defined area will do. It helps to mark out the dimensions of your schooling area on the ground, say 40 × 20 yards. You can then easily see if you are riding accurate figures.

The beginner should have been accustomed to riding the horse on the lunge line and have learned how to keep his seat at the walk and trot, before being asked to ride solo. So by the time he first takes the reins, he should be secure enough to avoid the common error of crouching forward and clutching at his horse in the effort to save himself from falling.

Schooling exercises for flatwork include the circle, figure-8, volte, half-turn, S-turn and serpentines, and changes of rein achieved in several ways, for example on the diagonal, or two semicircles, or a half volte, returning to the track on the same side but in the opposite direction. Sometimes you will be asked to "go large," which means using the whole schooling area.

Your aim should be to ride these exercises accurately, rhythmically and smoothly. To make accurate turns, it is necessary to prepare yourself well in advance, not leave it until the last minute and try to turn the horse abruptly. Look ahead to where you are going and adjust your position in readiness to give the required aids. When a good rider is in harmony with a well-schooled horse, this slight adjustment may be all that is necessary to indicate what is required and the horse will obey. It is sometimes said that a good rider only has to think of what he wants to do and his horse will understand and obey. Keep your aids as light and unobtrusive as possible, while still making them precise and effective.

Early work should be done at the walk, until the beginner is confident and secure enough to go into the trot. This phase does not usually last long and once the rider is happy at the trot, he can begin to make more progress.

To obtain the trot, the rider braces his back and pushes with his seat, while squeezing with his legs just behind the girth. The horse, if carrying himself correctly, will arch his neck more at the trot so that the rider needs to shorten the reins to maintain the same contact. At the walk, the horse's head nods with every stride and the rider's hands must follow this movement. At the trot, however, the horse's head remains steady and all the rider need do is maintain an elastic (flexible) contact.

Initially, the beginner will learn the rising or "posting" trot, letting his seat rise from the saddle at the thrust of the horse's inside hind leg and settling lightly back as that hind leg comes back down and the opposite hind leg leaves the ground. He will learn that the trot is a two-beat gait, the horse's legs moving as alternate diagonal pairs. The rider should sit to the left diagonal (left hind leg and right foreleg meeting the ground), when the horse is moving in a left-handed direction, and vice versa.

As the schooling progresses, the rider will learn to sit to the trot, which gives his seat more effective contact with the horse.

The canter is achieved by sitting to the trot, then simultaneously raising the inside hand with a quick give-and-take motion, moving the outside leg slightly back to ask for the strike-off and squeezing with both legs. The canter is a three-beat gait, the initial strike-off being with the outside hind leg, followed by the opposite diagonal pair and finally the inside front leg, known as the leading leg. When cantering to the right, the right foreleg is the leading leg and vice versa.

Leading with the outside foreleg in error is called cantering "on the wrong leg." Experienced riders sometimes ask horses to lead with the outside leg as a deliberate exercise to improve suppleness and balance. This is

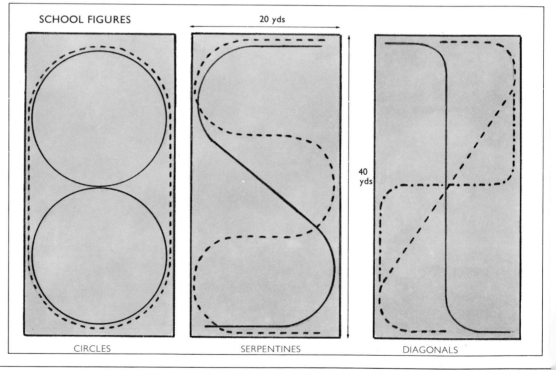

SCHOOL FIGURES

20 yds

40 yds

CIRCLES   SERPENTINES   DIAGONALS

HOW THE HORSE MOVES

WALK: leg sequence: off hind, off fore, near hind, near fore

TROT: legs move in diagonal pairs

WALK   TROT

Flatwork is best done in an enclosed school, but any defined area with a suitable surface makes a good substitute.

known as counter canter and requires considerable skill on the part of the rider to maintain it correctly.

To obtain a good trot, canter or even walk, with the horse working correctly and carrying himself well, the transition leading into the change of gait must be well prepared and correctly ridden, with plenty of impulsion, whether the transition is upward or downward. The change must be precise and balanced, with no running forward or unasked for change of speed and no evasion or escape from the rider's seat, hands and legs.

Turns on the forehand and on the haunches are the first steps toward lateral work and will be taught quite early to a rider who has understood the basic principles, as will leg yielding, which involves bending the horse around the inside leg and asking him to move forward and sideways simultaneously.

RISING TROT

The rider rises as the inside hind leg rises.

The rider settles back as the outside hind leg rises.

SITTING TROT

Rider remains in saddle with back upright but relaxed, legs maintaining constant position.

THE DIAGONALS

When a horse trots it raises and lowers diagonal pairs of legs in sequence.

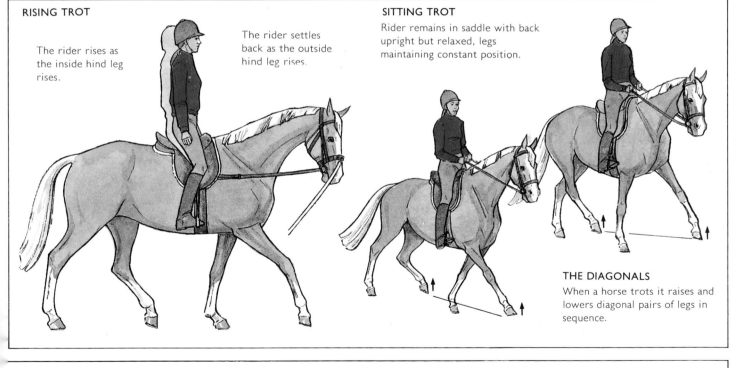

CANTER: a series of three bounds followed by all legs being clear of the ground

CANTER

JUMPING

If you want to hunt, or ride competitively, learning to jump will be high on your list of priorities and once you have mastered a good basic seat you can begin with confidence.

To begin learning to jump, however, you must obviously ride an obedient horse who is well schooled in jumping and will not be too upset when you make mistakes.

After all the trouble you took acquiring a good seat on the flat, the first thing you will learn about jumping is that your riding position must be adjusted, to allow for the athletic action of the horse going over the jump and to enable you to remain in balance. The main alteration is in the length of your stirrup leathers, which will have to be shortened between one and four holes, depending upon the leathers and the advice of your instructor.

The effect of this is to close the angles of your body, giving you more scope to follow the movements of the jumping horse and increasing your stability in the saddle, which now comes from your legs rather than from your seat. Your lower leg should be in close contact with the horse, ready to send him forward, and your toe may be turned outward a fraction to improve this contact. The widest part of your foot should be on the stirrup bar and your heel should always remain lower than your toe.

Your upper body bends forward from the hips, *not* the waist, and your back must remain flat and straight, *not* rounded. You should be balanced over your knee and foot, your seat displaced backward to counteract the effect of your upper body bending forward. Your reins will have to be shortened to keep a light, elastic contact with the horse's mouth and you should look ahead for the next fence, between the horse's ears, avoiding any tendency to look down as you go over a jump.

It is the horse who actually jumps the fence, but the rider is responsible for seeing that the approach is correct and for what happens when he gets to the other side.

On the approach you must take care to turn smoothly and accurately toward the center of the fence, so that your line toward it is straight. If you turn too soon or too late you will be coming in at an angle and be forced to make difficult corrections. When learning, it is best to circle away and

When jumping, bend from the hips, never from the waist, and keep your back flat and straight, not rounded.

make a fresh approach if this happens, rather than risk an upset.

On the approach you need to keep the horse balanced and going forward with plenty of impulsion. When he sees the fence in front of him, he will lower his head and neck in preparation for take-off. As he takes off, he raises his head and neck as the power of his quarters and hind legs propels him upward. In the air, he should tuck his forelegs up, stretch his head and neck and round his back.

As he lifts his hind legs to clear the fence, his forelegs extend to take the shock of landing, which is also aided by raising his head and neck. The leading foreleg takes the full force of the landing — an incredible pressure on such a tiny area of hoof and bone — which is

TROTTING OVER POLES

Your first jumping lesson will begin with trotting over poles on the ground, to give you the feel of riding in the jumping seat and help you develop the correct rhythm.

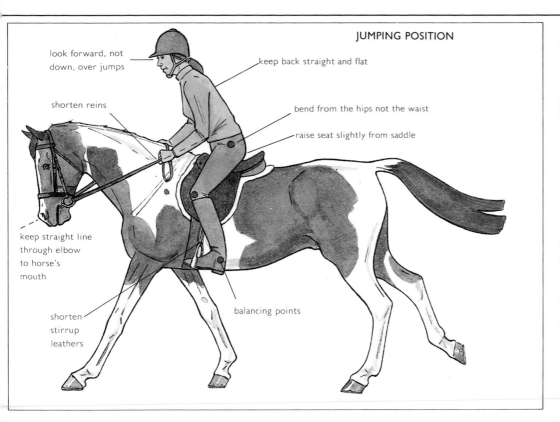

JUMPING POSITION

look forward, not down, over jumps

shorten reins

keep straight line through elbow to horse's mouth

shorten stirrup leathers

keep back straight and flat

bend from the hips not the waist

raise seat slightly from saddle

balancing points

THE JUMP

1 To jump a fence cleanly, the horse must take off at the correct point. If the takeoff point is too far back from the fence, the horse will catch the pole with his forelegs, and if it is too close to the fence the horse's hind legs will probably hit the pole.

2 When the horse is jumping you should be looking ahead, not down.

3 The horse lands on his leading foreleg, so good balance is very important during jumping.

JUMPING

PLACING POLES FOR JUMP

4 ft 6 ins   9 ft

The poles – three, four or five of them – are usually placed about 4 ft 6 ins apart, with a gap of 9 ft between the last pole and the 1- to 2-foot high fence.

why it is essential for jumping horses to have good, hard legs and feet.

Your job is not finished as the horse comes back to earth. While he is still in the air you should have been looking ahead to the next fence and as he lands, you must be ready to ride him on in the right direction. A skillful rider will have the horse land on the correct lead for his next turn, but when you are learning you will come back to trot between fences at first.

Your first jumping lesson will begin, not with fences, but with rails or poles on the ground. This both prepares the horse for the lesson and gives the rider the feel of riding in the jumping seat (also called the "forward" seat). It will help you develop a rhythm and remind you to look ahead and to think about turning your horse correctly for the approach. There should be three to five poles, set about 4 feet 6 inches apart, depending upon the size and stride of the horse. You will probably begin by just walking, then trotting over one pole, and your instructor will eventually increase the number.

When you are trotting your horse rhythmically over the poles, the instructor will typically introduce a small fence at the end of the line, 9 feet away from the last pole, and 1 foot to 2 feet high.

As the lesson progresses, if you are confident and riding well, a second fence can be added, 18 feet away from the first fence, with a placing pole on the ground in the middle. You then have your trotting poles, the first fence, one stride of canter over the placing pole, then the jump over the second fence.

Many variations on this theme can be arranged, to help both the rider and the horse. Cross poles, for example, will help you ride the horse to the center of the fence and will also encourage him to tuck up his forelegs and use his head and neck better. Schooling over this grid of fences is known as gymnastic jumping and your instructor may ask you to do various exercises, such as jumping with your arms folded, or even without stirrups. These are all designed to improve your balance and are not nearly as terrifying as they might initially sound.

When you have mastered jumping small grids, you will go on to jump a small course of fences, concentrating on making accurate turns and coming back to trot between fences. Later you will learn about combination fences and jump from the canter.

CROSS COUNTRY RIDING

Cross country riding as a sport can include anything from a day's hunting to international three-day eventing. Between these two extremes are all the sports of hunter trials, riding club events, team chasing and one- or two-day events – or horse trials, as they are now called.

The basic difference between show jumping and jumping across country is simple. Show jumping takes place in a confined arena, over colored fences which can be knocked down. Cross country jumping takes place over distances of up to several miles over solid fences, which are constructed to blend in with the surroundings and are often referred to as "natural" fences.

As a preparation for taking up competitive cross country riding, hacking will give you and your horse invaluable practice at riding across country. However, if your horse is young and inexperienced, and getting from the stables to where you want to ride involves

Hacking along quiet roads is a pleasant way to exercise your horse, but beware of traffic.

going onto roads or highways, you should first take time to accustom him to traffic.

Do this in easy stages. To begin with, either ride him or turn him out in a pasture alongside a road where there is traffic. Once he has learned to ignore the passing cars and trucks, you can start riding him along quiet roads. This is best done in the company of other riders, on experienced horses, who should ride outside, ahead of and behind you. Your horse will feel protected and reassured by the other horses.

When your horse becomes used to riding like this along roads, you can start riding him in more exposed positions within the group. First ride him on the inside of the lead horse, then on his own at the front of the group, and finally at the rear. Don't rush this training. If you move too quickly from one stage to the next, the result could be tragedy if your horse takes fright at passing vehicles.

You should follow a similar routine when you first introduce an inexperienced horse to riding in open country. The horse will

encounter many unfamiliar sights, sounds and smells, and the presence of one or more experienced horses will help him to cope with these. Keep away from difficult ground, ride slowly until the horse has learned to move confidently and with good balance, and never gallop an immature horse because that can damage his still-developing bones and tendons.

When you're out hacking, avoid trampling crops or pasture or disturbing livestock, and always close gates behind you. At first, you will probably need to dismount to open and close gates, but with practice it won't be long before you will be able to do this from the saddle.

Stop your horse parallel to the gate and facing the latch, then hold the reins in one hand and undo the latch with the other, moving gently so as not to disturb the horse. Push the gate open to about twice the width of your horse and ride through it. If you are holding the gate open for others to pass through, position yourself behind it to leave them plenty of room. When you close

it, line your horse up with it as you did when you opened it, holding the reins in one hand and fastening the latch of the gate securely with the other.

When you and your horse are experienced at hacking, you can begin cross country riding in a very simple way, by jumping natural obstacles that you encounter on your rides in the countryside. Fallen logs, low walls and ditches are the most obvious of these, but keep well away from barbed wire.

It is a good idea to inspect the landing side of any potential obstacle before you jump it, to be sure the ground is clear of rocks or other debris, and be especially careful to look for discarded wire, which is increasingly found lying on the ground, but is not always visible at first glance.

Shorten your stirrups to jumping length, adopt a light seat and approach your obstacle at a trot, with plenty of impulsion. Many horses used to hacking see no reason why they should suddenly start jumping something when they could just as easily go around it, so be prepared to ride strongly

forward and be alert for any inclination of the horse to run out around the obstacle.

Once they understand the idea, most horses take to cross country work and natural fences more easily than they do to show jumping, with its more artificial atmosphere. However, schooling over cavaletti will be helpful.

It helps to accustom your horse to as many different types of fence as possible – banks and drops, solid timber and steeplechase type brush fences, logs and walls and, in particular, ditches and water splashes. Many horses object to going into water and the sooner your horse learns there is nothing to fear, the better for your jumping career.

Cross country work is strenuous and your horse needs to be fit before you tackle a hunter trial or event. This takes about eight or nine weeks, starting from when you first bring your horse up from grass.

For the first month you should concentrate on walking, to harden off your horse's legs, and some schooling to make him supple. Towards the end of the month you can start some trotting and after five weeks, some slow canters. Fast work, to improve the heart and lungs, does not begin until the eighth or ninth week.

It is important not to ask too much of your horse when he first begins cross country work. Jumping him too often, over fences which are too big, will soon make him sour and could easily destroy his confidence. As in all forms of equestrian sport, progress must be made slowly, only moving on to the next stage when the previous one has been fully mastered.

Your first cross country event is likely to be a hunter trial. Arrive in good time and warm your horse up before the start, so that he is ready to go and not stiff and cold. A horse's muscles need to be stretched and warmed up gently, just as a human athlete does a series of warm-up exercises before a race.

In your first few events, con-centrate on completing the course safely and do not worry about your time. Approach fences at a trot if you wish, but try to maintain a rhythm and keep your impulsion, so that the horse is concentrating on his job and not on outside distractions. You will probably find it easier if you shorten your stirrups an extra hole or two from your show jumping length. Look ahead at your fences as you approach them, then look over and ahead, not down. If you need to check your horse between fences, try to use your body, bracing your back, and never pulling backwards with your hands – remember the lessons you learned about maintaining balance in your flatwork.

Once you have prepared a good approach to the fence, keep your horse straight and going forward and leave the rest to him, allowing him the freedom to stretch up and over the fence. Take care not to check him at the last moment, which could put him off his stride.

Riding in open country is good preparation for competitive cross country riding.

Jumping into water causes many problems. It is essential to avoid galloping too fast at a water jump, because if the horse cannot see what he is jumping into he will stop and that is the hardest thing to overcome. However, once you have committed yourself to the approach, your legs must be on the horse, your contact with the horse's mouth elastic and your hands "giving." Many riders are subconsciously wary of the water themselves and bring their hands back without realizing they have done so. Not surprisingly, the horse stops.

A novice horse unused to jumping must be given a chance to look at the fence, without actually stopping, but the rider must look over the fence and be determined to jump it. Remember the old adage, "Throw your heart over and the horse will follow."

WESTERN TACKING-UP & MOUNTING

The television and movie image of the cowboy, in his ten gallon hat and jingling spurs, with a rough and ready attitude to his horse, is one that true Western riding enthusiasts do not appreciate. In Britain, for instance, where Western riding is still in its infancy, the Western Equestrian Society is working hard to dispel the popular misconception that this and rodeo games are what Western riding is about. Rodeos undoubtedly have entertainment value and display the courage and prowess of the participants, but they bear no relationship to the sphere of Western riding concerned with horsemanship.

So what is the aim of Western riding? As with English riding, the goal is to have a well-trained, obedient horse, who is supremely supple, athletic and well balanced. The movements required differ in style, composition and speed from English school movements, but all have their origins in practical horsemanship and combine to produce a trained horse which is exceptionally light in the hand and a pleasure to ride.

However, the aspiring Western rider's first task is to understand his equipment and how to tack up his horse. The horse's initial training will be in either a snaffle bit, or, more traditionally, a bosal, which comprises a rawhide noseband with reins of braided horsehair and works on a similar principle to the hackamore. It should be fitted

WESTERN BRIDLES

The bosal hackamore is a bitless bridle which should only be used by experienced riders. The split ear bridle has a split that fits over one ear.

headpiece
browband
fiador
cheek piece
bosal
knot

bosal hackamore

split ear bridle

with the front of the noseband about four or five finger widths above the top of the nostrils and should hang just behind the corners of the mouth, with the knot under the chin. It must be neither too tight nor too loose – in the latter case the horse would feel the initial pressure on his jaw instead of his nose, which would result in his head being thrown up in the air rather than coming down as desired.

When riding with a bosal, which should initially be used in an enclosed area, the hands should be held slightly wider than with a bit and there should never be a steady pull on the reins, but rather a "check and release" motion. The horse should be encouraged to flex his head and neck, both downward and to both sides.

The great emphasis placed on softness in the horse's mouth makes it essential for him to be totally relaxed and obedient in the bosal or snaffle, before he progresses to the curb bit. The curb will be introduced using a jointed mouthpiece, and only when his training is complete will a ported mouthpiece be used.

Bridles are available in various styles – the usual browband type, or slip ear, split ear and one ear. The slip ear bridle has an adjustable earpiece which slides to the most comfortable position for the horse; the split ear bridle comprises a single piece of leather with a split for the ear, while the one ear bridle has a shaped earpiece. One ear bridles rarely have a throatlatch, nor is a noseband used for showing, although it will be used in training to discourage the horse from opening his mouth, which is considered a major fault.

There are various types of Western bridle. This horse is wearing a browband type.

TACKING-UP

I Place the saddle pad or blanket well forward and then slide it back into position. This will ensure that all the hairs beneath it are lying the right way.

2 Place the saddle on the blanket (or pad), with about an inch of blanket in front of the saddle. Pull the blanket up into the saddle gullet.

3 Take hold of the saddle horn and give it a gentle shake to settle the saddle down into the right position.

4 Fasten the cinch. If a flank (rear) cinch is used, the front cinch should be fastened first.

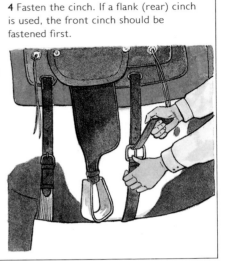

MOUNTING

I Stand facing to the front of your horse, at an angle of about 30 degrees to him and close to his side. Take a light contact to stop him moving forward.

2 Put your right hand on the horn or swell of the saddle (whichever is more comfortable), but not on the back of it. Then put your left foot in the stirrup.

3 Lightly spring to an upright position over the center of the horse, and quietly bring your right leg over the cantle.

4 Sink gently into the saddle, then put your right foot into its stirrup.

Saddle pads are used for comfort and to cushion the horse's back, but never as an attempt to compensate for a badly fitting saddle. They may be made of horsehair, felt, or fleece. Place the saddle pad or blanket well forward and slide it into position, remembering that the front of the Western saddle sits farther forward than the front of an English saddle, to allow for the swells and skirting, but maintaining the same seat position.

Place the saddle on the horse, with about an inch of blanket to the front, and pull the blanket up into the gullet. Take hold of the horn and give it a backwards shake, to settle the saddle down into the correct position. The saddle must not be placed farther back, or it will interfere with the horse's loins.

Cinches are attached by either buckles or open rings. If there is a single buckle, it should be on the offside, with the open ringed end on the near side fastened with a traditional tie knot. The remainder of the long latigo (the cinch strap) is carried in the nearside latigo keeper. The cinch on a Western saddle sits farther forward than

the girth on an English saddle and if a rear cinch is also used it must be the last thing to be fastened and the first to be unfastened, for obvious safety reasons. It must be neither so tight as to annoy the horse, nor so loose that he could get a hind foot caught if kicking at a fly.

The Western way of mounting is to face toward the front of your horse at an angle of about 30 degrees, standing close to his side. Take a light contact so he won't move forward — if his training has been correct he won't even consider it — and place your right

hand either on the horn or swell. Place your left foot in the stirrup, then lightly spring to an upright position over the center of the horse, quietly bringing your right leg over the cantle. Bending your left knee, slowly sink into the saddle and engage the right stirrup.

To dismount, the procedure is reversed. Disengage the right stirrup and stand up in the left stirrup, placing your right hand on the saddle horn and taking a light rein contact. Bring your right leg over and tuck it close into your left leg, stepping down and away.

BASIC WESTERN RIDING

The basic Western riding position is similar to the English riding position in that the rider should be balanced, sitting in the middle of the saddle and with a straight line through the shoulder, hip and heel. He should sit deep in the saddle, with his heels down, but in the effort to achieve this must avoid pushing his heels down by straightening his legs, or bringing the lower legs forward.

To achieve the correct position, the rider may be asked to stand in the stirrups, holding onto the saddle horn or swells, with his weight slightly forward and ankles and heels down. The knees are bent until the fork touches the saddle, then the rider rolls down the saddle to his seatbones, without allowing his legs to move forward. The stirrup length must be short enough for the rider to maintain flexibility of his knees and ankles without losing this position.

In competition riding, the reins are held in only one hand, but the beginner should use both hands in training. The arms should be relaxed, with the elbows comfortably bent, the hands held four to six inches apart, and the back of the hand following on from the back of the wrist, neither drop-ping down, nor rigidly turned out. The fingers should be closed on the reins, with the thumbs toward the top.

When the horse is trained to carry a rider, he must learn to adjust his balance so that his center of gravity is not over his shoulder, where most of his own weight is carried, but farther back. To do this he must stretch his neck, flexing at the poll, elevate his shoulders, round his back and loins and bring his hind legs underneath him, engaging his hindquarters. The trainer's job is to make the horse supple enough to do this with ease.

The beginner's aim is to learn to maintain this balance. To move off, the rider takes up a light contact with the bit and asks the horse to flex, easing his fingers back no more than a couple of inches. He uses his seat and leg aids to move forward in the usual way and if at any time the horse begins to lean on the bit, a quick give-and-take motion is used to ask him to flex again. If he slows down as a result of this, the seat and legs must drive him forward.

The main difference between Western riding and English riding is that in Western riding very little reliance is placed on the reins and it is a serious fault for the horse to open his mouth or resist the bit. Therefore, the rider must use his seat and legs to greater effect to control the horse's body. For example, if the horse drops to the inside when riding a circle, he should be pushed back out with the inside leg. This has the effect of elevating the horse's inside shoulder, which has dropped to cause the error. Pulling on the outside rein to bring him back to the circle will only twist his head, neck and body further, making the problem worse. Riding circles is an important part of training, to improve balance and suppleness.

Two more important exercises are the reinback and leg yielding. The reinback is started from the ground, with check-and-release movements, rewarding the horse when he takes a step back. It is important to release the bridle or halter as soon as the horse shows the inclination to move, not waiting until he has taken a full step. He will then begin to look forward to the release and associate it with taking the step. When mounted, lightly take the reins until the poll is flexed and the horse shifts his center of gravity backward, then release. If he takes the initial step, well and good, if not, tap lightly with the leg on the horse's shoulder, to encourage him to lift that leg and step back. As soon as he lifts the leg, release him. One step is enough to begin with and the horse can be asked to repeat it later in the lesson.

To reinback, the horse must lift his shoulders, so the rider should not stand up in the stirrups and lean forward, but rather stay in the center of the saddle, with his weight on his heels and his abdomen pulled in. When the horse can achieve several steps easily, he can be asked to turn his hips left or right and eventually to ride a circle backwards. At the beginning, however, each step must be rewarded and a good reinback is the basis from which canter departures and flying changes of lead will be developed.

Leg yielding is the start of sideways movement, teaching the horse to move away from the leg and again improving suppleness. A convenient hedge or fence may be used to avoid the need for too much rein pressure. Riding straight for a few strides with the fence on the left, the rider gently feels with the left rein, and applies pressure with the left leg to move the horse's body out. A slight bend and sideways movement is

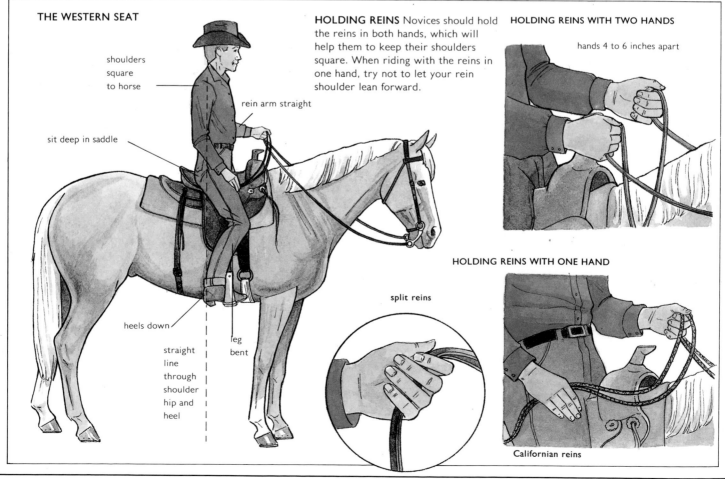

THE WESTERN SEAT

shoulders square to horse

rein arm straight

sit deep in saddle

heels down

leg bent

straight line through shoulder hip and heel

HOLDING REINS Novices should hold the reins in both hands, which will help them to keep their shoulders square. When riding with the reins in one hand, try not to let your rein shoulder lean forward.

HOLDING REINS WITH TWO HANDS

hands 4 to 6 inches apart

HOLDING REINS WITH ONE HAND

split reins

Californian reins

The correct riding position is to sit with a straight line through shoulder, hip and heel.

enough to begin with. If the horse simply bends his neck without yielding to the leg, take a little contact on the opposite rein, which will contain his shoulder movement and help encourage him to bring his inside hind leg across the outside hind leg, commencing the sideways movement. Keep your weight down through the seatbone on the side away from the direction of travel and avoid drawing your knee up in the effort to apply leg pressure, which will also have the effect of pushing your weight incorrectly to the other side.

Training exercises are begun at the walk, then at the trot and eventually the canter. At the trot, the horse is encouraged to adopt a low outline, with the rider giving and taking with the reins and never fixing the hands. Fixed hands encourage the horse to lean on the bit and when the reins are released he will immediately fall back on his forehand. The aim, however, is for the horse to learn to balance himself correctly at these paces before progressing to the slow, controlled, Western pleasure class paces of jog and lope.

REINING BACK

REINING BACK
1 Take the reins lightly until the poll is flexed and the horse shifts his center of gravity to the rear. Release as soon as the horse begins to move.
2 If the horse hesitates, tap your leg lightly against the shoulder of the leg you want him to lift.
3 and 4 At each step back, reward the horse by relaxing the reins and giving a word of encouragement.

LEG YIELDING

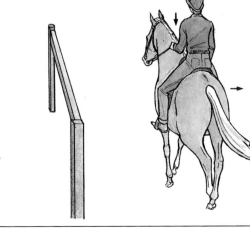

LEG YIELDING
1 Ride straight for a few strides alongside the fence. If the fence is on your left, gently feel with the left rein and apply pressure with your left leg to encourage the horse to move his body to the right.
2 Keep your weight down through your left seatbone. Avoid bringing your knee up as you apply leg pressure, because that will push your weight to the right. If the fence is on your right; use your right rein and leg to get the horse to move left.

RIDING SIDESADDLE

To ride sidesaddle must surely be the most elegant form of riding for a lady, and done properly it is a beautiful sight, especially in the hunting field or the show ring.

The sidesaddle, like any other saddle, must fit correctly. It must be completely flat on top and not tipped backward toward the tail, or forward toward the front. The saddle has a leather girth with a strap through which the balance strap and overgirth are passed, holding them neatly in position. The balance strap or girth is attached on the near side, under the flap, and is fastened on the off side toward the rear of the saddle. The overgirth is fixed to the near side flap and is fastened on the tiny off side flap with, usually, a clip running from the flap to the overgirth, holding everything neat and tidy.

There are two pommels on a sidesaddle, one facing upward and the other downward. The lower one is, in some cases, adjustable.

The elegant art of riding side-saddle is enjoying renewed popularity, especially for showing and hunting.

When sitting on a side-saddle, you face forward with your right leg around the top pommel and your left leg under the lower pommel. Your right leg can act as a stabilizer if you turn the foot toward the horse's shoulder. This will also help to keep you locked in position on the saddle.

Contrary to what the majority of people believe, it is the top leg (the right leg) that has all the weight, not the lower leg, and when you ride you should keep your hips level at all times. You should also keep your shoulders level, resisting the tendency to collapse your right hip and let your right shoulder swing forward.

The traditional sidesaddle out-fit, or habit, as it is known, consists of a cutaway jacket, a waistcoat

THE SIDESADDLE

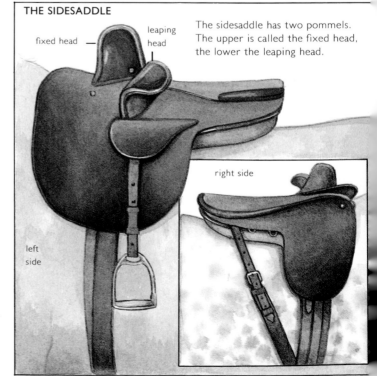

The sidesaddle has two pommels. The upper is called the fixed head, the lower the leaping head.

fixed head

leaping head

left side

right side

RIDING POSITION

The correct posture for riding sidesaddle is to keep your hips and shoulders level, your back straight and your weight on your top (right) leg. Turn your right foot toward the horse's shoulder for stability.

Common faults in riding sidesaddle are shown below.
1 The rider is leaning forward with her hands too low and her left leg held too far back.
2 The rider has let her right hip sag and her right shoulder swing forward, a natural tendency which you should try to resist.

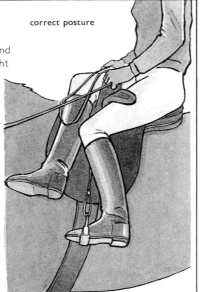

correct posture

COMMON FAULTS

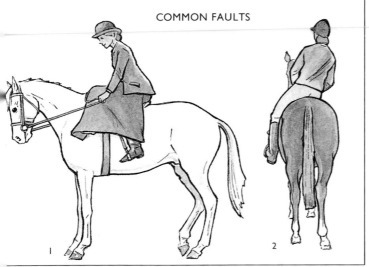

and a skirt. The skirt, which is known as an apron, is cut to the shape in which you sit on the horse. There is a little button on the back, toward the left-hand side, where you can attach the apron when not mounted, to allow you to walk about freely. Well-fitting breeches and boots are worn under the skirt (with a spur on the left boot only).

For mornings at shows, or even afternoons, the correct dress is a habit worn with a shirt and tie, a bowler hat and a veil. For hunting, show finals and afternoon shows, you may wear a top hat instead of a bowler, but it must also be worn with a veil and with a stock instead of a tie.

Another sidesaddle riding custom is to wear your hair in a bun, or to use a false one. Gloves are worn, preferably brown, and a stick may be carried. The stick may be a long one, held on the off side, or, if the horse is schooled, a short show cane; or, of course, a hunting whip.

Having got your horse a correctly fitting saddle and yourself attired in the proper gear, you then have to climb aboard. One way is to get on astride and then swing your right leg over into position, holding the reins in your left hand and keeping your right hand free so that you can steady yourself with it if the horse moves. This is an inelegant method, but a useful one if there is nobody around to help you into the saddle, which is by far the best way of mounting sidesaddle.

Have your helper stand by the horse's left shoulder with his or her back to its head. Your helper should clasp his or her hands together so that you can put your foot into them. You unhitch your apron and put it over your left arm, then, facing the horse's head, put your left hand on your helper's shoulder and your right hand on the saddle or the upper pommel.

Then you put your left foot into your helper's hands, so that they can lift you up and onto the saddle with both your legs on the near side.

Once you are in place on the saddle, you put your right leg around the top pommel, your left foot into the stirrup and your left thigh up under the lower pommel. Your helper can then pull the apron around your legs and under your right (upper) leg, and fasten the large piece of elastic (which is part of the apron) around your right boot.

To dismount, hold the reins in your right hand and pull your left foot from the stirrup. Carefully swing your right leg clear of the pommels and drop gently to the ground, keeping hold of the reins so that the horse remains under control.

When you are riding sidesaddle, remember to keep your weight on your right leg and your back very straight. Trotting is usually done sitting, for obvious reasons, and when you are cantering or galloping you should have the feeling that you are leaning backward slightly; in fact, this will only bring you into a properly upright position.

You use the aids in the normal way, except that your stick, cane or whip is used in place of your right leg. You should hold and use the reins in the normal way, and avoid using them to help you keep your balance. If you need to steady your balance, do so by holding the top pommel with your left hand.

To jump sidesaddle, bring your weight forward as the horse takes off, then bend forward (but not double) and stretch your hands and arms to follow the stretch of the horse's neck as it jumps. As the horse lands, sit upright again and use your left leg to absorb the impact of landing. During the jump your seat should not move far from the saddle, and you should avoid the natural but undesirable tendency to swing your right shoulder forward and downward.

THE APRON

The apron or skirt of a sidesaddle habit is cut to fit neatly when you are mounted, and is worn over well-fitting breeches and boots.

2 Swing the apron round behind you.
3 Fasten it to the single button at your left hip.

The 'spare' end of the apron is held by a loop of elastic hooked over your right foot.

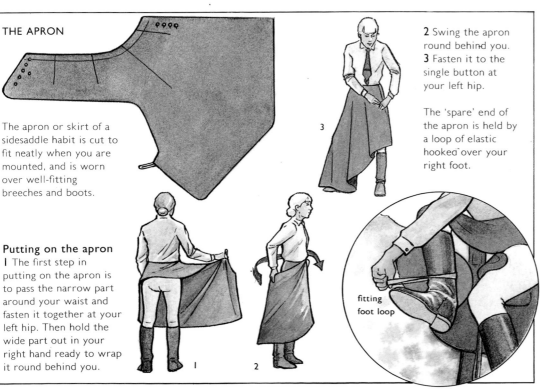

Putting on the apron
1 The first step in putting on the apron is to pass the narrow part around your waist and fasten it together at your left hip. Then hold the wide part out in your right hand ready to wrap it round behind you.

fitting foot loop

CARRIAGE DRIVING

Driving a horse has much in common with riding, but there are several differences which, for the sake of safety, must not be ignored. Use of the reins is similar, but instead of using your legs and body to pass on instructions to the horse, you use your voice and a whip. Knowing your horse, and watching its ears to judge what it is thinking, is also very important. And if you're driving on the road, remember that a horse and vehicle take up a good deal more space than a ridden horse, and you will need the same sort of road sense as you would if you were driving a car.

It's also important to ensure that the horse is correctly harnessed. It must be kept under control during this process by the use of a halter or head collar and lead rope which can, if you wish, be left on under the bridle. The first item of harness to go on is the collar which, if it is a full collar, is put on upside down, so that it doesn't rub the delicate skin above the horse's eyes. The hames, with the traces attached and coiled up out of the way, are strapped onto the collar, which is then turned right-side up.

The saddle and girth, back band, tugs, belly band, back strap, crupper, loin strap, breeching and breeching straps – already joined together – are lowered onto the horse's back as one unit, with the saddle in the middle of its back. The breeching is lowered over the horse's quarters, to lie about 12 inches below the dock, and the tail is lifted, folded in half and passed carefully through the tailpiece of the crupper. Next, the tailpiece is gently eased up to fit comfortably under the dock, making certain that no hairs are caught in it.

The saddle is now moved farther forward, but well back from the withers, and the back strap buckled (but not too tightly). The reins are threaded through the terrets (metal rings) on the saddle and on the hames, ready to be buckled to the bit, the ends you will hold, being tucked through the offside saddle terret to keep them out of the way but handy for when they are needed. Finally, the bridle is put on and the reins are attached.

The horse can now be led to the vehicle, which is then drawn up toward it with the shafts well clear. The shafts are lowered to pass through the tugs until the tugs rest against the tug stops on the shafts. The traces are uncoiled and attached to the trace hooks immediately, so that if the horse steps forward it is safely attached to the vehicle. The breeching straps are fastened by passing them around the shafts and traces and then through the breeching dees on the shafts. The belly band is now fastened, but more loosely than the girth.

Before mounting, walk around the turnout to make sure you haven't forgotten anything and that everything fits correctly. Mount the carriage from the off-side, moving quickly but quietly to avoid upsetting the horse. Hold the reins carefully to ensure control of the horse without inadver-

An elegant and well turned-out vehicle (below) is essential for Presentation and Dressage competitions, but a tougher vehicle. such as the one on the right is better for Marathons.

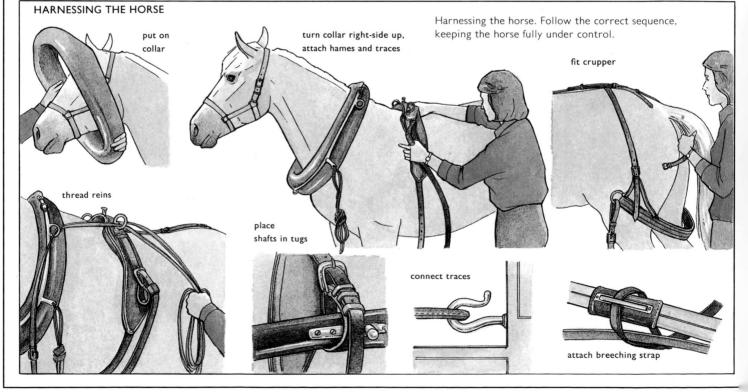

HARNESSING THE HORSE

Harnessing the horse. Follow the correct sequence, keeping the horse fully under control.

put on collar

turn collar right-side up, attach hames and traces

fit crupper

thread reins

place shafts in tugs

connect traces

attach breeching strap

HOLDING REINS

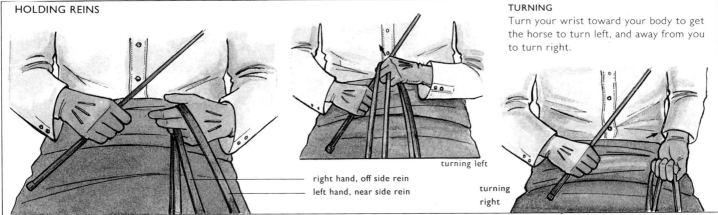

right hand, off side rein
left hand, near side rein

turning left

TURNING

Turn your wrist toward your body to get the horse to turn left, and away from you to turn right.

turning right

tently putting pressure on it mouth.

The correct way to hold the reins and whip for most types of driving is shown in the diagram. Both reins are always held in the left hand and the whip in the right. The whip is used, in place of the rider's legs, to keep the horse on the bit and to correct it if necessary by a light touch between collar and saddle.

When you are sitting comfortably, with both feet planted firmly on the floor or footrest, and have adjusted the apron, then the passengers (if any) can mount and the drive can begin.

Feel the horse's mouth gently before asking it to walk on. If it refuses, ask it again and touch it lightly with the whip. As it starts to move forward, ease the reins slightly to avoid pulling on its mouth, which can make it wonder whether you want it to move or not. Drive at the walk for a short distance, giving yourself a chance to check that everything is working properly.

The horse will be most comfortable and will tire less quickly if it is trotted at a constant speed, the ideal speed being that which comes naturally to it. Before turning a corner, check its pace so it

will be well-balanced and can turn without tipping the vehicle. To turn right, if the horse has a sensitive mouth, all that is needed is to turn your left wrist (which holds the reins) away from your body so as to slacken the nearside rein and pull on the offside rein. When turning left, the wrist is turned toward the body, which has the opposite effect.

If more pressure is needed on the horse's mouth, put your right hand slightly in front of your left, putting extra pressure on the appropriate rein. The only time it is permissible to hold one rein in each hand is when driving the

Marathon or Obstacle phases of combined driving, when speed and numerous changes of direction make it difficult to drive in the orthodox manner.

When taking the horse out of harness, the procedure should be exactly the reverse of that for harnessing it, again making sure that the horse is under control at all times.

Driving a pair, tandem or team of horses is basically similar, but considerably more difficult. It should certainly not be attempted until you have plenty of experience in driving a single horse, and then not without training.

SAFE RIDING

The need for safer riding has become increasingly evident in recent years, as statistics have shown an unacceptable number of injuries due to riding accidents. The image of the rider galloping free, hair blowing in the wind, may be captivating, but is hardly realistic in these days of increasing pressure on land use by many conflicting interests, heavy road traffic, growing numbers of horse riders and the overall better understanding of the dangers and how they can be avoided.

You may feel that if you want to risk your life by riding without a protective hat, that is your choice, but spare a thought for those who have to cope with the results of avoidable accidents — hard-worked doctors and your caring family.

A life can be ruined in less than a second and the cause is not always lack of skill or experience on the part of the rider. A moment's inattention, the carelessness of a third party, or some completely unrelated incident frightening a horse can all result in a fall.

A sensible rule is never to sit on a horse without wearing a properly fastened, safety approved hard hat. Since 1985, the American Horse Shows Association has required that anyone under the age of 18 wear a riding hat with a chin strap and a visor to protect the nose and head from injury.

Remember, most parts of the body can be repaired reasonably satisfactorily, but the same is not true of a damaged head. Landing on, or getting kicked on your head, can mean a fractured skull, epilepsy, brain damage and loss of basic faculties, or death. So don't take chances — wear an approved hard hat.

Another area of the body which often suffers from injury, in falls while riding cross country or at speed, is the back and if you are involved in these activities it is advisable to wear a back protector. These come in various styles, but they are all made of impact-resistant material which helps prevent the shock of falling, or of being kicked, from being transmitted to your body.

Safe footwear is a must. Conventional riding boots may not be practical or comfortable for all types of riding and many people prefer to wear short boots, but it is

Always wear a hard hat when you're riding, to protect your head if you have a fall.

essential that your footwear should have a heel, to prevent your feet from slipping right through the stirrups, should you lose your balance and fall. Training shoes are one of the worst types of footwear from the safety point of view, although they may be very comfortable.

If you have a genuine reason for wearing boots or shoes without heels (for example, endurance riders often get off to run alongside their horses and need soles that give traction on the ground) use guards over the front of your stirrups which prevent your feet from slipping through. Some Western stirrups are made with this design.

Also, your stirrup irons should not be too small, or again your foot might not slip free of the stirrup in an emergency. There should be no less than one quarter inch of stirrup bar on either side of your foot, when it is in the correct position for riding.

Pay careful attention to your tack. Clean it regularly — at least once a week — and as you clean, check all the stitching for strength, in particular girths, reins and stirrup leathers. The girth tabs on your saddle are also a vulnerable area — give each one a good tug to see that it is not coming loose.

If you are jumping or riding across country, when extra strain is put on your girth, always use a surcingle — a webbing strap, usually with an elasticated inset, which goes right over the saddle and around the horse's girth.

If your bridle has studs instead of buckles, check to see they have not been pulled loose and that the stud holes have not become over enlarged. For the horse's comfort, bits should have no sharp edges or worn places that may pinch its mouth.

All leather tabs are subject to wear. Keeping your tack clean and supple will help to avoid this and stirrup leathers should be shortened slightly whenever they are restitched, so that the iron will rest on a different area of leather.

Some of the worst accidents involve road traffic. When you are riding on a highway, stay alert for hazards and don't ride more than two abreast. On twisty roads where you cannot see oncoming traffic, stay in single file. Keep your reins short enough to have your horse under control and make clear signals when you want to turn left or right.

When taking out a young or nervous horse, it is sensible to have a quieter companion between it and the traffic. Riding on

ABOVE Clean your tack regularly, and check the stitching. LEFT If you ride on roads at night, reflective clothing is essential.

the roads after dark or in foggy weather is best avoided, but if you have no choice, use some sort of reflective clothing, such as bandages, vest, or hat cover, which show up in car headlights.

At times you may need to exercise a second horse by leading it alongside another. The led horse should be in a bridle and, if possible, in knee boots in case it should stumble. If the horse is to be led by the reins the far rein should be passed through the nearside bit ring. Otherwise a coupling and lead rope can be used.

Take the reins in the hand nearest the led horse, with one finger seperating them and keep a fairly short rein so that the led horse's head is alongside the ridden horse's shoulder or the rider's knee. It should not be allowed to get ahead of the ridden horse or to drag behind.

Finally, when you are riding in the countryside, be aware of the rights and safety of others. Close gates behind you and do not ride your horse at speed along public walkways, over crops or through livestock.

LEADING A HORSE

HOLDING REINS ONE-HANDED
When you're leading a horse alongside yours, hold your own horse's reins in the hand farthest from the led horse.

HOLDING REINS OF A LED HORSE
Hold the reins of the horse you are leading in the hand nearest it, with one finger between them. Keep the led horse on a fairly short rein.

keep led horse's head alongside ridden horse's shoulder

TREKKING & TRAIL RIDING

Pony trekking is a way of seeing beautiful countryside from the back of a horse, without too much emphasis on the techniques of riding. If you want a relaxing vacation, or just an afternoon's peace and quiet, away from the rat race, pony trekking could be the answer.

Trekking ponies are usually chosen for their placidity, rather than any considerations of performance or beauty. This is essential, since most trekking centers cater to everyone down to the complete beginner and the object of the exercise is to get you out into the country without preliminaries. Obviously the combination of an unbalanced, uncoordinated rider and a lively mount would not be a happy one.

A trekking pony needs a strong constitution to cope with hard work all through the summer season and with carrying many different riders, all of varying ability. In Britain, the various native breeds make ideal trekking ponies, the Highland being especially popular for his steady gaits and his stamina. Welsh Cobs can be lively, but crosses are frequently found trekking and the influence of other breeds can be found.

Some trekking centers do provide livelier riding and if you have some experience and want more than just a quiet meander, inquire closely as to the type of animals provided by the center, before you make reservations. If you have no experience whatever with horses or riding, make sure you choose a place that caters to beginners. In some areas you will find the local Tourist Offices or National Park authorities helpful and there are also useful associations in most areas that will give advice and information on trekking vacations.

It is not essential to have proper riding clothes for pony trekking. However, you might find jodhpurs or stretch trousers more comfortable than jeans. Your boots or shoes should be sturdy and well fitting and must have heels. Trainers are therefore unsuitable and you should also avoid flimsy fashion footwear. A hard hat is mandatory, but you might be able to rent one if you don't want to go to the expense of buying one.

Most trekking takes place at a slow pace, enabling you to enjoy the countryside as you ride, but you can quickly become chilled on an open mountain or on other

exposed terrain, so a warm top is advisable. Also take a lightweight waterproof jacket, which can be rolled up and tied to the saddle when not in use.

You will usually be shown how to tack up your pony, with a halter worn under its bridle, and mounting will be explained, together with the basic requirements of how to balance and hold the reins. Treks are usually arranged on a half-day or whole day basis, returning to the trekking center afterwards. A whole day trek will have a stop for lunch en route, during which time your pony's bridle and saddle should be re-

moved; it should be offered a drink and possibly some feed will have been arranged. It can be tethered, using a quick release knot, while you have your own lunch.

The riding will be geared to the time available and the ability of the riders, which the trek leader

Most trekking is done at a leisurely pace, and is suitable for inexperienced riders. Trail riding is more strenuous, and riders should be experienced.

day. Of course, the levels of riding and the type of horses vary. In Scotland, for example, you might find the Highland pony in use. However, some of the more ambitious trail riding organizers use horses with some Thoroughbred blood, to improve speed and stamina, and you should go prepared to control and look after your own mount.

Trail riding vacations are widely available in many countries. Spectacular scenery is to be found in the Canadian Rockies and in the western United States. Dude ranches are very popular with families because of the wide variety of activities they offer. Some of the best riding is to be found in France, where many trails are marked for riders' benefit, and Spain's Andalusian mountains are also popular.

Trail riding is not for the fainthearted — you will be expected to care for your horse before yourself — and overnight stops vary too. It is sensible to find out, before you book, if you will be camping under a tree or staying in four-star accommodation, and to take the appropriate clothing and equipment. On the most rugged trail rides you might camp and carry all your gear with you on pack horses. In Britain, overnight accommodation at farmhouses is usual and while you are riding, your baggage is transported by car from stop to stop.

Trail riding parties are usually small, but this should not be a deterrent to going on your own, if none of your friends want to come along. By the time you have spent a week riding with a like-minded small group of people, you will come to know each other very well.

To summarize, before you make reservations here or abroad, ask the following questions: What are the horses like? What is the overnight accommodation? How far will we ride each day? What equipment should I bring?

Then aim to get yourself as fit as possible before you leave. Even if you are a regular rider, you will feel the effects of several days nonstop in the saddle. Swimming, running and skipping are all fitness training methods that horse riders find useful. Finally, enjoy yourself.

will assess during the early part of the trek. Usually, ponies follow one behind the other, a leader in front and another at the rear to cope with any problems or stragglers. Most of the trek will be at a walk, but if the riders are able, some trotting and cantering may be included. Scotland, Wales, the West Country and some parts of Ireland are the main centers for trekking in the British Isles, taking advantage of beautiful scenery in wide-open spaces.

Riders who are more experienced, but want the pleasure of seeing different places and a "holiday on horseback," should try trail riding. Various combinations are available, from a day's outing returning to the starting point in the evening, to two weeks or more of continuous travelling, with different overnight stops.

Both riders and horses need to be fit for this, where you will probably cover 20–25 miles a

COMPETITIVE RIDING

Once modern weapons and firepower had made the employment of horses in warfare an irrelevance, and when the internal combustion engine had superseded their use in transport, agriculture and haulage, it was inevitable that the survival of the species in significant numbers, outside of the firmly established industry of racing, would depend upon the extent to which horses could be used for recreation and leisure.

The levelling effect of social change, and the greater affluence which followed World War II, provided the answer to that, contributing materially to what amounted to an explosion in horse interest and all things equestrian. But it also changed the traditional pattern of horsekeeping.

In the days before World War II, the ownership of horses was largely the prerogative of the country dweller and in Britain, which may be taken as a good example in this instance, many horses were kept solely for the purpose of hunting between late September, when the season opened with cub hunting (or cubbing), to the end of the season proper in April. That is no longer the case.

Hunting still thrives, possibly as never before, in both Britain and the United States and in a more stylized form on the Continent, but increasingly the emphasis has shifted over the past forty years to competitive riding. There are still people who are content to keep a horse for no more than quiet hacking, and thousands whose ownership of horses is concerned entirely with hunting.

For many more, however, a large number of them keeping horses in urban or suburban areas and having neither the opportunity nor perhaps the inclination, to go hunting, ownership and equestrian participation is about competition, for which there is ample opportunity the whole year round, and which sets standards of achievement against which the individual can measure his or her progress.

As a consequence, the growth of riding clubs and Pony Club branches, many of them urban-based, and all arranging inter-club competitions, as well as staging instructional clinics and events confined to their own membership, have added very largely to the spread of competitive horse sports. Further encouragement has been given by television coverage, particularly of show jumping and eventing.

Racing is endemic to the human condition and probably began early in the domestication of the horse. One can imagine the young men of the nomadic steppe tribes matching their horses against each other. Many more competitive sports, however, derive from military practice as practical training exercises. This is certainly so in the case of mounted games, horse trials, jumping and, to a large degree, endurance riding. Genghis Khan, for instance, used the Great Hunt, lasting over four months and involving thousands of warriors, as a regular training campaign.

Even dressage has its roots in warfare, the movements performed in the *manège*, in particular the High School airs, being those practiced by the knights in battle. The pirouette, for instance, was an essential maneuver when fighting on horseback and even the most resolute infantry would be deterred by an energetic *croupade* or, perhaps, a soaring *capriole*.

Harness racing, in chariots, was an enormously popular spectator sport in the classical civilizations of Greece and Rome, horses being bred for the purpose as they are today.

In the United States, where there is a division between English and Western style riding , competitive events acquire a new dimension. American riders go hunting and racing, they showjump, compete in horse trials and dressage, play polo and take part in the world's toughest long-distance endurance rides, the Tevis Cup being the most severe. (The tradition of endurance riding, so strong in America, started when the US Cavalry staged 300-mile rides, carrying 200 pounds of weight to test horses used as remounts.) Additionally, however, Western riding has its own sports, demanding just as much skill and dedication. Indeed, the rodeo, the larger events held under the rules of either the Rodeo Cowboys Association or the International Rodeo Association, is a multimillion-dollar business attracting large and enthusiastic audiences and providing a livelihood for numbers of professionals.

The principal rodeo events, like bareback bronc riding, steer and calf roping, bull riding, team roping and barrel racing, are virtually extensions of the early cowboy's working life and began as informal contests held while the cowboys waited for their cattle to be loaded onto trains. The first commercial rodeo, held before a paying audience, was on July 4, 1886 at Prescott, Arizona, and nowadays many rodeos are held on Independence Day.

Competitive riding, of course, provides a direct encouragement to horse breeding and in Europe, as a consequence, breeding policies are almost entirely aligned to the production of the "competition" horse, specially bred for one or other of the major disciplines.

Every nation concerned with horse sports has its own national association responsible for the encouragement and organization of events. The world governing authority, responsible for rules and the conduct of international events, is the *Fédération Equestre Internationale* (FEI), through which the national associations are all represented.

The three major horse disciplines – show jumping, horse trials and dressage – are included in the Olympic events and all three stage World Championships, as well as events such as the European and the Pan-American games in the years between the Olympic Games. Individual countries also stage their own national championships.

Although international competition represents the highest level of achievement, competitive riding in all spheres is carried on throughout the horse world from a beginners' level upward and on all types of horses.

PONY CLUB GAMES

The Pony Club was founded in England in 1929 and the United States Pony Club Inc. was created in 1953. (The movement has spread to 22 other countries, including Australia and New Zealand). Mounted games have always been a feature of the clubs, and such games are often known by the Anglo-Indian word *gymkhana*. (*Gymkhana* is a combination of the Hindi word *gend-khana* – a ball-house or a racquet court – and *gymnastics*.) These gymkhana games were introduced into Britain by Army officers returning from India, where there was a long tradition of mounted sports that still survives today in both military and civilian riding.

The first people to play games on horseback were the mounted nomads of Central Asia, people such as the Scythians whose territory extended north of the Black Sea, in the Caucasus.

The games played today by their descendants, as well as by steppe people in many other parts of the Soviet Union, are not much different from those which were part and parcel of the life of those Scythian warriors. In the past

there were no set rules, but nowadays mounted sports in the Asian republics of the USSR are highly organized, if still somewhat robust, affairs.

Much later, the cavalries of the world were to follow the example of the early Asian horse peoples and to encourage their troopers to compete in mounted sports. The games were certainly an enjoyable and often exciting form of relaxation but they also fulfilled an important practical purpose as a training exercise. Not only did they increase the rider's suppleness, agility and general proficiency, they also did much the same for the horse too.

That, of course, applies to the Pony Club rider and pony and the advantage of this kind of competition is that the everyday rider can achieve a high standard on an "ordinary" pony – given that he or she is prepared to put in quite a lot of practice. Indeed, the topclass mounted games or gymkhana pony is far more likely to be a sagacious, streetwise mongrel than an expensive well-bred aristocrat of faultless conformation. The secret of success in mounted

ing a specialized technique on the part of the rider and a cooperative pony who will run alongside on a loose rein. A similarly skilled pony is needed for the stepping stone dash where the rider must hop from one "stone" to the next as the pony trots by his side.

The dragon race and the balloon bursting race are both based on a form of tent-pegging reminiscent of the military skill-at-arms exercises, while team coordination is tested to the full by those events calling for the ponies to carry two riders. Examples of these are the sharpshooters' race, in which one of the riders has to dismount to demolish an "Aunt Sally" with a supply of balls, and the more simple race when one rider and one pony gallops down the course to pick up a second rider and gallops back to the finish.

The variety of ingeniously contrived races is almost endless but all of them put the emphasis on riders and ponies working as a team, which, of course, along with the encouragement of good sportsmanship, was Prince Philip's intention when he presented his trophy.

The Prince Philip Cup represents the highest level of Pony Club mounted games and many of the games played at "rallies" emphasize the team aspect, but there are many individual competitions put on at hundreds of local shows. At most of them there will be some form of musical chairs; a sack race certainly; a walk, trot and canter race, with penalties for breaking the pace; pole bending races and sometimes an apple bobbing race, when the rider has to seize an apple in his teeth as it "bobs" in a trough of water. At one time this was a certainty at every gymkhana, but in recent years has appeared less often.

Mounted games are sometimes criticized on the grounds that they encourage rough riding. Certainly, it is possible for children to become rough in the excitement of the moment, but if the games are properly supervised, and the children and ponies well-trained, they encourage effective riding and are an opportunity for even the most ordinary pony to compete at a national level.

The Pony Club also stages its own polo tournament, an event inaugurated in 1958. Obviously, it does not attract the same number of entries as the Mounted Games Championship, but good standards are reached.

There is an endless variety of Pony Club games, but they are all intended to be fun as well as to help children develop their riding skills and to encourage the riders and ponies to work together as teams.

games is less concerned with speed than with handiness, immediate obedience to the aids and a good temperament. There is no place in a mounted games team for the highly-bred and highly-strung pony who may be able to gallop but throws a tantrum at the sight of a sack on the ground or a row of upturned buckets.

It was with the average sort of Pony Club pony in mind that HRH Prince Philip presented his trophy for a national mounted games championship. This was

first competed for in Britain in 1957. Then in 1985, Philip donated a similar perpetual trophy to be given to the top mounted games team in the United States. This presentation is now a featured event at the National Horse Show. Even though, as standards have risen, the games have become more sophisticated, the competition remains virtually unaltered.

Each year, teams from hundreds of Pony Club branches compete at area meetings. Important shows are held at Fairfield, Devon, Harrisburg, Culpeper, and at the Washington International. In Britain, the top six are then eligible for the national championship which is an exciting and very popular feature of the world-famous Horse of the Year Show at

Wembley Arena, London.

Teams consist of five members, who must be under sixteen years old, and a nonriding captain who is usually the trainer. The ponies, which must be turned out in conventional saddles and snaffle bridles, mustn't exceed 14.2 hands.

The games are devised to test the skill, timing and agility of the riders as well as the ponies' adaptability and standard of training. The team relay bending is a "basic" event of the competition which puts a premium on suppleness and accurate riding. Competitors have to weave in and out of a line of poles and then gallop back down the arena to make the critical baton change.

Another favorite is the ever popular relay sack race, demand-

SHOW JUMPING

Although show jumping is a comparative newcomer to the field of equestrian activity it has, nonetheless, lost no time in becoming established as a major world sport with a spectacular rate of growth.

A minor reference to jumping appears in a French cavalry manual of the late 18th century, but not until the 1860s is there any record of organized competitions. In 1865, the Royal Dublin Society staged a high and wide leaping competition on Leinster Lawn, Dublin, which was intended as a test for hunters. (In Britain, even up to the Second World War, "leaping" was commonly used to describe what we now call a jumping or show jumping competition).

In the year following the Royal Dublin competition, a jumping class (*Concours Hippique*) was held at the Paris Show, but this was more of a cross country event and did not involve a course of fences erected in an arena. Indeed, after a preliminary parade indoors the competitors were sent out to jump over mostly natural obstacles in the countryside.

The sport then spread rapidly on the Continent, particularly in Germany and France, and in 1900

jumping competitions were included in the Olympic Games in Paris. Two years later, cavalry officers from Germany and Switzerland competed against their Italian hosts, now riding in accordance with the theories taught by their innovatory guru, Federico Caprilli, at the first Turin *Concorso Ippico Internazionale*.

In that same year at Howard Willett's farm in Richmond, Virginia, the latter's Thoroughbred, Heatherbloom, ridden by Dick Donnelly, jumped 7 ft 10½ ins; two years later, at White Plains, New York, they jumped 8 ft 2 ins. Although these jumps were not ratified officially, noone has jumped any higher since then.

Upperville, Virginia, claims that its show – first held in 1853 – is the oldest in America, a claim hotly disputed by Lakefield, Connecticut, and Springfield, Massachusetts, where a show was held indisputably on November 12, 1853. Whether jumping competitions were included in those early shows is not known, but they certainly formed a significant part of New York's first National Horse Show held at Madison Square Garden in 1883.

The accent in those initial com-

petitions was on the high jump and most horses competing were entered as hunters also. At the first show the competition was won with a jump of 6 ft; five years later George Pepper's 14.2½ hands mare cleared 6 ft 10 ins and in 1901 S S Howland's Ontario set a record at 7 ft 1 in.

By the turn of the century show jumping, in its higher reaches and in international terms, was increasingly dominated by the military teams. The National opened its doors to foreign riders in 1909 when a team of five British officers led by Major J G Beresford, 7th Hussars, divided the honors with the American team. The British returned in the following year, along with the French and Dutch, and in 1911 an American team made its first appearance at the International Horse Show, held at Olympia, London.

By then, the Nations Cup competition at the International was celebrating its second anniversary and the show itself was four years old. Originally, the competition was for teams of three officers of the same country riding in uniform, the prize being a gold challenge cup, value £500, presented by King Edward VII. The first contest, in London, was won by the French; Britain had to wait until 1921 to win its first Nations Cup at the same venue, with a team led by Major-General Geoffrey Brooke, who rode a horse called Combined Training, the first title given to the sport of horse trials or eventing. The United States did not have a win until 1929 when it scored a victory on home ground, at Boston, with a team led by one of the greatest American horsemen, Colonel Harry D Chamberlin. The most successful of the prewar Nations Cup teams was that of the Irish Army, which won 23 competitions around the world from 1928 to 1939.

A crack Russian team, which included Paul Rodzianko, who was to become trainer of the Irish team, won the Cup outright by victories in London in 1912, 1913 and 1914. The Cup, following the Russian Revolution, was never seen again and was replaced by the Edward, Prince of Wales Cup.

At least one reason for the popularity of jumping as a spectator sport is the uncompromising clarity of the rules concerning

Show jumping is one of the few sports where women compete on equal terms with men.

penalties, which makes it easier for the onlooker to follow the fortunes of a competition. But it was not always so, nor was there any uniformity in the rules applied by different countries or, indeed, within a single country.

Slats, or in American terminology, slip fillets, were rested on the top of the fences, their dislodgement attracting a penalty. Faults were given for these touches, for knockdowns and for landing on or within the demarcation lines of spread fences, while a fence hit by the forelegs cost twice as many faults as a knock with the hind legs. Time, too, was unimportant and at smaller shows riders could be seen circling in front of a fence so as to get the right stride.

After the formation of the FEI in 1921, the rules were standardized, but slats were still used in Britain under national rules until after World War II and until comparatively recently in America also.

Today, audiences know the rules almost as well as the judges: four for a knockdown, three for a first refusal, six for the second and elimination for a third. The use of a digital time clock to record time faults is an additional help to the spectator and essential for timed jump-offs or in those speed competitions when faults are expressed in seconds.

The high jump has now disappeared from world show jumping, its place being taken by the Puissance competition in which an initial course of six fences is reduced to two, usually a triple bar and a final wall. These are raised for each round, usually restricted to three, until all save the winner have dropped out.

Every nation has a system of grading horses, and courses are built according to the experience and grading of the entry. In Britain, for instance, grading is based on the amount of prize money won. A Grade A horse only reaches that level after winning £1000. In France, grading is mostly based on a horse's age. Here in the United States, the system is extremely flexible, beginning with Schooling Jumpers and progressing to Prelimary, Intermediate and Open Jumpers, and eventually to Grand Prix.

American horse shows include a very wide variety of classes, from hunters and Western classes to Saddlebreds and Walkers, but the Jumper Division is probably the strongest sector of all.

A competitor at Hickstead, one of Britain's top show jumping venues.

EVENTING

The sport of horse trials or eventing, which the French describe so accurately as *concours complet* – the complete test – has its origins in military competitions designed to test the endurance, speed, stamina and obedience of the horse, exactly the same objects as those of the modern event.

It all began with the Greek soldier-author-horseman, Xenophon (c 430–355 BC), who wrote in one of the first ever cavalry manuals a direction for cavalry commanders which runs like this: "The duty will devolve on you for seeing, in the first place, that your horses are well-fed and in condition to stand their work, since a horse which cannot endure fatigue will clearly be unable to overhaul the foeman or effect escape; and in the second place, you have to see to it that the animals are tractable since, clearly again, a horse that will not obey is only fighting for the enemy and not for his friends."

From the 17th century until the beginning of the 20th the armies of France, Germany, Sweden and the USA were running "endurance rides" as part of their systems of cavalry training. These rides varied between $18\frac{1}{2}$ miles to something around 450 miles. The pace was fast but no jumping was involved, the emphasis being on stamina and endurance.

It was left to the French to develop a more comprehensive test. They staged the *Championnat du Cheval d'Armes* in the country around Paris in April 1902 as a purely military exercise. It comprised four phases: a dressage test, followed by a steeplechase, then a 30-mile ride over roads and tracks and finally a jumping competition.

The exercise developed and a three-day event for military riders was included in the 1912 Olympics. It was won by Sweden, a nation which remained a powerful force within the sport for many years.

Only after World War II was civilian participation allowed and from that point the sport grew with remarkable speed, although few could have foreseen at the time how dominant the female influence would become in what is recognized as the toughest and most demanding of horse sports.

It was much encouraged, and not only in Britain, by the interest of the Duke of Beaufort, who allowed his estate at Badminton, England, to be used for an annual three-day event.

Eventing has now become complex and sophisticated. Event horses are graded according to performance records and there is a carefully devised progression all the way from the novice one-day event right up to the full-blown three-day championship event, which will usually be run, in fact,

LEFT *Virginia Leng on Beneficial at Holker Hall, 1988.*
ABOVE *Rachel Hunt and her mount Friday Fox take off for a difficult jump at the 1988 Badminton Horse Trials.*

over four days, the entries now being so large that two days have to be devoted to the dressage phase.

In one-, and usually in two-day events also, the dressage test is held first, followed by the show jumping phase and then by the cross country. Horses eliminated in the jumping phase are automatically disqualified from starting on the cross country course.

In the three-day event dressage still comes first; on the following day the cross country course is ridden; the course, which is at the very center of the event, being preceded by a roads and tracks

section leading to the steeplechase course, after which there is another section of roads and tracks before the competitors tackle the cross country fences. The whole is classified as the speed and endurance phase. On the final day, after a veterinary inspection, the show jumping test completes the competition.

The philosophy of the event, harking back to the qualities required of the military horse, is this: the dressage test proves that the horse, though at the peak of fitness necessary if he is to perform across country, is nonetheless obedient and sufficiently submissive to the rider to perform a series of controlled movements in a small arena.

It is also, of course, a test of supple athleticism and a horse that performs *very* badly, revealing the shortcomings in his training, may

very well be persuaded by the Jury (which judges the test and is the event's ultimate authority) from continuing further. It rarely happens but there have been occasional instances.

The speed and endurance test is designed to display just those qualities and is a test of the ability and courage of both horse and rider in negotiating a variety of pretty formidable obstacles.

The last jumping phase over a relatively straightforward course is to show that after all his exertions the horse is sound and "fit for further service."

In theory the relative influences of the three tests should be in the ratio of Dressage 3: Speed and Endurance 12: Show jumping 1. To attain this ideal, or to come very close to doing so, the cross country must be demanding enough to sort the men from the

boys (or, perhaps, the women from the little girls).

Lest the dressage exert too great an influence, which may have occurred in the earlier events, there is, however, a built-in safeguard known as the Multiplying Factor. It is decided in advance by the Ground Jury on their assessment of the severity of the cross country. It varies between 0.5 and 1.5, the more demanding the cross country the higher will be the Multiplying Factor and consequently the greater will be the spread of dressage penalties between the highest- and the lowest-placed competitor.

The dressage test poses difficulties which do not occur in pure dressage. An obvious one is the state of fitness which is essential for the speed and endurance phase but is not always conducive to

calm behavior within the restrictive confines of the dressage arena.

The test is not, of course, as demanding as the pure dressage tests and judges will be more forgiving of occasional lapses in accuracy, so long as the horse is going forward energetically throughout the test while remaining submissive to the rider and is straight in the movements required – which is more difficult to achieve than might be thought.

At Badminton, the endurance test covers about 16 miles and calls for something like $1\frac{1}{2}$ hours of sustained effort. The first roads and tracks section is $3\frac{1}{2}$ miles long. The 2-mile steeplechase section needs to be completed in $4\frac{1}{2}$ minutes, which means an average speed of around 26 mph, and that is followed by a further 6 miles of roads and tracks.

After that, there is a compulsory 10-minute break before competitors set off on the $4\frac{1}{2}$-mile cross country course and its 32 fences. In fact, because there are a number of combination fences the horse makes considerably more than 32 jumps.

The severity of the jumping test depends to a large degree on what transpired on the previous day, and is made more or less difficult in order to preserve the correct proportion.

It can, however, be a nerve-racking experience for riders, however straightforward the course. Horses are bound to feel the effects of the previous day and sympathetic allowance has to be made for slower reactions and a reduced level of energy in the performance. It all adds up to being the "complete test" of horse and rider.

DRESSAGE

The word *dressage* comes, like so many of our riding terms, from the French, deriving from the verb *dresser*, which is used to describe the training (the "dressing") of the riding horse, or even of a harness horse.

As with eventing, the discipline has its roots in the progressive systems of training described by Xenophon, who in his book *Peri Hippikes* discussed riding as both a science and an art. When the riders of the Renaissance period began to school their horses in the "classical" airs and movements, it was to Xenophon that they turned for inspiration. He was certainly

familiar with the collected movements of *passage* and *piaffe*, which form part of our modern Grand Prix test; he wrote lucidly about the riding of voltes and serpentines and he discussed the *levade*, the "half-rear" which is included in the High School airs.

The first of the classical Masters was Federico Grisone, the Neapolitan nobleman who founded what might be termed the first modern riding school in Naples in 1532. Fifty years later the Spanish Riding School was founded in Vienna and from that point the Italian influence diminished, giving way by the end of

the century to the French schools which culminated in the École de Versailles and the École de Saumur.

First of a succession of French Masters was Antoine de Pluvinel (1555–1620), tutor to King Louis XIII. His was a far more humane system than that of the Neapolitans and it incorporated progressive gymnastic suppling exercises which prepared the horse for the more advanced movements. Pluvinel was the inventor of the pillars, still in use in the classical schools. He included work on two tracks in his system and he provided an altogether more enlight-

ened approach to school riding.

His work was extended by his pupils and by others who followed his teaching, but the greatest figure in the advance of educated horsemanship was without doubt François Robichon de la Guérinière (1688–1751), the director of the royal *manège* of the Tuileries from 1730–1751. His *École de Cavalerie* remains to this day as the equestrian bible of the Spanish Riding School and retains

Modern competitive dressage is descended from 19th-century military riding school tests.

its relevance for dressage riders throughout the world.

Using more active and better-bred horses, Guérinière perfected gymnastic exercises which enhanced the natural paces. He it was who invented the supreme suppling exercise, the shoulder-in (*l'épaule en dedans*) as well as "head-to-the-wall" and "tail-to-the-wall," *travers* and *renvers*, and many of the school figures we ride today.

During the 19th century the military riding schools of Europe, which based their instruction on that of the classical schools, dominated the equestrian thinking of their day. Indeed, it was their "best trained charger" tests which were the forerunners of competitive dressage.

Dressage was not included in the Olympic disciplines until the Stockholm Olympics in 1912. The Swedes, who won the team show jumping and three-day event, also produced the first three in the dressage, for which there was no team competition. Sweden repeated that performance in 1920 at Antwerp and they headed the dressage line-up at Paris four years later.

The 1912 competition was held in an arena measuring 20 meters × 40 meters (66 feet × 131 feet) and was at what would now be considered an elementary level. No lateral movements were included, no flying changes of lead and, of course, no *piaffe* or *passage*. There was, however, a jumping test over five fences as part of the competition and this practice persisted in some tests until after World War II.

Considerably more was asked for at the Antwerp Olympics. The test included half-passes at the trot and canter, and flying changes of leg up to one-time, and a system of coefficients was introduced for the more difficult movements.

Piaffe and *passage* formed no part of the Olympic test until the Los Angeles Olympics in 1932 and canter pirouettes were not included until the Berlin Games of 1936. (The classical High School "airs above the ground" *levade*, *courbette* and *capriole*, form no part of the competitive dressage tests but are still practiced at the Spanish School and by France's *Cadre Noir*.)

As the armies of Europe became increasingly mechanized, and the cavalry schools closed, so the military influence declined, and after World War II participa-

Stephen Clarke on his horse Becket at the 1988 Goodwood International Dressage Festival, Sussex, England.

tion in dressage was almost wholly civilian. The classical precepts remained inviolate, but dressage, perhaps inevitably, moved closer to becoming a sport discipline. At its best, competitive dressage could still be looked upon as an art-sport, but few would accord it the accolade of an art-form in the spirit and execution of the Spanish School. Nevertheless, it became the recreation of thousands and it certainly did no harm to the furtherance of equestrian knowledge.

Very quickly, the Germans acquired an awesome superiority, largely on account of the tradition of school riding which obtains on the Continent and because climatic conditions there during the winter months discourage outdoor riding.

The British, whose traditions remained firmly anchored in the hunting field, excelled at eventing as might be supposed, but they were slow to enter competitive dressage. The United States and Canada, however, both learned more quickly and produced some talented combinations.

Today, dressage is practiced all over the world, the tests varying from the simplest, suitable for Pony Club and riding club level, to the ultimate Grand Prix ridden at international meetings and in the Olympics.

Every nation produces tests suitable to the grades in which the sport is divided. These range from a preliminary level to an advanced standard. The four tests ridden at international meetings, in an arena measuring 20 meters × 60 meters (66 feet × 197 feet), are: the Prix St George, the lowest international test; the Intermediate I and II; and the Grand Prix.

At major competitions the first 12 riders in the Grand Prix qualify to compete in the Special, a shorter test involving more concentrated work and with movements performed in difficult areas of the arena. A *Kur*, or free-style test, may also be included and increasingly this is ridden to music of the rider's choice. It adds another dimension to the sport and goes some way to restoring the art content.

FLAT RACING & STEEPLECHASING

The first historical record of racing was at the 33rd Olympiad in 624 BC, but the matching of one horse against another must have begun long before that.

The establishment of organized racing in Europe and thereafter throughout the world was concerned very closely with the evolution of the world's superhorse, the English Thoroughbred, which began in the 17th and 18th centuries with the importation of the Arab sires the Godolphin Arabian, the Darley Arabian and the Byerley Turk.

Racing, however, had for long been a part of the British scene and the Royal studs, founded by Henry VIII in the 16th century, were much concerned with producing "running horses." Many of these would carry Oriental blood as well as that of Spanish and Neapolitan imports which were interbred with the native Hobbies and Galloways.

Racing in Britain has traditionally enjoyed Royal patronage, hence its claim to be "The Sport of Kings." James I of England, who enjoyed both racing and hunting, was responsible for putting Newmarket on the map in the 17th century as the future headquarters of British racing. Regular spring and autumn meetings were held there in the reign of James' son, the ill-fated Charles I. Following the English Civil War and the

Restoration, Charles II, indulging his passion for the Turf, continued the development of the town.

The Jockey Club, British racing's governing body, was founded in about 1752 by a group of interested aristocrats, although an official list of its members did not appear until 1835. Similar organizations, following the British pattern, now exist in all countries in which racing is carried on. *An Introduction to a General Stud Book* appeared in England in 1791 and the first volume of the GSB was published in 1808.

During the first half of the 18th century, the emphasis was on distance races of up to 4 miles (6.5 km), which took the form of several heats followed by a final. Breeding policies were therefore directed to this end. However, far shorter races were the norm in the latter part of the century, a trend reflected in the British Classic races for three-year-olds: the St Leger, first run in 1776 over 1 mile 1320 yards (2.8 km); the Oaks (founded in 1779) and the Derby (1780), both of which are run over 1 mile 880 yards (2.4 km). The two 1 mile (1.6 km) Classics, the 2000 Guineas and the 1000 Guineas, were first run in 1809 and 1814 respectively. The last-named, together with the Oaks, is for fillies only.

In Britain, the Triple Crown comprises the 2000 Guineas, the

Derby and the St Leger and is regarded as the ultimate accolade of the British Turf. Twelve horses have won the Triple Crown since the inauguration of the races, the last being Nijinsky in 1970.

British breeders, therefore, concentrated on middle-distance horses, as they continue to do today, and that policy was followed by the European studs.

In modern times the most influential racing nations in Europe, other than Britain, have been France – which dominated the European scene following World War II through the studs owned by the millionaire Marcel Boussac and the pervading influence of the stallions Pharis, Tourbillon and Asterus – and Italy, a country which had a profound influence largely through Federico Tesio's Dormello Stud and horses bred there including Donatello II, Nearco and Ribot. Leased to the United States, Ribot became the world's best Classic sire.

In the Southern Hemisphere, Thoroughbred racing thrives in both Australia and New Zealand, both of which have developed their own type of race horse.

Racing began in the United States almost as soon as the first settlers set foot in the New World and could clear "race paths." The first racecourse was laid out on Long Island (close to the site of the present-day Belmont Park) in

Flat racing is one of the world's most popular and competitive equestrian sports.

1664 by the first British Governor of New York, Richard Nicolls, and in time racing and breeding, based notably in the Blue Grass country of Kentucky, was to become one of the greatest multimillion-dollar industries in the Thoroughbred world.

Initially, Americans followed the British pattern of 4-mile races, but eventually American racing accomplished a U-turn, placing the breeding emphasis on precocity, with two- and three-year-olds sprinting over short distances. The Kentucky Derby, run at Churchill Downs, Louisville, at $1\frac{1}{4}$ miles, is 440 yards shorter than the Epsom prototype. The United States, having bought carefully, still produces middle-distance horses and a lot of American-bred Thoroughbreds have done exceptionally well in the European Classics.

The legendary Man O'War is still considered America's greatest racehorse, despite the more recent records of sires like Bold Ruler, who topped the sire-rating list between 1963 and 1969 and again in 1973; and horses of the caliber of Secretariat, winner of America's Triple Crown in 1973, Seattle Slew who won it in 1977, and Affirmed, the 1978 winner. The

resemblance to Britain's "winter game" (in terms of the kind of obstacles jumped) is the Czechoslovakian Gran Pardubice Steeplechase. It is run over four miles but is really more like a cross-country race, for it includes numerous and formidable natural obstacles.

America's big jumping race is the Maryland Hunt Cup, but this is over post and rail fences and held in open country without benefit of grandstands.

The first recorded match, and there have been many similar ones in the sporting annals of Britain and Ireland, took place in the latter country in 1752 when Messrs O'Callaghan and Blake settled a difference of opinion regarding the respective merits of their hunters by racing over the $4\frac{1}{2}$ miles separating Buttevant Church from St Leger Church — from steeple to steeple, hence "steeplechase."

The most famous of all the English chases is the Grand National, first run in 1837 and held in March at Aintree, Liverpool, over a distance of 4 miles 856 yards (7.22 km) and 30 big and stout fences.

Just as Newmarket is the center of British flat-racing so Cheltenham holds the same position for steeplechasing. The most prestigious of the season's events, the Gold Cup (instituted in 1924) is staged there, as well as the Champion Hurdle, first run in 1927, the Champion Chase and a whole bunch of top-class races.

Steeplechasing in the United States does not have the same enormous following it has in Britain and Ireland. Even so, it too has its Triple Crown: the Grand National, the Temple Gwathmey and the Colonial Cup.

ABOVE Churchill Downs, home of the famous Kentucky Derby.

RIGHT The Chair, one of the English Grand National fences.

superb Man O'War, whose statue surmounts his grave at Lexington, Kentucky, appears in the pedigrees of a host of winners, including the English Derby victors Never Say Die, Sir Ivor and Relko.

The American Classics are the Kentucky Derby, the Preakness Stakes, the Belmont Stakes and the Coaching Club American Oaks. The Triple Crown comprises the first three of these.

Although steeplechasing takes place in Europe and America, its spiritual home is in Britain and Ireland where it attracts a large and enthusiastic following.

The only race bearing some

HARNESS RACING

Harness racing, or trotting, is the second most popular sport in the United States next to Thoroughbred racing. It attracts a following of about 30 million, a figure considerably in excess of that estimated for football.

In Italy, more trotting horses are bred than Thoroughbreds. The sport is well established and popular in France where the French Trotter has been developed to a point where it can take on and sometimes beat the world's top harness-racing horse, the Standardbred. In many European countries trotting attracts more spectators than Thoroughbred racing, and in Russia this is certainly so.

The Russian Trotter (the result of crossing between the purpose-bred Orlov trotter and the Ameri-

can Standardbred) is raced outside the country of its origin with great success and appears in strength in Sweden, Norway and West Germany, all trotting countries, as well as in countries of the Eastern bloc where the sport is carried on.

In New Zealand, trotting is recognized as a national pastime and it falls little short of this standing in Australia. In fact, the Southern Hemisphere produced one of the great champions of the sport, the gelding Cardigan Bay, foaled at the Mataura Stud, Southland, New Zealand, in 1956. He was the winner of 80 races in New Zealand, Australia and America, the holder of two world records, the first Standardbred to win a million dollars and the only one whose return to his native New

Zealand was marked by the issue of a commemorative stamp.

The Standardbred traces back to the English Thoroughbred Messenger, exported from England to Philadelphia in 1788. Additionally the blood of the Norfolk Trotter is a significant factor in both the American Standardbred and the French Trotter. And although that is by no means insignificant, it is nearly the sum total of British involvement in the harness sport. Trotting takes place on a minor scale in Britain in North Wales, the Midlands and Lancashire and at grass tracks elsewhere, but is not included in the national horse disciplines, nor is it ever given press coverage.

A possible reason why trotting is almost completely ignored in

Britain is that at the time when Americans were concerned with the development of an early trotting horse, the English, particularly members of the landowning squirearchy and nobility, for whom the "Sport of Kings" represented the equestrian ideal, were far too preoccupied with the development of the Thoroughbred race horse to be concerned with an activity which was outside their traditional sporting interests.

The modern Standardbred goes either in the conventional diagonal trot or at the pace. At the pace, the right foreleg moves simultaneously with the right hind and is then joined by the opposite lateral pair.

Initially in the United States, which is regarded as the world's

A trotting race on a snow-covered track at St Moritz, Switzerland.

leading nation in the sport of harness racing, pacing was the less popular gait, but today the pacers outnumber trotters by four to one. In Europe, too, pacers are increasingly evident but conventional trotters still retain a numerical supremacy. (Trotters and pacers never race against each other.)

The reason why pacers are so much preferred in the States, where heavy betting is a feature of the sport, is that their action, assisted by hobbles, is less prone to "break" than that of a trotter. Any horse that breaks the pace and gallops in a race must move to the outside and lose ground. When that happens it is virtually impossible for the horse to win.

It is also easier to train and drive the slightly faster pacer with the assistance of those gait-inducing hobbles. Harness men, whichever gait they are concerned with, are far more involved in the niceties of shoeing, bitting and so on than the average horseman, but to balance the action of a trotter precisely demands a greater degree of expertise.

The original "standard" for the mile, the distance over which harness races have always been run, was a flat 3 minutes and the first horse to improve on that time was Yankee, who trotted the distance in 2:59 on June 11, 1806. He

was followed by a succession of mostly female champions. One of the most famous in the annals of the sport was Lady Suffolk, who trotted the mile in 2:29½ in 1845 when she had already trotted the distance under saddle in 2:26.

In the early contests ridden races were commonplace, probably because the vehicles of the day were of the strong, and therefore heavy-duty sort. As a result the ridden races were faster. Modern trotters race in lightweight two-wheeled "sulkies" which weigh in the region of 30 to 40 pounds. Trotting races under saddle are no longer held in the United States; the only country still staging them to any extent is France and the races are held to encourage an aspect of a deliberate breeding policy.

Pacers began to make their mark in the mid-1800s. Aggie Down, a mare, broke the existing record with a paced mile of 2:29 in 1844 and another mare, Pocahantas, brought the standard down to 2:17½ in 1855. Thereafter, however, pacing, unlike trotting, has been dominated by the males and the standard time has been lowered consistently.

In 1897, Star Pointer returned the remarkable time of 1:59¼, and after him, at the turn of the century, came the Midwest horse who captured the imagination not

just of the trotting world but also of the whole American nation. He was Dan Patch, whose record of 1:55¼ stood for 33 years until it was broken by Billy Direct in 1938.

Dan Patch became a celebrity in a way that would probably not be possible outside America. All sorts of products were named after him, from cigars to washing machines, and baking soda to children's toys. Even children were given his name, and a dance, a railroad and buildings were also named after him.

The fastest trotting horse of all time, Prakas, went the mile against the clock in 1:53⅖ in 1985. The fastest pacer, Niatross, won $2,000,000 in two seasons' racing and in 1980 broke the record with a stunning 1:52⅕ and time-trialed at an unbelievable 1:49⅕.

Night racing, now a feature of the sport, was introduced at the opening of Roosevelt Raceway on Long Island, New York, in 1940, and it was there that the mobile starting gate made its first appearance and solved forever the problem of starting the field in a perfect line.

The starting gate, invented by the Ohio horseman Steven Phillips, comprises a set of retractable wings mounted on an ordinary truck. The horses are led up to the starting point by the vehicle,

In trotting (above), the horse's gait is a diagonal trot. In pacing it is a lateral trot.

which then accelerates and pulls off the track.

Despite Roosevelt's popularity, it is the Meadowlands which is regarded as America's leading raceway. An oval mile in East Rutherford, New Jersey, it was opened in 1976 and stages the world's most valuable harness races, heading the list with the $2,000,000 Woodrow Wilson Pace and $1,000,000 Hambletonian Trot. (On a 10-race card at the Meadowlands there is a minimum of eight pacing races, and the same practice is followed at the other 50-odd raceways throughout the country.)

Like flat racing, the harness sport has its own Triple Crowns, one for trotters and one for pacers. The trotting Triple Crown, which began in 1955, comprises the Hambletonian (Meadowlands), the Yonkers Trot (Yonkers Raceway, New York) and the Kentucky Futurity (Lexington's Red Mile).

The pacing Triple Crown, inaugurated a year later in 1956, consists of the Cane Futurity (Yonkers), the Little Brown Jug (Delaware, Ohio, County Fair) and the Messenger Stakes (Roosevelt Raceway).

COMPETITIVE DRIVING

The sport of Combined Driving owes its existence largely to the efforts of the Duke of Edinburgh who, when he was President of the International Equestrian Federation (FEI), attended the 1968 International Horse Show at Aachen, West Germany, and was most impressed by the competition in which teams of four horses were driven around a course of obstacles. The Secretary-General of the Polish Equestrian Federation suggested that international competitions of this type should be planned, and the Duke not only made arrangements for this immediately – the first international event taking place in 1970 – but determined to take up this sport himself.

The format of combined driving is based on that of the three-day event, with one extra phase – Presentation. In this phase, Competition AI, marks are awarded for the following:

1. Driver, groom and passengers: Position, dress, hat, gloves, holding whip and handling of horses
2. Horses: Condition, turnout, cleanliness, matching and condition of shoeing
3. Harness: Condition, proper fit and cleanliness
4. Vehicle: Condition, cleanliness, height of pole and spare equipment
5. General impression of the whole turnout.

The Dressage, Competition AII, aims to test the freedom, regularity of paces, harmony, lightness, ease of movement, impulsion and correct positioning of the horse(s). Judges also look at the competitors' style of driving, accuracy and general command of the horse(s).

The arena for a single horse or a pair is usually 80 × 40 meters (88 × 44 yards), and that for teams and tandems 100 × 40 meters (109 × 44 yards) with marker letters set up as for ridden dressage. The test takes 8 minutes in the smaller arena and 10 minutes in the larger. There are usually three judges (five at the more important championships) and they sit at various points around the arena so that all movements can be closely scrutinized.

The tests are made up of a combination of movements, which are of course more limited than in ridden dressage. These movements are the walk, the trot, turns and circles, and the reinback.

Competition B is the Marathon, the counterpart of the speed and stamina phase of ridden events. It tests the fitness and stamina of the horse and the judgment of pace and horsemanship of the competitor. A full Marathon of five sections is 27 km (17 miles) long, and consists of:

Section A: 10 km (6 miles) at the trot at 15 km/h (9 mph)
Section B: 1200 meters (1300 yards) at the walk at 7 km/h ($4\frac{1}{4}$ mph)
Section C: 5 km (3 miles) at the fast trot at 20 km/h ($12\frac{1}{2}$ mph)
Section D: as B
Section E: as A

Lower speeds are set for ponies; speeds are maximums and may be reduced by the Technical Delegate if the going is particularly difficult.

There are compulsory halts of 10 minutes after Sections B and D, during which the horses are inspected to see that they are fit to continue.

The three trotting sections always include natural hazards, such as water crossings and narrow gateways, and Section E includes between five and eight specially-constructed (and very solid) obstacles. Penalties are awarded in each section if a competitor takes longer than the time allowed, for breaks of pace and for the dismounting of a groom. Going through the "gates" of an obstacle in the wrong sequence leads to elimination, as does failure to complete any obstacle

RIGHT A team of Lipizzaners tackle a water crossing.
BELOW Carriage driving enthusiast the Duke of Edinburgh in action at the 1986 World Driving Championships.

within a 5 minute time limit.

The final phase, Competition C, is the Obstacle Competition which, like the show jumping it replaces, tests the fitness, obedience and suppleness of the horses after the Marathon, and also the skill and competence of the drivers.

The horses are driven around a tightly twisting course between pairs of plastic cones with balls set on top, which are only slightly farther apart than the carriage wheels. The course is between 500 and 800 meters long (550 to 875 yards), and besides the simple pairs of cones it may include a water splash, a low bridge, a serpentine, U-turns or L-turns, and there are exact specifications covering the number and measurements of obstacles and the distances between them.

Penalties are awarded for balls dislodged, for stopping, stepping back or circling before an obstacle, for grooms dismounting, for refusals and for exceeding the allowed time.

Many local clubs have been set up to organize similar events at a lower (and less expensive) level and for them there are various alternatives to a full-blown driving trial. Many one-day and two-day events are held, which include all phases, but the five-section Marathon may be reduced to three sections or even to one, which will in that case usually be longer than 10 km (6 miles) and will include the specially-built obstacles.

The Obstacle Competition can also be held on its own, even at national and international levels, and this is known as "scurry driving." This competition can be easily set up at very little cost, and is a spectacular display of driving skill enjoyed by drivers and spectators alike. Clubs often arrange other driving competitions, mainly lighthearted and less competitive.

For the simple competitions at club level, any experienced driver with a fairly fit horse or pony can take part with little expense or preparation, the only slight problem being that the Marathon, and to a lesser extent the Obstacle Competition, don't do an elegant vehicle much good. So if you have only one vehicle, and it's elegant or expensive, get an exercise vehicle for the tougher sections.

The trotting sections always include hazards such as water crossings and gates.

WESTERN RIDING EVENTS

Showing in Western classes gives the competitor considerably more scope to show his riding and horsemanship abilities than in conventional English showing. The classes vary in content, but there is far greater emphasis on performance and correct training than on the conformation of the horse. Thus Western riding may appeal to many who own well-schooled riding horses which would have no chance of winning in an English style show class.

The classic Western mount is the Quarter Horse, and it does have the ideal requirements for the job. It is compact and well muscled, particularly in the hindquarters, with a strong back, good bone and a forward-going yet amenable temperament. However, almost any horse can be trained to perform satisfactorily in the basic pleasure, trail and riding classes. There are also showmanship classes, where the judging is based purely on the handler's ability to produce and show a horse in hand, and not on the merits of the horse, while horsemanship classes are judged on the competitor's riding ability and he may be asked to change mounts with other competitors.

However, it is perhaps the novice pleasure class which is of the greatest interest to the beginner in Western showing. The movements required in this class are simple – changes of lead at the walk, jog and lope, all on a reasonably loose rein, and a stop and a reinback. Horses may also be asked to extend the jog. The jog and lope are the acquired gaits of the Western trained horse, adapted from the trot and canter. The jog is a smooth, rhythmic, two-beat diagonal gait, with the horse on a loose rein but in a collected outline. The pace is slow and controlled, but active, with the hindquarters engaged and the horse balanced, so that it appears to float over the ground.

The lope is an easy canter, with the horse in a lower outline than for English riding. The three-beat gait must be maintained and performed in a rhythmic and smooth manner. The stride should be natural and relaxed and the speed appropriate to the horse, his level of training and the work he is being asked to do.

The Western horse's head carriage should be relatively low and never forced, but he must stay balanced and active, rounding his back and bringing his hocks well underneath his body.

Novice pleasure classes may be ridden two-handed in a snaffle or hackamore or one-handed in a curb bit, depending upon the horse's level of training. There are two types of bridle reins, each carried differently in one-handed riding. Romal reins are closed reins with an extension, or romal. The rein is carried from the horse's mouth through the bottom of the hand and over the top, with the thumb uppermost, the romal being carried in the free hand. Texas split reins should be carried with the reins passing through the top of the hand, the free end hanging down on the same side as the rein hand.

There are also pleasure class categories for junior and senior horses and youth riders. The class is judged on the performance and conformation of the horse, with

faults given for errors such as changing hands on the reins or holding them incorrectly; being on the wrong lead; excessive speed or excessive slowness at any gait; breaking gait; failure to take a required gait; touching the horse or saddle with the free hand; a head carriage that is too high or too low; the horse's nose going in front of or behind the vertical; the horse opening his mouth, stumbling or falling; and using the spurs or romal forward of the cinch.

The requirements of a pleasure horse are that it should give a smooth, relaxed and comfortable ride, while remaining alert and responding easily and quickly to its rider's commands.

The next major category of Western showing is the trail class, again reflecting the various levels

ABOVE The spectacular sliding stop.
RIGHT When working a cow, the rider must be able to anticipate the horse's movements.

of training. The aim is to show a competent trail horse, and the class is judged on the horse's performance over various obstacles, with emphasis on good manners, responsiveness and attitude. Good style and a degree of speed are desirable, but must not be at the expense of accuracy. Horses must work at all three gaits in covering the course.

Three mandatory obstacles are included. First, the rider must open, pass through and close a gate. He must not change hands on the gate or let go of the gate until the exercise is completed. Second, he must ride over at least four logs or poles, which may be in a straight line, curved, zigzagged, or raised. Third, he must perform a reinback exercise, either through an "L" shape, or around markers.

There will also be three optional obstacles which may include a water hazard; hobbling or ground tying the horse; carrying an object from one part of the arena to another; riding over a wooden bridge; putting on and taking off a rain slicker; removing and replacing items from a mailbox; a side pass which may be over an obstacle; and a 360-degree turn inside a measured square. Two attempts at each obstacle are allowed, with penalties being given for refusals.

The reins must be held in only one hand and must not be changed over, except when necessary to negotiate an obstacle, and the rider's hands must be clear of the horse and saddle.

Marks in the trail class will be awarded for the horse's willingness to accept the obstacles, while approaching them with care; the horse's expression — it should lower its head to look at obstacles on the ground as it negotiates them; light rein contact; obedience; smooth paces; overall per-

formance. Penalties will be incurred for stepping out of obstacles; lack of caution; obvious aids to encourage the horse to look at the obstacles; knocking or touching obstacles; double stepping or overstepping when negotiating obstacles on the ground; and leaving a wide opening when going through a gate, which on the trail might allow stock to escape.

Related to the trail class is the Western riding class, which, however has the emphasis on straight riding rather than on handiness. The aim in this class is to show a smooth, calm ranch horse who is sensible, well mannered, free and easy moving and giving its rider a comfortable and pleasant ride. The class follows a set pattern, including a gate and a small log, with the first part ridden in the walk, a second short section in the jog and the remainder in the lope. Reasonable speed is expected and depending upon the level of the class, there are either simple or flying changes of lead. Finally, there is a stop and reinback. Judging is on the quality of the gaits and lead changes and the horse's manners, disposition and response to the rider.

The epitome of Western riding is the reining class, best compared

with English riding as a variation of dressage, but performed at speed. As an introduction to reining there are arena test classes, which at the lower level may be ridden two-handed in a snaffle or hackamore, but at the next stage must be ridden single-handed, with a curb bit.

The arena tests take the form of a dressage test, with set movements showing the three gaits and including rollbacks — 180-degree turns on the haunches — and progressing at the higher level to 360-degree spins, best described as very fast, flat pirouettes. The test, or pattern, must be ridden accurately, halts must be square, with the horse's hocks underneath it and pivots and spins must be performed with the inside hind leg moving as little as possible from the central spot.

The fully trained reining horse is an equine athlete *par excellence*, performing circles, rollbacks, reinbacks, flying changes, spins and sliding stops at incredible, breathtaking speed, yet with apparently effortless ease, its body balanced over its four legs, without using its head and neck as an extra "prop," its rider upright, but relaxed in the saddle, the reins held lightly in one hand — the

horse and rider forming two components of a completely harmonious whole.

To achieve such a level of horsemanship takes patience and careful, progressive training, never asking more of the horse than it is capable of giving and never allowing a situation to develop where the horse becomes frightened or resistant. Since minimum rein contact is used, speed must be controlled by body position and direction mainly by leg aids.

A number of different patterns are used and scoring is based on the correctness of the maneuvers including straight, controlled "run downs;" size and speed of the circles; fluidity of movement of the horse; accuracy; minimum contact between horse and rider and correct lead changes. Spins should be executed without resistance and at the same controlled speed in both directions, the pivoting foot remaining planted in position. Rollback turns should be flat, without resistance from the horse, stops should be smooth and straight without excessive contact, and in the reinback lightness of contact should be maintained. The horse should show a relaxed attitude at speed.

The sliding stop is one of the most spectacular movements in the Western reining class and it is developed progressively through training, starting from the walk. In a correct sliding stop the front legs continue to move normally, with the shoulders elevated, while the hind legs come underneath the horse, as it drops its hindquarters down and slides. Collection and controlled movement are essential for a correct stop and special shoes or "sliding plates" enable the horse to slide more easily, while a well-prepared ground surface is an essential safety requirement for training.

Finally, there are the cutting and working cow horse classes, developed, of course, from the cowboy's ranch work with cattle and the need for the horse to be able to separate any particular animal from the herd. Much of the ability to work cattle seems to be bred into the horses who excel at these sports and experts maintain that a good cow horse will 'work anything that moves'. When working a cow, the horse moves at lightning speed, turning low to the ground, and the rider must be fit, supple and able to anticipate the movement of the cow as does the horse, in order to avoid being left behind the movement or jarring his back and neck.

POLO

Just when the first game of polo was played is unclear; it was certainly played in Persia as much as 2500 years ago. There is indeed much pictorial and other evidence of its being played there and in neighboring areas, and by both men and women, as in ancient China. In the Persian tongue the game was called *changar*, meaning mallet, but the word *polo* itself derives from the Tibetan word *pulu* – a ball.

Without doubt it was an Eastern game of great antiquity and one that assumed varying forms according to the area in which it was played.

The first Western contact with the game was made by British soldiers and civilians serving in India in the 19th century. They learned it from the people of Manipur, that small mountainous state which is squeezed between Assam and Burma. The Manipuris copied and perhaps adapted the game from their northern neighbors the Tibetans, and used the Tibetan word *pulu* as well as their own name, *Kán-jāi-bazèè*.

In Manipur it was the national game, with villages and groups of villages having their own teams. In 1854, the British were establishing tea plantations in Manipur's Cachar valley and the first European polo club was formed there in 1859, after the Indian Mutiny, by Lt Joseph Sherer of the Bengal Army and Capt Robert Stewart, the Superintendent of Cachar. Sherer, later Major-General Sherer, became known as the "Father of Modern Polo" and he and his friends encouraged the formation of clubs elsewhere in the subcontinent. By 1870, the game was being played throughout British India at every station and cantonment.

The Indian example inspired the adoption of the game in Britain, and the first tentative game of "Hockey on Horseback" was played by the 10th Hussars at Aldershot in 1869. The first "inter-regimental" between the 10th and their friends of the 9th Lancers took place later in the year at Hounslow with eight players on each side. This marked the beginning of polo in the Western world and it was to develop in England

into a highly fashionable game which quickly became integral to the "London Season."

An early and lasting influence on polo was the Anglo-Irish cavalry officer, John Watson. He applied himself so assiduously to improving the tactics, style and technique of the game that he has been dubbed the "Father of *English* Polo." It was Watson who first perfected the backhand stroke which was to do so much to speed up the game.

Polo was first played in America in 1878, following the visit to Hurlingham in 1876 by James Gordon Bennett, the newspaper tycoon who became, in the words of the historian of American polo, Newell Bent, "one of the best and most liberal patrons of the sport our country has ever known." Four years later, a group of Long Island enthusiasts formed the legendary Meadow Brook Club, which became the headquarters of American polo in the same way as Hurlingham filled that position in Britain.

The initial match for the Anglo-American Westchester Trophy, the top prize of the game, took place in 1886 and was won by the British team captained by Watson, and by then the number of players forming a team had been reduced to four.

America did not win the Westchester until 1909 when its team, under Harry Payne Whitney, defeated the English on their home ground. Thereafter, supremacy in the Westchester began to pass inexorably to the well-drilled and superbly mounted American teams. The competition was discontinued in 1939 at the outbreak of World War II in Europe, but has since been revived in the shape of the Coronation Cup, which since 1971 has been competed for annually in England at either Windsor Park or at Cowdray.

There is no doubt, however, that the leading polo nation of the world since the 1930s has been Argentina, where ponies and men play the game as part of a way of life. Polo was introduced to that country and first played there in 1877 by Englishmen, who were responsible for the formation of the numerous clubs.

The Argentinians are natural ballgame players as well as horsemen (qualities which do not always go together; many very good polo players are not very good horsemen, while the opposite is also true), while the Argentine ponies, the result of a Thoroughbred cross with the handy little Criollo, are second to none.

The ponies first used by the British in India, and for some time after the game was established in England, were real ponies, no bigger than perhaps 13.2 hands, while those early Manipuri ponies were often no more than 12.2 hands.

In 1899 the English brought in a height limit of 14.2 hands, and because of the availability in Britain of good-quality ponies of this size they virtually cornered the market. The rule was abolished (largely by the Americans) in 1916, and the average height of ponies increased to 15—15.3 hands. Although small horses in reality, polo ponies, whatever their height, are called "ponies."

The American handicapping system was universally adopted in 1909, players being graded from −2 to +10 goals. "High goal" polo is when the team

Prince Charles (no. 3) playing in a match at Windsor Park, one of England's top polo grounds.

aggregate handicap is around 19 and upward — a medium-goal competition would involve aggregates of from 15 to 18.

Polo, which is played almost entirely at the gallop, is the fastest game in the world and one in which it is difficult to excel. Played with teams of four the object, in simple terms, is to score more goals than one's opponents, and that involves hitting the 3-inch diameter willow ball with a bamboo mallet, through 10 foot-high goalposts placed 24 feet apart.

The ground, usually enclosed by low boards, is on grass and measures 300 yards by 200 yards. There is a white line across the center of the ground and penalty lines at 30, 40 and 60 yards from each back line. A match lasts something under an hour and is divided into *chukkers* of seven-and-a-half minutes duration. At the big high-goal tournaments the match is divided into five or six chukkers, at smaller events into four. Ponies are changed after each chukker and no pony plays more than two chukkers in a match.

The four players are numbered 1 and 2 (the forwards), 3, and 4 (the Back). Number 1 marks the opposing Back and in attack tries to hold off the latter and create an opportunity for his number 2 to score. Number 2 is the "striker," the principal goal-scorer, while number 3 is the pivot of the team, a position often taken by the captain who can best control the run of play from that position. Number 4, the Back, marks the opposing number 1, hits the ball through to his number 2 and must be a reliable, strong hitter in defense and particularly effective with his backhand play. The opposing numbers 2 and 3 mark each other.

There is no offsides rule in polo, but stiff and immediate penalties (free hits) are given for infringements such as crossing another player's right of way, for deliberate bumping, zigzagging or improper use of the stick.

When a goal is scored teams change ends. When the ball goes over the sideline another is thrown in by an umpire (there are two of them) between the lined-up teams. When the ball crosses the back line it is formally hit in by the defenders. If a defender knocks a ball over his own back line the opposing side is awarded a free hit at goal 60 yards in from the point where it crossed the line.

HUNTING & POINT-TO-POINT RACING

Hunting in Britain, a country in which the sport is carried on more extensively than anywhere else in the world, has been practiced since the Norman Conquest in the 11th century. Indeed, its beginnings belong firmly to *la vénerie française* and the deep-tongued Gascon, Talbot and St Hubert hounds. The traditional quarry of the hunt 800 years ago were the stag, the boar and the hare. It was only towards the end of the 17th century that the English began to hunt the fox, which though classed as vermin ran straighter and stronger than the hare, and because its scent was not as powerful as that of the stag presented a greater challenge to the huntsman and hounds.

Within a hundred years fox hunting flourished as no other sport in England. To begin with, hunting the fox, in common with other forms of hunting, was a very slow business. Hounds were bred more for their tongue and scenting prowess than for speed, and before the enclosures of farm land there was little opportunity to jump, even had those early sportsmen been so inclined.

By the second half of the 18th century, matters had changed. Hugo Meynell was hunting the Quorn in 1753 with young thrusters pressing his hounds and testing his temper, the Earl of Yarborough at Brocklesby was breeding an English hound that combined speed with stamina and nose, and the land was becoming enclosed with every sort of fence. Horses were faster, too, because of the increasing influence of the Thoroughbred, and there was no shortage of young bloods willing to ride against their peers and risk their necks over the big fences of

the English Shires.

Initially, packs of foxhounds were kept privately at the expense of the great landlords, men like the Dukes of Beaufort and Grafton and the Earls of Berkeley, all of whom hunted vast areas of the country. As the sport developed, however, subscriptions were increasingly taken from followers to defray costs.

The Golden Age of British fox hunting is looked upon as being that period between 1820 and 1890. The great estates were still intact; there were no cars or super highways and none of the fumes concomitant with the internal combustion engine; there was no wire in the fences and artificial fertilizers were unknown.

But even in those halcyon days hunting could feel itself threatened. The Industrial Revolution brought with it the canals and railways that were necessary to shift the produce of England's "dark, Satanic mills," and many thought the steam train was sounding the death knell for the sport. In fact, the railways did just the opposite, opening up the country and making meets accessible as they had never been before.

Few thought that the sport would survive a World War, let alone two within the space of a quarter of a century. That it did so is proof of its strength as a traditional part of country life.

In Britain today, and in Ireland, hunting has more participants than any other horse sport. Upward of half a million people hunt during the season (November–April), 50,000 of them turning out each week, and a sizable industry revolves around the activities of nearly 400 packs of hounds. The

Pony Club, founded in 1929, was based on the hunt countries and the majority of branches carry the name of the local hunt and maintain close associations with it.

In many ways, hunting remains the bastion of British equestrianism and certainly is directly responsible for the increasingly popular sport of point-to-point racing. Every hunt holds its own point-to-point meeting for horses that have been "regularly and fairly hunted" and these properly organized race meetings provide a very considerable source of revenue for hunt funds.

Originally, the point-to-point was just that – a headlong gallop across country, from point to point, over natural fences. Today's point-to-points are held over properly built steeplechase

ABOVE A huntsman in traditional scarlet hunting coat, top hat and white breeches.
RIGHT Point-to-point racing is an increasingly popular amateur sport in Britain.

fences and courses of some three miles in length. The horses competing are Thoroughbred and there is really no room for the old sort of halfbred hunter, but the riders are decidedly amateur and must be members of a recognized hunt (one recognized by hunting's governing body, the Masters of Foxhounds Association). Racing, nonetheless, takes place under the control of the Jockey Club.

The English point-to-point classics are the Lady Dudley Cup at the Worcestershire point-to-point, which can be regarded as

the sport's equivalent of Cheltenham's Gold Cup; the Ralph Grimthorpe Gold Cup over $4\frac{1}{2}$ miles at the Middleton meeting in Yorkshire, which is on a par with the Grand National; and the four-mile Heythrop race, the Lord Ashton of Hyde Cup.

The great thing about the point-to-point, now open to riders of both sexes, is the two-way traffic between the amateur sport and professional racing over fences. At the one end there are the young hopefuls making their way from the preparatory Hunt point-to-point to National Hunt racing proper; at the other the

LEFT The Quorn Hunt, one of the oldest in Britain.

former steeplechasers and ex-hurdlers who came down to the point-to-point race via the hunting field.

The US is enthusiastic about hunting, the American Masters of Foxhounds Association being affiliated with its British counterpart in 1914, but point-to-point racing hasn't developed the same way.

American hunting originated in the richly historical states of Virginia, Maryland and Pennsylvania, where the early colonists were quick to establish the sport and style of the English squirearchy.

Thomas, the sixth Lord Fairfax, went to Virginia in 1747 and was probably the first to own a pack of hounds in a country which abounded with deer and gray foxes, and George Washington was another keen hunting man who kept his own hounds. The gray fox, predominant in America, is not as straight-running as the red English fox, which seems to have been imported early in American history and established in the area of Chesapeake Bay. Most eastern states have a population of red foxes but the gray, despite a regrettable tendency to run in circles and climb trees, provides good sport elsewhere.

Middleburg, Virginia, 50 miles from Washington DC, is the Melton Mowbray of American hunting and the Red Fox Inn there dates from 1728, so it can be said that American hunting is nearly as old as the English tradition. Hunting, with either the red or the gray fox as the quarry (or, in the West, the coyote), is widespread and varied in its form but it is a popular sport and there are about 150 packs in the United States.

The organization of a hunt is similar in England, Ireland and the US. There is a Master (or Joint-Masters) who arranges and controls the Hunt activities and who employs hunt servants who look after the hounds in kennel and hunt the pack in the field. The hunt servants are the Huntsman, or Kennel-huntsman if the Master hunts his own hounds, and his assistants the whippers-in. Only the Huntsman carries and blows the hunting horn with which communication is maintained with the hounds and the members of the field.

Masters, hunt servants and members who are invited to wear the Hunt button turn out in the traditional color of the hunting field which, with the exception of some packs, is scarlet.

ENDURANCE RIDING

Endurance riding is the main competitive branch of long distance equestrian sport and is becoming increasingly popular throughout the world. The main difference between endurance riding and its sister sport, competitive trail riding, is that endurance rides are always races, the winner being the first horse past the finish line, and which also passes all the veterinary judging. In competitive trail rides participants aim for a set standard, for example 30 miles at a speed of between 7 and 8 mph.

Endurance rides may be any distance from 25 miles to 100 miles in one day. Some rides are divided, to cover 100 miles over two or more days, in which case the winner is the horse with the fastest average time. If you are unfamiliar with the sport, you may be surprised that horses can cover these distances in a racing situation, with speeds of over 10 mph regularly recorded in one-day 100-mile rides. However, before the age of the internal combustion engine, horses were accustomed to working far harder than we expect of them today and a properly trained and fit horse is

capable not only of completing such distances at speed, but also of passing the final veterinary judging with flying colors and maybe winning the coveted Best Condition award.

Veterinary inspections are an integral part of the sport of endurance riding and every year the pool of knowledge of managing and caring for endurance horses is being extended. Inspections take place before, during and after rides and failure to pass the inspection means elimination.

To pass a veterinary inspection during or after a ride, the horse's pulse rate must be below 64 beats per minute within 30 minutes of arriving at the inspection point or the finish. Lameness also means elimination. The important criterion in all situations is that in the veterinarian's opinion the horse is "fit to continue." A badly bruised mouth, girth or saddle sores, or excessive dehydration may all be reasons for elimination. There will often be spot checks on the route in addition to the official inspections.

It is this strict veterinary surveillance which has raised the

sport to its current high standards of horsemanship, and everything possible is done to assure the safety and well-being of the horses, with the result that the sport has fewer casualties than any comparable equestrian activity.

The United States is the home of endurance riding and of the world's toughest ride, the Tevis Cup (also called the Western States Trail Ride). Founded in 1954 by Wendell T Robie, the Tevis covers 100 miles of trails once used by Pony Express riders through the Sierra Nevada Mountains in California. There might be snow on the mountains above Lake Tahoe near the start of the ride, while by midday in the deep canyons the temperature can rise to as much as 120°F. The Tevis Cup, named after a President of Wells Fargo, goes to the winner, while the reward for those further down the list who complete the distance is a buckle embossed with a Pony Express horse and rider.

The International Equestrian Federation (FEI) took an interest in the sport in the early 1980s and in

Endurance riding is a sport for experienced riders and fit horses with plenty of stamina. Veterinary inspections ensure the well-being of the horses.

1985 the first official European Championships were run at Rosenau in Austria, followed by the first World Championships in Rome in 1986. Endurance riding is now firmly entrenched as the fourth equestrian discipline.

From 1979, European rides were organized under the auspices of the European Long Distance Rides Conference (ELDRIC), with a trophy awarded each year, based on a points system, for rides completed in more than one country. ELDRIC remains a powerful influence in international endurance riding and works closely with the FEI to further the interests of the sport.

Endurance riding has almost as strong a history in Australia as in America, the Tom Quilty being the premier Australian ride. In Britain the Golden Horseshoe (which is not a race and therefore not technically an endurance ride) began in 1964. Since then, Great

on with the job. A horse which is unwilling at the start will never give you that little bit extra that gets you home in time at the finish. A horse which is sociable, and likes human company, is preferable to one that would rather keep itself apart. Purebred or partbred Arabian horses are often the preferred choice of experienced endurance riders, as well-bred specimens should possess all these qualities.

Getting your horse fit for endurance riding is an entire subject in itself. It must be healthy when you start – its feet must be trimmed and well shod, its teeth must be checked and it should be wormed regularly. It should live out as much as possible to avoid the common equine susceptibility to dust allergies. Its food must be of good quality and, since you will be working it hard, a multiple vitamin and mineral supplement might be advisable.

Your training program will depend upon what level of ride you are aiming for and the golden rule is to build up gradually. It takes two to three months to prepare a normally fit riding horse for a competitive ride of 40 miles. This should be adjusted progressively as you aim for higher speeds and distances. Top endurance riders say that it takes three seasons of steady competition for a horse to reach top level 100-mile racing condition. Once fit, the horse needs only to be kept in condition between competitions, but no horse should be asked to tackle more than two or three major rides in one season. At the end of the season, turn your horse out for a couple of months – by then it will need a good break to offset the intensity of its work.

Britain has played a major role in the sport, winning the ELDRIC Trophy six times, plus medals at several championships and running two or three one-day, 100-mile rides each year.

If you decide to take up endurance riding you will certainly make many friends and find much help and companionship in the sport. You will also get to know your horse better than you ever thought possible.

What kind of horse do you need? Obviously, one that can cover the ground well, but does not carry too much bodyweight, is essential. It must have strong, sound limbs, plenty of heartroom and stamina and the kind of well-proportioned conformation that lends itself to good natural balance. It must also have a good temperament and be eager to get

GLOSSARY

A

Aids The means by which the rider gives instructions to the horse. The natural aids are the body, hands, legs and voice, and the artificial aids include whips and spurs.

Air Also called 'air above the ground': a High School movement in which the horse's forelegs, or fore and hind legs, are lifted clear of the ground.

Albino A horse with unpigmented, pure white hair, pale skin and pale eyes. The albino is a color type, not a breed.

Alter To geld a stallion.

Amble A slow, two-time gait. The horse's hind and foreleg of the same side move forward together.

Ambler Obsolete term for a pacer.

Ass Either of two members of the horse family, the African wild ass (*Equus asinus*) or the Asiatic wild ass (*Equus hemionus*); another name for the donkey (see also Donkey, Hinny, Kiang, Mule, Onager).

Atlas The first vertebra of a horse's neck.

Axis The second vertebra of a horse's neck.

B

Back The part of a horse's body, between the withers and the loins, on which the saddle is fitted; to make a horse carry the weight of a rider for the first time; to move a horse backward; to place a bet on a horse.

Ballotade A High School air. The horse half rears then jumps forward, bringing its hind legs up below its quarters before landing on all four legs.

Bareback riding Riding without using a saddle or blanket.

Barrel The part of a horse's body between its forearms and its loins.

Bit A metal or rubber device attached to the bridle and placed in the horse's mouth so that it can be controlled by means of the reins.

Bitless bridle A bridle used without a bit. With a bitless bridle, the reins control the horse by pressure on the nose and curb groove, instead of by pressure on the mouth as is the case when a bit is used.

Blacksmith A craftsman who works with iron; a popular term for a farrier.

Blinkers A pair of leather eyeshields positioned to prevent the horse from looking anywhere except directly ahead.

Bloodstock Thoroughbred horses, especially those used for racing and breeding.

Body brush A short-bristled brush used for removing dirt from horse's coat.

Bone The circumference of the foreleg of a horse, measured just below the knee. In a horse described as having good bone, this circumference will be large.

Bran The husks of cereal grains, separated from the flour during milling and used as a feed supplement.

Breaking The initial training of a horse.

Bridle The part of a horse's tack or harness which is fitted over its head.

Bronco A wild or partially tamed horse.

Brood mare A mare kept for breeding.

Browband The part of a bridle which lies across the horse's forehead, below and in front of its ears.

C

Calf roping A rodeo event in which the rider ropes a calf, then dismounts and ties it.

Cannon bone The shin bone of a horse, the bone between the knee and the fetlock.

Canter A three-time pace in which the horse's hoofs strike the ground in the sequence of either: near hind, near fore/off hind together, then off fore (leading leg); or off hind, off fore/near hind together, then near fore (leading leg).

Capriole A High School air. The horse half rears, then jumps up and forward, kicking its hind legs back before landing on all four legs.

Castor Another name for the chestnut on a horse's leg.

Cavaletti A small jump, usually consisting of a pole mounted on X-shaped supports and used in the basic training of a riding horse.

Cavesson A type of noseband, such as the lunge cavesson worn by the horse for lungeing.

Chaff Green oat straw or meadow hay cut finely and used as a feedstuff.

Cheek piece Either the leather part of the bridle between the bit and the crownpiece, or the side pieces of a bit to which the reins are attached.

Chestnut A small, horny callus on the inner surface of a horses's leg, just above the

knee. Also called a castor.

Clear round In show jumping or cross country competitions, a round which is completed without the competitor incurring jumping or time faults.

Cob A type of horse, not a breed, with short legs and the bone and substance of a heavy hunter. Capable of carrying a rider of substantial weight, the cob has a maximum height of 15.1 hands.

Coldbloods The heavy horses, such as the Shire and the Percheron.

Colic Sharp abdominal pains in horses, caused by flatulence, constipation or other digestive problems. Requires veterinary attention.

Collection Shortening of a horse's pace by light hand contact and steady pressure from the rider's legs. The horse flexes its neck and relaxes its jaw, and brings its hocks well under to maintain its proper balance.

Colt An ungelded male horse under four years old.

Combined Training Competition Another name for horse trials (eventing).

Conformation The physical shape and lines of a horse.

Contact The connection, via the reins, between the rider's hands and the horse's mouth.

Coronet The boundary between the horny part of a horse's hoof and the skin of the pastern.

Corral A pen or enclosure for animals.

Country The area over which a particular hunt may operate.

Country bred A horse or pony that has been bred unselectively, and is usually a crossbreed.

Cowboy (cowgirl) A man (woman) who tends and herds cattle on ranches, working mainly on horseback.

Cow horse The horse used by a cowboy or cowgirl when working cattle. Also called cow pony.

Courbette A High School air. The horse rears up and hops forward on its hind legs.

Crest The part of a horse's neck from which the mane grows.

Crossbreed A horse or pony bred from parents of different breeds.

Croup The region of a horse's back between its loins and its tail.

Croupade A High School air. The horse rears and then jumps

vertically, drawing its hind legs up toward its belly.

Curb bit A type of bit used with a snaffle bit in a double bridle.

Curb chain A metal chain fitted to a curb or Pelham bit and lying in the curb groove of the horse's jaw.

Curb groove The groove, just behind the lower lip, of a horse's lower jaw.

Curry comb A piece of grooming kit used for cleaning the dirt from a body brush.

Cut To geld a male horse; to separate an animal from a herd.

Cutting horse A horse trained for cutting cattle from a herd.

D

Dam The female parent of a foal.

Dandy brush A brush used for removing surface dirt or mud from a horse's coat.

Dock The bony root of a horse's tail; to cut the tail short by cutting through the dock.

Donkey A small, long-eared, domesticated relative of the horse, descended from the African wild ass (*Equus asinus*). (See also Ass, Mule.)

Double bridle A bridle with two bits — a curb and a snaffle — which are attached to two cheek pieces and may be operated independently.

Dressage The art of training horses to perform artistic movements in a perfectly balanced and disciplined manner.

Drover An Australian horseman who herds cattle or sheep.

E

Elbow The joint of a horse's foreleg between the humerus and the forearm.

Enteritis Inflammation of a horse's intestinal lining. It may be caused by bacteria, toxins or fungi contained in moldy or damaged feed.

Equestrian Of or relating to horses and riding; a male rider or performer on horseback.

Equestrienne A female equestrian.

Equine A horse, donkey, ass, mule or zebra; of or relating to the horse.

Equitation The theory and practice of riding and horsemanship.

Ergot The horny outgrowth at the back of a horse's fetlock; a fungal disease of cereals and grasses, especially rye, which is harmful to horses if it contaminates their feed.

Event horse A horse trained to compete in horse trial events.

Extensor A muscle that stretches or extends a limb or other body part (see also Flexor).

F

Farrier A person who makes and fits horseshoes.

Fault In show jumping and horse trials, a penalty incurred by a competitor for any knockdown, refusal or other offense.

Feather Long, often silky hair found on or near the fetlocks of some horse breeds, usually coldbloods.

FEI The Fédération Equestre Internationale (International Equestrian Federation). Based in Brussels, Belgium, the FEI is the international governing body for show jumping, eventing, dressage and carriage driving. All international events in these equestrian sports must comply with the FEI rules.

Fence Any obstacle to be jumped in competitions or races.

Fetlock The lower end of the cannon (shin) bone of a horse's leg; the joint between the cannon and the pastern.

Filly A female horse under four years old.

Flexor A muscle that contracts to bend a joint or limb (see also Extensor).

Foal A young horse less than 12 months old.

Forearm The upper part of a horse's foreleg, between the elbow and the knee.

Forchand The part of a horse that is in front of its rider: the head, neck, shoulders, withers and forelegs.

Forelegs The front legs of a horse.

Forelock The part of a horse's mane that grows forward between its ears.

Frog The shock-absorbing, V-shaped area of horny material on the underside of a horse's hoof.

Full mouth The mouth of a horse at about six years old, when it has grown all its permanent teeth.

G

Gag A type of bridle, with rounded leather cheek pieces that pass through holes at the top and bottom of the bit rings and are then attached directly to the reins.

Gaited horse A horse that naturally, or through training, has distinctive gaits.

Gaits The paces of a horse, including the walk, trot, canter and gallop. Some breeds, such as the Saddlebred, have additional or different gaits.

Gall A skin sore or abrasion caused by friction from the saddle or girth.

Gaskin The lower part of the thigh of a horse's rear leg, between the hock and the stifle (also called the second thigh).

Gate An upright obstacle used in show jumping.

Gelding A male horse that has been gelded (castrated).

Gestation The period of about 11 months between the conception and birth of a foal.

Girth The circumference of a horse as measured around the deepest part of the body behind the withers; a leather, webbing or nylon band passing under the horse's belly to hold the saddle in place.

Good mouth A term used to describe a horse with a soft, sensitive mouth. A horse with a good mouth will be very responsive to the reins.

Go short A horse which is lame or restricted in its action is said to go short.

Green A broken but inexperienced horse; a trotter or pacer that has not yet been raced against the clock.

Groom To clean the coat, feet, mane and tail of a horse; a person responsible for looking after a horse.

Grooming kit The brushes, combs and other items used in grooming a horse.

Ground To let the reins of an unmounted horse touch the ground, so that it will stand without having to be tethered.

Gymkhana An event consisting of mounted games, usually for riders under sixteen.

H

Habit The formal outfit worn by women riders when, for example, hunting or riding side-saddle.

Hackney A compact, high-stepping horse type, not a recognized breed, used originally as a coach horse.

Halter A rope or leather crownpiece used for leading a horse not wearing a bridle, or for tying up a horse in a stable; a head collar.

Hand A measurement of 4 inches (just over 10 cm) used to measure the height of horses from the ground to the top of the withers. The figures after the decimal point are inches, for example 14.2 hands is 14 hands 2 inches.

Handicap A race in which the horses carry weights that are calculated so as to give each horse an equal chance of winning; the weight carried by a horse in a handicap race.

Haunches A horse's hips and buttocks

Haute école The classical art of equitation (French for 'high school').

Hay Grass cut and dried for use as fodder.

Head collar A leather crownpiece and noseband used for leading a horse not wearing a bridle, or for tying up a horse in a stable; a halter.

Heavy horse A horse belonging to any of the large draft breeds, such as Shire, Percheron or Holsteiner. A coldblood.

Heel The rear of a horse's foot.

High School The classical art of equitation (also called Haute école).

Hinny The sterile hybrid offspring of a male horse and a female donkey (see also Mule).

Hitch up To harness a horse or horses for driving.

Hock The joint between the thigh and the cannon of a horse's hind leg.

Hog's back A show jumping obstacle consisting of a spread of three poles, the first near the ground, the second the highest point of the obstacle and the third slightly lower than the second.

Hoof The horny part of a horse's foot.

Hoof pick A metal hook used for removing dirt or stones from the feet of horses.

Horseshoe A shaped piece of metal nailed to the base of a horse's hoof, to protect it against damage.

Hotbloods Pure breeds, such as the Arab.

Humerus The bone between a horse's shoulder and its elbow.

Hunt button A button carrying the symbol of a particular hunt.

Hunter A horse bred and trained for hunting.

Hurdles The obstacles the horses jump in hurdle racing.

I

Independent seat The ability of a rider to maintain balance and position without relying on reins or stirrups.

In foal Term describing a pregnant mare.

J

Jiggle The standard gait of a cow horse.

Jog A trot with short, irregular steps.

Jowl The flesh in front of a horse's throat, between and below the branches of the lower jaw.

Jugular groove A groove at the side of a horse's neck, just behind the windpipe.

Jumper A horse trained to jump.

K

Keep Pasture used for grazing.

Kiang A variety of Asiatic wild ass (*Equus hemionus*) originating in Tibet and the surrounding regions (see also Ass, Onager).

Knee The joint between the forearm and the cannon bone of a horse's foreleg.

L

Lad A stablehand; a groom.

Laminae The tender layers of a horse's hoof, lying between the hoof wall and the pedal bone.

Laminitis A very painful inflammation of the laminae.

Leathers Stirrup leathers.

Levade A High School movement. The horse rears, standing on its hind legs and drawing its forefeet in.

Livery or **livery stable** A stable where horses are boarded.

Loins The part of a horse's body between the croup and the back.

Lorimer Someone who makes the metal parts of saddlery and harness.

Lungeing Exercising or training a horse on a lunge line.

Lunge line A long cotton or nylon rein attached to the cavesson to control the horse during lungeing.

M

Maiden A racehorse which has not won a race.

Maiden mare A mare which has not had a foal.

Maiden race A race for horses which have not yet won a race.

Mane The long hair on a horse's head and neck.

Mane comb A metal comb for grooming a horse's mane.

Mare A female horse; a female horse aged four years or more.

Martingale A strap or straps connecting the reins, noseband or bit to the girth. Its purpose is to help keep the horse's head in the correct position.

Manège The art of training horses and riders; a riding school.

Master The person with overall responsibility for the running and organization of a hunt.

Meet A hunt meeting; the place where a hunt assembles.

Muck out To remove

droppings and soiled bedding from a stall.

Mud fever Inflammation of a horse's skin, caused by exposure to wet and muddy conditions.

Mule The sterile hybrid offspring of a male donkey and a female horse (see also Hinny).

Muzzle The lower end of a horse's head, surrounding and including the lips and nostrils.

N

Nap In racing, an allegedly good tip; also, a horse is said to nap (or to be nappy) if it is obstinate or uncooperative.

Natural aids The rider's body (or weight), hands, legs and voice as used to give instructions to the horse.

Near side The left-hand side of a horse.

Noseband The part of a bridle that lies across the horse's nose.

Numnah A saddle pad. The word is derived from *namda*, an Urdu word for a type of felt from which saddle pads were once made.

O

Oats A type of cereal crop which may be used as part of a horse's feed.

Off side The right-hand side of a horse.

Onager A variety of Asiatic wild ass (*Equus hemionus*) originating in southwest Asia (see also Ass, Kiang).

One-day event A combined training competition with dressage, showjumping and cross country phases that are all held on the same day.

Oriental A term used to describe breeds from the 'Orient', including the Arab and the Barb.

P

Pace A two-time lateral gait in which the fore and hind legs on the same side move forward together; also another word for 'gait'.

Pacer A horse (especially a harness-racing horse) whose gait is the pace (see also Trotter).

Paddock A grassed enclosure, usually near a stable or house, into which horses can be turned out; the racecourse enclosure in which the horses are paraded before they race.

Parimutuel In the USA and continental Europe, a form of horserace betting in which the total amount wagered is divided, after deduction of operating costs, among the holders of winning and place tickets; known in Britain as the Tote.

Passage A High School air. The passage is a slow, elevated trot in which the raised pair of legs are briefly held still in the air while the other pair remain on the ground.

Pastern The part of a horse's foot between the hoof and the fetlock.

Pelham A bit which combines the functions of the snaffle and the curb bit.

Piaffe A High School air. A spectacular, elevated trot performed on the spot.

Pirouette A dressage term for a turn within the horse's length.

Place To finish second (and sometimes also third or fourth) in a horserace.

Points The external features of a horse.

Poll The top of a horse's head.

Post To rise from the saddle at the trot; the starting or winning post of a racecourse.

Prepotent A term used to describe a sire (or dam) that tends to pass on more of its characteristics to its offspring than the other parent does.

Q

Quarters The hindquarters of a horse. They extend on either side from the rear of the flank to the tail root and down to the top of the leg.

R

Racehorse A horse, usually a Thoroughbred, bred and trained for racing.

Racing plate A lightweight horseshoe for racehorses.

Rack The most spectacular gait of a five-gaited American Saddlebred horse. Each foot strikes the ground separately in rapid succession.

Rein back To make a ridden or driven horse step backward.

Reins The pair of thin straps, attached to the bit or bridle, that help the rider or driver to guide and control the horse.

Renvers A dressage movement in which the horse, with its tail to the wall, moves sideways at an angle of not more than 30 degrees (see also Travers).

Ringer A horse illegally entered in a race under the name of another (usually inferior) horse.

Rub rag A rectangular sheet of cloth used for rubbing down a horse at the end of grooming. Also called a stable rubber.

S

Saddle furniture The metal fittings of a saddle.

Saddle pad A shaped pad fitted between the saddle and the horse's back. Also called a numnah, it may be made of natural or synthetic fabrics, horsehair, felt, sheepskin or fleece.

Saddler Someone who makes or sells saddles and harness.

Saddlery The saddle, bridle and other tack used on a riding horse.

Second thigh Another name for the gaskin of a horse.

Servicing Mating a mare with a stallion.

Shoulder The joint between the foreleg and the body of a horse.

Sire The male parent of a foal.

Slow gait One of the gaits of a five-gaited American Saddlebred horse. Each foot in turn is raised and held briefly in the air before being brought down.

Snaffle The simplest form of bit, consisting of a single bar with a ring at each end to which the reins are attached.

Splint A bony growth that develops between a horse's cannon bone and one of the splint bones. Caused by excess strain or impact.

Spur A metal device strapped to the heel of a riding boot. Used to encourage the horse to move forward.

Stable rubber A rectangular sheet of cloth used for rubbing down a horse at the end of grooming. Also called a rub rag.

Stallion An ungelded male horse aged four years or more.

Standard event Any of the five recognized rodeo events, which are bareback riding, bull riding, calf roping, saddle bronc riding and steer wrestling.

Steeplechase A horserace in which there are a series of obstacles to be jumped.

Stifle The joint in a horse's rear leg between the thigh and the gaskin.

Stirrup iron The loop of metal, wood or leather into which the rider's foot is placed.

Stirrup leather The adjustable strap to which the stirrup iron is attached.

Stock A white neckcloth worn, for example, for hunting; the handle of a riding whip.

Stock class A Western show class for stock or ranch ponies.

Strangles A very infectious disease of horses, causing fever and abscesses under the jaws. Veterinary attention is essential.

Stud A place where horses are kept for breeding; a collection of racehorses belonging to one owner; a male horse used for breeding; a metal projection screwed into a horseshoe to give better grip.

Surcingle A webbing strap which goes over the saddle and girth to give them additional security; also used to hold rugs or blankets in position.

Sweat scraper A curved blade, with a handle, used to scrape sweat from a horse's coat.

T

Tack Another name for saddlery and harness.

Tail comb A metal comb for grooming a horse's tail.

Tetanus An infection, often fatal, caused by a baccillus which lives in the soil and can enter a horse's body through an open wound, especially one in the foot. Veterinary attention is essential.

Thigh The part of a horse's rear leg between the hip and the stifle.

Three-day event A combined training event (horse trial) held over three successive days.

Throatlatch The part of a bridle that passes under the horse's throat. Also called the throatlash.

Thrush An inflammation of the frog of a horse's foot, accompanied by a foul-smelling discharge.

Tote The British version of parimutuel betting. Short for Totalizator.

Travers a dressage movement in which the horse, with its head to the wall, moves sideways at an angle of not more than 30 degrees (see also Renvers).

Trot A pace in two-time in which the legs move in diagonal pairs.

Trotter A harness-racing horse whose gait is the trot.

U

Unbacked A term used to describe a horse that has not yet been ridden.

Unbroken Wild or untamed.

Unsound Term describing a horse with any acquired or congenital defect that reduces its ability to work.

V

Vertebra One of the bony segments (vertebrae or vertebras) of a horse's spine.

Volte In dressage, either a full turn on the haunches or a movement in which the horse walks in a small circle of predetermined radius.

W

Walk A four-time pace. The hoofs strike the ground in the sequence of near hind, near fore, off hind, off fore.

Warmbloods Horse breeds that are neither as pure as hotbloods (such as the Arab) nor as heavy and slow as the coldbloods (such as the Shire). They are used for riding, competitions and driving.

Water brush A brush used wetted to groom a horse's mane and tail.

Windgall A soft swelling around the knee or fetlock of a horse, often caused by strain of the tendons or joints.

Windsucking The harmful habit of swallowing air, which gives the horse indigestion and results in loss of condition.

Withers The region at the base of a horse's neck, between its shoulder blades. It is the highest part of a horse's back, and the point at which its height is measured.

X

Xenophon Greek general, historian, horseman and author (430–355 BC).

Y

Yearling A horse between its first and second birthdays; a Thoroughbred racehorse is counted, for racing purposes, as being one year old until the second 1 January after its birth.

Z

Zebra Any of several wild members of the horse family, such as *Equus burchelli* (the common zebra). They have distinctive black-and-white stripes, and are found in southern and eastern Africa.

Zebra marks Stripes on the legs, neck, withers or hindquarters of a horse.

ASSOCIATIONS & SOCIETIES

American Driving Society,
P. O. Box 160
16 East High Street
Metamora, MI 48455

American Endurance Ride
Conference
701 High Street, Suite 216
Auburn, CA 95603

American Horse Council
1700 K St, NW
Washington, DC 20006

American Horse Protection
Association
1038 31 Street, NW
Washington, DC 20007

American Horse Shows
Association
220 East 42 Street
New York, NY 10017

US Combined Training
Association
292 Bridge Street
South Hamilton, MA 01982

US Pony Clubs
893 South Matlack Street,
Suite 110
West Chester, PA 19382

US Trotting Association
750 Michigan Avenue
Columbus, OH 43215

Canadian Equestrian Federation
1600 James Naismith Drive
Gloucester, ON K1B 5N4

Canadian Pony Society
13 Caie Crescent
Yarmouth, NS B5A 1N5

Canadian Trotting Association
233 Evans Avenue
Toronto, ON M8Z 1J6

BIBLIOGRAPHY

Ainslie, Tom and Ledbetter, Bonnie *The Body Language of Horses* (1980)

Baker, Jennifer *Saddlery and Horse Clothing* (1982)

Blazer, Tom *Natural Western Riding* (1979)

Bongianni, Maurizio *Simon & Schuster's Guide to Horses & Ponies of the World* (1988)

Dossenbach, Monique and Dossenbach, Hans D *The Noble Horse* (1985)

Drummond, Marcy *Long Distance Riding* (1987)

Drummond, Marcy *The Horse Care and Stable Manual* (1988)

Dunning, Al *Reining* (1983)

Foreman, Monte and Wyse, Patrick *Monte Foreman's Horse Training Science* (1983)

Hartley Edwards, Elwyn *Paddock to Saddle* (1972)

Hartley Edwards, Elwyn *Standard Guide to Horses and Ponies* (1975)

Hartley Edwards, Elwyn *Horses — Their Role in the History of Man* (1988)

Hayes, M Horace *Veterinary Notes for Horse Owners* (17th rev ed 1988)

Jones, Dave *Practical Western Training* (2nd rev ed 1985)

Kays, John *The Horse* (3rd ed 1982)

Kellon, Eleanor M *The Older horse: A Complete Guide to Care and Conditioning* (1986)

Kunffy, Charles de *Dressage Questions Answered* (1983)

Lose, M Phyllis *Blessed Are the Broodmares* (1978)

Lose, M Phyllis *Blessed Are the Foals* (1987)

Madden, Frank and Cooney, Bill *Fit to Show* (1985)

Morris, George H *Hunter Seat Equitation* (rev ed 1979)

Müseler, Wilhelm *Riding Logic* (5th ed 1984)

Price, Steven D, et al, (eds) *The Whole Horse Catalog* (1983)

Richter, Judy *Horse & Rider: From Basics to Show Competition* (1982)

Richter, Judy *The Longeing Book* (1986)

Roth, Charlene *Driving the Light Horse: Training for Pleasure and Competition* (1984)

Scott, Brough and Cranham, Gerry *The World of Flat Racing* (1984)

Steinkraus, William C and Stonebridge, M A *The Horse in Sport* (1987)

Stoneridge, M A *A Horse of Your Own* (rev ed 1980)

Stoneridge, M A (ed) *Practical Horseman's Book of Horsekeeping* (1983)

Sutcliffe, Anne *Breeding & Training a Horse or Pony* (1981)

Vernan, Glenn R *Man on Horseback: The Story of Mounted Man from the Scythians to the American Cowboy* (1972)

Wells, Ellen B *Horsemanship: A Bibliography of Printed Materials from the Sixteenth Century to 1974* (1985)

INDEX

Page numbers in bold type (eg **134**) indicate main entries, and those in italics (eg *74*) indicate photographs or diagrams.

CREDITS

AUTHORS:
Jenny Collier
Marcy Drummond
Elwyn Hartley Edwards
Frances Gayther-Martin
Ann Green
Georgie Henschel

EDITORIAL:
US Consultant Editor Madelyn Larsen
UK Consultant Editor Elwyn Hartley Edwards
Editor Ian Wood
Art Director Steve Leaning

PHOTOGRAPHY:
Tack & Equipment photography John Darling, with additional photography by Kit Houghton

All other photography Kit Houghton

ARTISTS:
Horse breeds John Francis
Technical artwork Maggie Raynor

DETAILED CREDITS:

Pages 6–7: *photo* Kit Houghton
8: *photo* Houghton
10–11: *illustrations* Maggie Raynor
12–13: *photo* John Darling, supplier Polegate Saddlery
14–15: *photo* Darling, supplier Polegate Saddlery
16–17: *photo* Darling, supplier Polegate Saddlery
18–19: *photo* Darling, suppliers Polegate Saddlery (English bridles and bits), RPM Western (Western bridles and bits)
20–21: *photo* Darling, supplier RPM Western

22: *photo* Darling, supplier Polegate Saddlery
23: *photo* Kit Houghton, supplier Paragon
24–25: *photo* Darling, supplier Polegate Saddlery
26–27: *photo* Darling, supplier W E Vine
28–29: *photo* Darling, suppliers Mr & Mrs Latham
30–31: *bottom photo* Darling, *other photos* Houghton
32: *photo* Darling
33: *photos* Houghton
34: *photo* Darling, supplier Polegate Saddlery

35: *photo* Darling, supplier RPM Western
36–37: *photo* Darling, supplier Polegate Saddlery
38: *photo* Houghton
40–41: *illustrations* John Francis
42–43: *illustrations* Francis
44–45: *photos* Houghton, *illustrations* Maggie Raynor
46–47: *photos* Houghton
48–49: *photos* Houghton, *illustration* Raynor
50–51: *photos* Houghton
52–53: *photos* Houghton
54–55: *photos* Houghton

56: *photo* Houghton
58–59: *photos* Houghton
60–113: *illustrations* John Francis
114: *photo* Houghton
116–145: *photos* Houghton, *illustrations* Raynor
146–161: *photos* Houghton
162: *photo* Darling
163–169: *photos* Houghton